George Lacon James

Shall I try Australia?

Or, Health, Business, and Pleasure in New South Wales

George Lacon James

Shall I try Australia?
Or, Health, Business, and Pleasure in New South Wales

ISBN/EAN: 9783337151874

Printed in Europe, USA, Canada, Australia, Japan

Cover: Foto ©Lupo / pixelio.de

More available books at **www.hansebooks.com**

Shall I Try Australia?

OR,

HEALTH, BUSINESS, AND PLEASURE IN NEW SOUTH WALES.

Forming a Guide to the Australian Colonies for the Emigrant Settler and Business Man,

BY

GEORGE LACON JAMES.

WITH TWO ILLUSTRATIONS.

LONDON:
L. UPCOTT GILL, 170, STRAND, W.C.
1892.

CONTENTS.

CHAP.		PAGE
	Introduction	1
I.—	The City of Sydney	5
II.—	The Suburbs—Parks—and Public Buildings of Sydney	12
III.—	Sydney Restaurants, Hotels, and Boarding Houses	21
IV.—	Houses in Sydney—House Rent and House-keeping—The Butcher's Bill—Furnishing—Cost of Living generally	29
V.—	Consumption of meat—The Live Stock Resources of the Colony—The Sydney Meat Supply—Its Imperfections—The Frozen Meat Trade	39
VI.—	Fruit, Vegetables, and Milk in New South Wales—Their Cost—Supervision of Dairies ...	50
VII.—	"The Harvest of the Seas"—Salt and Fresh Water Fisheries—The Fish Market in Sydney—Oyster Culture	58
VIII.—	The Liquor Trade—Are Australians Temperate? What they Drink—The Licensing Laws ...	67
IX.—	The Railways—Tramways and Roads of New South Wales	74
X.—	Australian Scenery—"The Bush"—"Bush" Townships and Cities— Swagmen — Sundowners—"On the Wallaby"	85
XI.—	Sheep-runs—What has to be done upon them—A Woolshed in Working Order—Droving...	95
XII.—	Art in New South Wales—The National Gallery. Native Artists and Local Exhibitions—Music—The Theatre—Literature	106

XIII.—Wages in Town and Country—The Prospects of Professional, Clerical, and Working Men, and also of Women, in the Colony 113
XIV.—Sport in the Colony—Sporting Proclivities, and Sportsmen—Horse-racing and Racecourses—The Totalisator—"Sweeps"—Games and Pastimes 123
XV.—Trades Unionism in New South Wales—The Great Strike—The Shearers' Grievance—Labour Troubles generally 132
XVI.—By Steamship to Australia—The Suez, Cape, and American Routes—Ports of Call, and What They are Like—Oriental Traders—Life on Board Ship 139
XVII.—The Sailing Vessel Route—The "Roaring Forties," "Trades" and "Doldrums"—The Monsoons—Bird Life at Sea—Hints upon the Voyage 154
XVIII.—The Climate of New South Wales—The Coast, Table Land, and Plains—Heat and Rainfall.—Health Resorts, and Cost of Living—What to Wear... 171
XIX.—The Steerage, and How to Make it Comfortable—The Several Classes Compared, with Special Information for Steerage Passengers both by the Suez and Cape Routes 184
XX.—Animal Life in the Colony—The Marsupials: Will they soon become Extinct?—Birds, Reptiles, and Insects 193
XXI.—How to Acquire Land—The Land Laws of the Colony—What to Do—Business Openings—The Small Capitalist—Undeveloped Industries 204
XXII.—Forestry in the Colony—Native Woods—The Wattle Tree and Its Cultivation—Irrigation and Conservation of Water—Mining—Broken Hill—"Prospecting," "Reefing," and Alluvial Working 219

III.

XXIII.—A Chapter for Business Men—The System of Import Business—The Appointment and Choice of Agents—Rents of Offices, Warehouses and Shops—Government Contracts—The Wharves of Sydney—Wharfage and Other Charges—Customs and Excise—Protection of Patents and Trade Marks ... 229

XXIV.—Disease and Epidemics in New South Wales—Sanitary Questions—Municipal Shortcomings—Sydney Hospitals 241

XXV.—Types of Australians—The Rising Generation—How They Talk in Australia—Education—The Cadet Corps 249

XXVI.—An Idle Man in Sydney—Horses and Carriages, and their Cost—Amusements—Newspapers—Excursions from Sydney, Near and Far—Tasmania—New Zealand—The South Seas—China and Japan 257

XXVII.—New Chums—Their Prospects in Australia—What Can They Do—Letters of Introduction 264

XXVIII.—Sydney Social Life—Larrikins, and Larrikin "Pushes," and other matters 269

XXIX.—The Mode of Government—The Legislative Council and Assembly—Legal and Ecclesiastical Matters—The Police Force—The Imperial and Local Forces in the Colony ... 275

XXX.—Concluding Remarks—Centralization—Life in Cities—Technical Education—The Aboriginal—"John Chinaman"—Alien Communities 286

LIVERPOOL
EDWARD HOWELL CHURCH STREET

INTRODUCTION.

ALTHOUGH, day by day almost, something is being done to render ocean travel, if possible, more speedy and luxurious and, it may be added, less expensive; it is, even yet, somewhat of a "far cry" to Australia, and less is known, I am inclined to think, by English people generally, about the country and its resources than is excusable in these present days of progress.

It is true that I have confined the following pages, mainly, to one colony, but much that I have written, upon what I might term the most essential points, which, the intending emigrant, whatever his position may be, should first consider; will, I think, apply to Australia generally. A brief sojourn in a new country has before now induced a visitor to regard himself as competent to write a book upon it; but during no small experience of foreign travel I have endeavoured to learn how misleading first impressions too frequently are; as well as the great mistake of seeing things, through the eyes, as it were, even of the most experienced of cicerones. In the present instance I hope that two visits to the Antipodes, and more than two years varied experience of life in the city and "Bush" alike—with my object constantly before me—may have enabled me to do some justice to at least one great division of a vast continent, viz., New South Wales.

First of all, there must be many whose thoughts, for diverse reasons, must often turn towards founding a new home in a new country, finding or extending a market for their productions, or seeking a suitable field for the remunerative investment of capital.

Again, there is, I fear, an increasing number of premature "breakdowns" in the pace at which the race of life must now be run—the "pace that kills," which call urgently for rest and change of scene. While, lastly, there are many who, having the means to enable them to fly from the vagaries of an English winter, might for once, at least, exchange the Riviera for the Antipodes, to the benefit of health and pocket alike.

For all the foregoing I have endeavoured to provide some useful information in the following pages, and, at the same time, I trust they will not be devoid of interest, if not instruction, to those fortunate beings who are healthy, happy, and contented "at home."

Briefly reviewing my work, I would first ask those—for unfortunately there are not a few that do so—who would tempt fortune in Australia without having been brought up to any particular trade, profession, or calling, to glance at a chapter headed "New Chums," No. XXVII., as well as at "Wages in Town and Country," No. XIII.

The cost of eating, drinking, housekeeping, and living generally, are but prosaic items; but they are, I think, very necessary to those who have to weigh carefully the cost of a new venture.

For the consideration of the invalid and the robust alike, I have submitted three chapters on ocean travel, based upon a long experience thereof; while my notes under the heading of "The Climate of New South Wales," No. XVIII., for the benefit of the first-named, have been kindly reviewed by a medical friend of wide experience.

After a long acquaintance with Australian business, I have ventured upon Chapter XXV., which may possess some interest for business men; while a resumé of the land laws, business openings, &c., will, I hope, be of interest and use to those who contemplate emigration to the Antipodes.

The chapters on "Art and Sport" in the colony, and "An Idle Man in Sydney," are more for the pleasure seeker. Finally, I have, after very careful enquiry, submitted chapters on the "Live Stock Resources of the Colony, &c.," "Forestry Irrigation and Mining," and cognate questions; concerning which, I would remark, that I hope rather to prove the means of exciting some curiosity or desire upon the part of my readers, to learn something of the resources of the vast continent of Australia, than pose as an authority upon the several subjects.

The works I have consulted have all been purely statistical. My best thanks are due to Mr. Coghlan's* "Wealth and Progress of New South Wales," Parliamentary Reports, &c., and "The Year Book of New South Wales," compiled from official sources: while, in confirming my gossip on the Fauna of the Colony and the marvellous bird-life of the Southern Ocean, I have to

* The Government Statistician of New South Wales.

acknowledge the great courtesy extended to me by the officials of the South Kensington Natural History Museum.

Correctness has been my aim throughout. If I have in any way erred, being but human, I claim that forgiveness which is proverbially divine.

CHAPTER I.

THE CITY OF SYDNEY.

Two furrowed, weatherworn headlands—the northern falling in a grim precipice of some four hundred feet—the southern stretching out with more gradual slope to stay the long rollers of the Pacific—are passed: and we are soon in the far-famed Sydney harbour, perhaps after months of sea and sky, fair and foul weather; or, it may be, fresh from the flat, unlovely, shores of Port Philip.

A succession of bays and inlets of every shape and size open out on either hand, and a most varied, if not unrivalled, panorama of wooded heights, now abrupt, now sloping gently to the water's edge, dotted here and there with tasteful mansions and terraced gardens, reflected in the bright waters of the harbour, charm the beholder almost to the verge of bewilderment.

But mail steamers wait not for scenery, so we are soon alongside Circular Quay, perhaps in a crowded tender, or, if there is room, our steamer takes up her position at the quayside, where the largest ocean-going giants that have as yet appeared in Australian waters find depth enough and to spare. Here we make our first step ashore, where, in 1788, Captain Philip landed to form the nucleus of the City of Sydney; to use his own words, "at the head of a cove, near a run of fresh water, which stole silently through thick wood."

The cove is here, but changed indeed. The "run of fresh water and thick wood" are now no more. An old-world quay, overshadowed by huge prosaic warehouses and solidly-built buildings, has taken their place; and singularly home-like all appears. Less grimy, however—in fact, infinitely brighter, and by no means depressing—is even the meanest and ugliest building, but there is at first sight scarcely the smallest detail that smacks of a foreign land.

There are, perhaps, fewer pleasanter hours than the first one spends on shore after a long voyage, however much we liked our ship, we are rarely sorry to leave her and see fresh faces and fresh surroundings. How refreshing is the first toilet in a comfortable room, instead of in a cramped cabin; and what a pleasure it is to sally forth for our first walk ashore.

The shops we see are undeniably smart, and there is no lack of fine substantial buildings, but with the exception of the brightness before referred to, and the fact that many of the side walks are protected from sun and rain by light iron verandahs, there is still little or nothing of a foreign element. The streets, perhaps, are not too wide, nor are the side walks too spacious, especially by contrast with Melbourne. The pavement, however, and roadwork is good, wood blocks being generally used for the latter.

The traffic in the streets is much the same as in those of the Mother Country, the gondola of London, the hansom cab, is much in evidence, and so also is the buggy, *the vehicle of Australia*. Very English-looking omnibuses ply for hire, and if we turn into Elizabeth Street we will see train after train of noisy, jangling steam trams—several carriages linked to a powerful motor—which make one wonder how any horse that ever "looked through a bridle" can be brought to " stand tram," which is a very necessary condition when purchasing horse-flesh for city use—for the rest, an orderly trooper may dash past, smart in his Kharkee uniform, and eminently workmanlike rig-out, or equally smart, a well mounted, well set up trooper of the police, in his neat uniform of dark blue kepi (exchanged for a black helmet with white puggaree when in " full dress "), serge jacket of blue, spotless "cords," and irreproachable riding boots. While lastly, telegraph boys, who do all their delivery work on horseback beyond a certain radius, scurry about in a fashion which suggests the care of a special providence. The police, we notice, are dressed in dark blue, with helmets of London pattern ; during the summer the latter are covered with white, and the wearers rejoice in white "ducks." Now and again we see an individual in semi-uniform with the badge M.T.C., he is in the service of the Metropolitan Transit Company, and is charged with regulating the traffic of the city.

But it is perhaps about that hour in the afternoon when the youth and beauty, rank and fashion, of Sydney assemble to do "the block," otherwise to promenade certain portions of George, King, Pitt, and Hunter Streets, and this will afford us an excellent chance of seeing what manner of men and women, physically speaking, our Australian cousins are—at least in Sydney.

We miss, no doubt, the exceedingly well-groomed men we are used to see in Piccadilly, and we may perhaps not consider that the clothes of the Sydney "masher" are quite up to London form in point of "cut." As we are some twelve hundred miles nearer the Equator than we were in London, we almost expect to find some material difference in the garments worn by the sterner sex, but it is not so. Not a few "chimney pot" hats are to be seen, and save for the light fabrics, worn by the fairer sex, there is nothing much beyond our own feelings to tell us that the temperature is over eighty degrees in the shade. The men, perhaps, seem, as a rule, to be thinner than we have been used to; while in Pitt Street we see the business men with the same anxious pre-occupied look, in many cases, that is so familiar to us in the streets of London city, on the Liverpool "flags," and elsewhere where "merchants most do congregate. The complexion of the fairer sex show somewhat of a pallor and less of freshness than we have been wont to observe at home; but we are reminded that we are in a land where an earlier development of the race is a rule by certain precocious young damsels, whose abbreviated skirts display a somewhat startling solidity of what our American cousins, with commendable modesty, term "limbs." A smart-looking Chinese merchant, minus his beloved pigtail, and in European garb, passes by. A Bushman, with sunburnt face and the unmistakable air of a man unused to the bustle of crowded streets, lounges diffidently along. The bright turbans of a few swarthy Lascars, from a "P and O" liner, add a bit of colour to the scene, while a sleek, dressy, dark-eyed, full-lipped gentleman, with a nasal organ of a shape familiar to us, betokens that some of the "chosen people" have made a home, and we should guess, a very comfortable one, in the colony of our choice.

But, though the proper study of mankind be man, and womenkind also, I presume, we tire for the while of them and of the bricks and mortar, and wish for a view of the glorious surroundings of which we had a vision, all too short, during our passage up the harbour. From the top of the Grosvenor or Metropole Hotels, or better still from the lantern of that tall slender tower which springs from the General Post Office, we have Sydney and its suburbs at our feet—but rather let us cross Macquarie Street and enter a portion of the beautiful "lungs" of Sydney—the Palace Gardens, and looking eastward try to describe what we see before and around us.

A luxuriant carpet of greensward is beneath our feet, and, in the immediate foreground carefully tended beds of brightly-hued flowers add colour to the scene. In front, the grounds run, verdure clad, in terraced slopes down to the Botanical Gardens, one of the many joys of Sydney, relieved here and there by statuary of gleaming white. From where we stand, the gardens look a tangled mass of greenery, of graceful palms, and all the varied forms of semi-tropical and tropical forest life—high over all of which there rises, tall and graceful, the lordly Norfolk Island Pine.

To the left, and far below us, are the wavelets of Farm Cove, dancing and shimmering in the sunlight, and through the tree-tops we catch glimpses of trim-built men-of-war, and a bugle call, the roll of a drum, or the shrill pipe of the boatswain breaks upon the ear. Still further to the left are the turrets and battlements of Government House embosomed in well-grown trees.

Beyond the Cove rise the green and well-wooded sides of the Domain, over which peep the waters of the harbour, and beyond, from out of the northern shore thereof, runs Bradley Head, shutting out from our view the bold precipice of the North Head; while straight in front, closing in the picture and some half dozen miles away, the South Head slopes down to the fatal "gap," where, early in the "fifties," the "Dunbar" was lost, with all on board, save one.

To the right, above the tree-tops of the Outer Domain, are the terraced houses of Darlinghurst, and from thence, sloping northwards to the water's edge, are Potts and Darling points, with their burden of many mansions.

Dot the blue waters of the harbour with the white sails of tiny craft, and the majestic forms of ocean-going ships, imagine the deepest hued of cerulean skies, light up the whole with radiant sunshine, and we return from our first experience, our first few hours stroll in Sydney, satisfied that we have at length seen something to prove to us that we are in a foreign and a favoured land.

At eventide, during a tour of observation through the streets, we are likely to see comparatively little. Those devoted to business during the day have the deserted look common to the haunts of commercial men in our own cities after business hours. The remainder are for the most part quiet, but on Saturday and Sunday evenings some portions, as well as several arcades, which are a distinct and pleasant feature of Sydney, are fairly well thronged, and the manners and customs of a certain class of young Sydney may be studied with ease as far as amplitude of material is concerned. We may notice that the electric lighting has, as yet, been taken up to a very slight extent only in the city, though in more than one township in the Colony it has been successfully installed.

The "almond-eyed Celestial," as it is usually the fashion to term the Chinaman, is to be found in several quarters of Sydney, where quaint characters over the shop windows and doors betoken his name and calling. Hereabouts he smokes his beloved opium, and, no doubt, encourages certain of his virtuous Caucasian brethren to do the same, while we may also find, if we are inclined thereto, an establishment where the forbidden game of "fan-tan" is played; and here assemble young and old, who have no fashionable club or private residence whereat to gamble, to back their favourite number at the afore-mentioned game.

Generally there is no great temptation thrown in the way of erring mankind in Sydney streets at night-time. Private bars and billiard rooms, apart from the theatres and a few minor places of amusement, seem to be the sole attractions. If it be the summer time, when we court the open air as much as possible, the new arrival will almost expect some outdoor forms of amusement, music, and open-air cafés or beer gardens, but no. Of this, however, we will take further notice.

But after our casual look at Sydney, what is it that we miss in a city so thoroughly English in many details, so far as we have seen, and we might search still further? How does it very materially differ from most cities, nay, from all large cities in Great Britain? Slums? Yes, there are none worthy of the name in Sydney.

Chapter II.

THE SUBURBS, PARKS, AND PUBLIC BUILDINGS OF SYDNEY.

Such fair promise as our first glimpse or two at the surroundings of Sydney gave us, we shall find borne out in full by a few walks, rides, or drives in the suburbs, or by availing ourselves of an occasional ferry boat, to see more of the beauties of the famous harbour.

It is far from my wish to weary the reader with descriptions; so, briefly sketching one surburban trip will, I think, be sufficient, and this shall be by what is known as the New South Head Road. A splendidly kept roadway it is, too, and free, thanks to the numerous steep hills or "pinches," as I have heard them termed in the bush, from invasion by the demon steam-tram. Furthermore, it affords a charming and fashionable ride or drive to those of the Sydney folks who have the means and leisure in the afternoon. The distance to the South Head Lighthouse from Sydney is about six miles, and the road, for the most part, skirts the south side of the harbour, running about due east.

Turning to the left from Macquarie Street, we leave the Domain on our left, Hyde Park on our right, and commence our descent into William Street, Woolloo-mooloo, the which somewhat weird combination of l's and redundant o's, I have heard explained as being an effort upon the part of a black-fellow in byegone days to pronounce the word "windmill." As a triumph of articulation, it may be urged, without doing injustice to native talent, that it is not a marked success. However, theory is useless. I need only add, for the benefit of these who have occasion to use the word, that the accent is on the final syllable.

A steep pull brings us into Darlinghurst, and we soon descend into another furrow, as it were, this time coming upon Rushcutter's Bay, on the shore of which is the prettily situated "Oval" Cricket Ground, the low lying ground running up to a gully on our right being carfully tilled by Chinese gardeners. Another ridge, the aristocratic Darling Point, upon which a very English-looking spire crowns some fine trees, and we descend more gradually to the charmingly wooded shores of Double Bay, where are many dwelling-houses to suit all pockets. A more level stretch of beautifully kept road at length opens up Rose Bay, the view of which I think will induce the visitor to pause a few moments, however satiated he may have been with earth's natural beauties. It is the most extensive of the bays in Sydney harbour, and its blue waters are fringed by a perfect semicircle of yellow strand. Here we get views of the North and Middle Harbours, and skirting the edge of the bay we begin to ascend the bulk of the South Head; and, passing the magnificent lighthouse with all its appliances for furnishing the revolving electric light it flashes between sunset and sunrise so many miles around, we finally arrive at the signal station where we have a magnificent view seawards, northwards, and, to the west, one over the harbour, with Sydney in the background, and the Blue Mountains above all, and far away, that I will not attempt to describe.

Hence the pedestrian can go by an easy descent past the " Dun bar Gap " into the pretty little harbour resort known as Watson's Bay, and take the steamer to Sydney ; but those that ride or drive had best "hark back," and turning to the left at Rose Bay, return by the Old South Head Road, skirting the somewhat dreary sand dunes of Bondi Bay. By this road one passes through the elevated and pleasant suburb of Waverley, and looks down across the extent of Centennial Park, towards Randwick with its racecourse, the Flemington of Sydney, Botany with its smoky chimneys; and beyond, the somewhat historic bay of that ilk, sadly lacking the beauties with which its near neighbour, Port Jackson, as "our harbour" was first termed, is so richly endowed.

On through the suburbs of Woollahra, with its many handsome, substantial mansions, standing in trim well-kept grounds, we come to the next suburb to the city from the eastward, familiarly named Paddington, and thence within the confines of the city itself. Coogee Bay lying beyond, and to the eastward of Randwick, is a pretty spot, it boasts an aquarium and concert hall, and on Sundays is a great resort of Middle Class Sydney, when an immense quantity of "all sorts and conditions" of vehicles and horses may be seen, and next to attending a race meeting perhaps nothing pleases young Australia better than to drive a fast horse in a neat buggy, with what the Americans sometimes term "his best Sunday girl" by his side.

Of the remaining suburbs on the south, the Sydney side of the harbour, some are prosaic enough; among them are Redfern, where the Railway terminus is situated, Eveleigh, McDonald Town, Camperdown, Newtown, Stanmore, Marrickville, Petersham, and Lewisham. Farther away, a few miles on the south coast line, are Tempè, Arncliffe, Rockdale, and Kogarah, while on the Parramatta line are Ashfield, Croyden, Burwood, and others, almost every mile on the way to Parramatta—itself fourteen miles from Sydney. Westward of Sydney is the pretty and convenient suburb of Glebe, also Balmain, and Five Dock, each situated on promontories running out into the harbour.

The north shore, which includes St. Leonards, St. Leonards East, and North Willoughby, affords beautiful sites and views, and being extremely convenient to the city, by the swift and frequent ferryboats available, is much sought after as a place of residence by business men. A service of cable tramways, similar to those in use in Melbourne, is at the disposal of the North Shore residents, and they are also being connected by railway with the Northern line.

The various harbour resorts, such as Manly and Watson's Bay, are well worth a visit, though each of them are somewhat hot and perhaps relaxing in summer, being sheltered from the cool southerly winds. Clontarf, in the middle harbour, is beautifully situated, and is the favoured haunt of the multitude of picknickers, as also is Chowder Bay. Mossman's Bay is another pretty inlet, and it has a ferry to Circular Quay. While those that desire to explore further westward, should take the steamer to Lane Cove or Parramatta. In short water excursions Sydney is well off. In rough weather, by the way, the Manly boat, when crossing the opening between the Head, is exposed to the full " fetch " of the Pacific, and has sometimes quite a " bit of weather " to contend with, otherwise the trips generally are not of a nature calculated to upset the most timid " sailor."

In the matter of parks, Sydney is also blessed in abundance. The Botanical and Palace Gardens, the Inner and Outer Domain, Hyde Park, the Centennial Park, and a host of lesser reserves are open to the public, for, throughout the Colony, there is, in such matters at least, solicitude exhibited on behalf of the public weal. Many of the small parks and reserves have also "pitches" for cricketing, which has not been eclipsed as yet by football in New South Wales, but is undoubtedly *the* national game.

The Botanical Gardens are a host in themselves, and no tyrannical order to "keep off the grass" prevents the visitor from wandering at will over a thick, well-kept carpet of greensward. On Wednesday afternoons, the band of the Permanent Artillery usually discourses sweet music to a large crowd of listeners; and, if tired of the immense and beautiful variety of tropical and semi-tropical vegetable life of all kinds, a small collection of, for the most part, native birds may serve to interest the visitor. From out of these gardens we stroll into the Domain where the gum tree preponderates, though here and there the Moreton Bay fig tree affords a grateful shade. At Lady Macquarie's chair, the extreme north point, a beautiful view of the harbour is to be had, and here, when a hot wind makes Sydney streets well-nigh unbearable, those that can escape from them assemble, and loll and lie about to court such cool airs as may be forthcoming.

Further south, the paltry building which contains the Art treasures of the Colony greets us, of which more anon, and across the way is a hideous concoction of galvanized iron, a production so fatal to the picturesque throughout the Colony, which we shall find upon enquiry, does duty as the outdoor department of the Sydney Hospital, combined with a well-stocked technological museum. Midway between these two architectural gems lies the Domain cricket ground, where, during the luncheon hour, there is always keen practising at the national game, and excellent matches upon holidays and Saturday afternoons.

Hyde Park, with its well-laid walks, good turf, and rows of shade trees, comes next. Here is a fine statue to Captain Cook, and on Friday afternoons an hour or so is devoted to military music. Then we pass on to Moore Park, with its racecourse and splendid Association cricket ground, and adjoining it is Centennial Park, once known as the Lachlan swamp. A fitting monument of the centenary of the colony. Its years are, of course, very tender, and it is only just possible to estimate what it may become in course of time. It is, I believe, over six hundred acres in extent, has well laid drives, is a splendid place for horse exercise, and is ornamented by statuary, some from the antique, others representing famous men, some of which, the statues, not the men, the too fastidious art critic may class as being more of an entertaining than highly artistic nature, which, however, may be what was

B

aimed at in their production. The Zoological Gardens hard by the southern end of the Centennial Park are fair of their kind, but hardly equal to those in Melbourne ; of the remaining parks and reserves in the city and suburbs it is hardly necessary to make particular mention.

A feature in the Domain and Hyde Park especially, are the homeless dogs which one sees in great numbers, and to "class" a dozen of them would puzzle an expert. They are in many cases covered with mange, and a pitiable sight generally. They are abjectly miserable for the most part, and have a sort of "throw-myself-upon-the-mercy-of-the-Court" look about them at the best of times. Nowhere but Sydney would they be allowed to wander as they do.*

I should not omit to mention the National Park of New South Wales, a magnificent reserve of not less than thirty-six thousand acres, 17 miles south of Sydney by rail. It has a frontage to the Pacific of nine miles, is composed of table land for the most part, varied by deep and picturesque gullies, and, with the exception of its roadways, presents the features of some of the wildest parts of the Australian bush. It is well watered, and special efforts have been made to stock its various creeks with trout from New Zealand waters, where the "spotted

* In certain parts of Sydney also, apparently nomad goats will be noticed, whose haughty and independent bearing is in strong contrast to that of the homeless, ownerless dogs. Their adopted dietary scale, is, like Sam Weller's knowledge of London, "extensive and peculiar." I have, on one occasion, remarked an aged goat, presumably of a literary turn, stripping advertisement posters off a board, and eating them with infinite relish, though there was green food at hand.

beauties" have flourished so well. A lengthy description would fail to do justice to the Park, which should form one of the first trips out of Sydney and its immediate suburbs.

There is not a plethora of fine public buildings in Sydney, as far as my humble ideas go. The city, as I have said, preserves a homelike aspect, with little to wonder at or especially admire in the way of architectural beauty, such at least as one might expect to meet with in a new country.

The Town Hall, the scene of civic festivities, with the exception of its concert-room possessing the largest organ in the world, has nothing particularly attractive about it, while, hard by, is the Protestant Cathedral of St. Andrew, a fine building, the effect of which is somewhat marred by its nearness to the Town Hall. The Roman Catholic Cathedral is in College Street, opposite Hyde Park, a fine open site. The building is upon a very grand scale, but very far from complete as yet. The other churches, chapels, and places for public worship call, I think, for no special comment. Government House is by no means so prominent a figure in Sydney as it is in her sister city on the oderiferous Yarra, and last, though by no means least, is the University of Sydney, which stands on high ground in the suburb of Newtown, a very conspicuous figure in the southern view of the city. But perhaps the Sydney General Post and Telegraph Office, lying between George and Pitt streets, may be said to be the finest building in the city.

It has, now that the buildings which stood immediately in front of it have been removed, an exceedingly fine appearance, though the immense height of the slender tower which springs from the centre, rather dwarfs the building itself, while its depth is not great. On the Pitt street front the visitor must not fail to notice the famous Post Office carvings, which are to Sydney what the Elgin Marbles or Treasures of Nineveh are to the British Museum; Venus of Milo, to the Louvre; Thorwaldsen's Works, chaste and cold as the Icelandic snows amongst which their sculptor first drew breath, to quaint, quiet Copenhagen; or the Art Treasures of the Hermitage to the capital of the Great White Tsar. They are simply unique.

Chapter III.

SYDNEY RESTAURANTS, HOTELS, AND BOARDING HOUSES.

Eating and sleeping are somewhat necessary though perhaps prosaic items in the programme of life, and, to those who travel with but slender purses, the expense thereof is a matter of grave importance. So I trust to be excused for giving details which may be useful, if not exactly artistic, with respect to such matters.

Now I think the man would, indeed, be hard to please who is dissatisfied with the fare and accommodation generally provided for him in Sydney, or with the price he is asked to pay for it: whether he patronises the leading hotel, or pays the modest sum of sixpence at such restaurants as provide a substantial meal at that figure.

It may be that in our first essay of Sydney restaurants, we would prefer to look in at one more of the middle-class style, where we might observe how a large portion of the community lunches or dines, as the case may be, and study both the eaters and what they eat. Certain peculiarities, at least they may seem so to the travelling Briton, attach to both in America. One is curious, therefore, to see whether, in this new country, new habits and new ideas as to food have been formed; whether, for instance, in the summer heats, they discuss beef and mutton in orthodox English style, and the production of

Bass or Guinness, or favour fish, fowl, salads, fruit, and such like, and drink their native wines.

It is a summer's day we will say, and the thermometer indicates well over 80° in the shade. Here is a middle-class, indeed you ought to call it a superior, restaurant — where your dinner will cost you one shilling, whereas you can dine well for ninepence, and also, as I will show you later, for sixpence. The bill of fare is a plenteous one, and you learn from it that you can have soup, a choice of fish, joint, entrèe, or grill, pie or pudding, with tea, coffee, and frequently aerated waters, all good of its kind, for, as I have already stated, one shilling *

But on this hot day, one more provocative of thirst than even the semblance of hunger, you are likely to notice no lack of appetite amongst the diners. They dispose of what they have before them right manfully, and go through the bill of fare in workmanlike fashion, and yet you may venture to make a shrewd guess that the majority had a more substantial breakfast than the English business man eats, or can perhaps always afford to eat, say a steak, or chops with a delicate accompaniment of sausages or eggs, and when their business is done, the majority will likewise take tram, 'bus, or rail for the Sydney people have a holy horror of wearing out shoe leather by walking, to their respective homes, there to recruit exhausted nature by a little delicate attention in the shape of a dinner, or a "thick" tea, which general method of recuperation will make you understand, perhaps, when we come to deal with the question of the meat supply, how so much meat is

* "Tipping" or feeing in restaurants is not usual in Sydney.

consumed in the Colony, as statisticians say is the case. The drinking of tea with all meals, as a rule, does not find favour in the eyes of the Britisher, at all events at first sight, but it is an exceedingly general habit. A fair number drink beer with their dinner—half-a-pint of "British" on draught being threepence: many also would perhaps patronize their native wines, but salaries in Sydney, outside of Government "billets," are not princely, so all "extras" have to be watched with a careful eye; hence the drinking of tea, though many take it from choice—the native born especially—may in some cases be induced by a desire to economize.

Another matter, I think, is to be noticed with pleasure, after American experience, and that is that even in the hottest weather the Australians do not consider it necessary to swill their internal economy with glass after glass of iced water, neither are they addicted to the consumption of vinegary pickles in profusion, both of which habits, the former I humbly consider as silly and culpable as it is unnecessary, must tend largely to produce the dyspeptic wrecks which may be not unfrequently noticed amongst our American cousins.

To finish our day, if not inclined for a heavy meal, we can get an excellent cup of tea with scone or muffin for as low a sum as threepence, and later on, if disposed to try the oysters of New South Wales or New Zealand, a small plate of the bi-valves with roll and butter will only cost us sixpence, or we can experiment upon capital prawns or crayfish at a small cost.

To run the gamut of eating-houses we will, having risen early this bright morning, see what can be done for sixpence, as far as breakfast is concerned, at one of the restaurants referred to in the opening lines of this chapter, which I may term a special feature in Sydney.

The external appearance of most of such establishments as bear on their windows the legend "all meals sixpence," is, perhaps, not particularly inviting, but the table at which we take our seat is covered with a fairly clean, if coarse, cloth, and we must not be over particular. We can commence our meal with good porridge and fresh milk, and, having selected tea or coffee, as our tastes incline, we listen, somewhat bewildered, to the verbal avalanche in which the brusque waiter rehearses the delicacies which await us, for printed bills of fare there are not. We select say a chop and sausage, and when all is finished it is impossible to deny that we have had a substantial and wholesome meal; here also we can dine for three courses, and have tea on the same substantial lines as breakfast, on each occasion, as I have said, being only required to disburse the small sum of sixpence.

One other gastronomical feat we can achieve for sixpence. At noon or earlier, for there is a great "rush" towards the luncheon hour, we will go to Chinnery's, in Hunter Street, and there taste some Australian fish, it is always of the best, and freshest, and beautifully cooked, a small plate with roll and butter, neatly served, will cost us only the aforementioned coin. And now, having seen what those with slender purses can obtain for a small sum, we can fly higher, and at the Café Français, Günnsler's, Paris House, and other restaurants, will, I think, have no reason to complain of what is set before us, or what we are called upon to pay.

Next, as to good hotels, whatever there might at one time have been, there is now no lack of them. The Grosvenor may perhaps be said to take the lead, then follow Petty's, the Imperial, Pfahlerts, the Exchange, the Empire, the Oxford, the Royal, Roberts' Hotel, and others; all have their admirers, and with nearly all, the rule is, to make a charge of so much per day to include everything, the meals being generally served in *table d'hote* style. The minimum charge for first-class hotels is about ten shillings per day, though perhaps twelve may be nearer the average; this includes bedroom, attendance, and three excellent and ample meals; for a stay of any duration special terms may be made. Then again there are numbers of less pretentious hostelries in the city and suburbs, where good accommodation is to be had at prices of from two guineas weekly downwards, the lowest price at which a bed of any kind is obtainable in Sydney is one shilling; the sixpenny restaurants, already alluded to, in nearly all cases have beds on hire at the price in question. The Australia, by the way, a large and imposing hotel, in Castlereagh street, was not opened when I left the "Harbour City."

Last and not least there are the coffee palaces, as they are termed in Australia; we should very probably call them temperance hotels in England. At their head I should place the Metropole Hotel; then comes the Grand Central Coffee Palace, and others. At these hotels the minimum price for a single bedroom for one night is half-a-crown to three shillings inclusive, no stupid charge for attendance, and a bedroom may be secured at a low weekly rate, if any stay is meditated. On the ground floor there are excellent restaurants where all meals can be had, well and cleanly served, for about one shilling each, at the Metropole rather more, and bars whereat single cups of tea or coffee with light refreshments may be obtained. At upstairs restaurants the boarders dine, &c., and such of the public as may elect to do so. The accommodation at these coffee palaces is extremely clean, and one is apt to think that they might do well in this country, and do some real good in the cause of temperance as well.

No doubt, however, many will desire to obtain as soon as they can, some permanent lodging at the least possible expense, and even the married couple may shrink at first from housekeeping. To such is open an endless variety of boarding-houses, furnished apartments being not nearly so general as they are in England. No doubt the high rents asked for houses in Sydney prevent people in most instances from taking a larger house than they can decently squeeze their belongings into, thus they have no superfluous rooms. As I have said elsewhere they frequently, if they have a room to spare, have one or more boarders, who live to all intents and purposes on the same footing with the members of the family.

Of boarding-houses there is an ample choice, both in the heart of the city, and throughout the suburbs. There is no lack of accommodation advertised in the daily papers, to which anyone desirous of securing quarters at once, can refer, but anyone strolling about in the most casual manner in the city, cannot fail to notice the frequent card denoting "Vacancies" which, of course, shows that the establishment is a boarding-house, such being the case, I need not say more than briefly add that if any special accommodation is required, a short advertisement will not fail to elicit numerous replies.

To begin at the bottom of the scale of charges, the working-man can get good, clean sleeping quarters, and washing for about five shillings weekly, at the lowest, and board at the rate of nine shillings and sixpence weekly, for three substantial meals daily. Very good board may be obtained at one pound or one guinea weekly (I use the word as meaning meals and bedroom). For twenty-five shillings very superior accommodation may be had, while for thirty or thirty-five shillings everything of the best, including a well kept table, is to be obtained The laundry charges in Sydney are not particularly dear, while the work is for the most part exceedingly well done. Of course anyone in delicate health would probably require certain surroundings, and in advertising, he had better, as indeed had anyone, state the style of accommodation he requires, separate room for instance, or whatever is wanted, and the price he is prepared to pay.

The breakfast bell at most boarding houses rings at a tolerably early hour, but the late comer will mostly find wherewithal to satisfy himself. Luncheon is also an elastic meal, but at dinner, those who wish to enjoy it, should endeavour to be punctual. As to the company one meets, there are of all sorts, but in time, the gentlemen who like ladies' society, and those who do not, and likewise those who are "musical," as well as those who are not much given to "concord of sweet sounds," suit themselves either in mixed, cheery, lively company, or in the greater freedom and comparative quiet of bachelor quarters. Taken altogether, I think boarding house life is far better for a young fellow than existence in "diggings," as bachelor apartments are not unfrequently termed.

There may be many, however, who do not care for boarding houses, and may, owing to the nature of their engagements, be unable to keep up the regular boarding house meal hours. Such I would advise to look out for a neat balcony room, and arrange to have breakfast therein, taking the remainder of their meals at restaurants, the tariffs of which, I think, I have given at sufficient length. For the rent of such a room they would have to pay not less than ten shillings weekly. The married couple, also "without encumbrance," might follow this plan, and make such terms as they think will suit them. They would be able to arrange for use of kitchen, and cater and cook for themselves if it is desirable for them to economise.

Chapter IV.

HOUSES IN SYDNEY—HOUSE RENT—HOUSE-KEEPING—THE BUTCHER'S BILL—FURNISHING—COST OF LIVING GENERALLY.

It is estimated, I believe, by those exceedingly clever people who make up all manner of statistics concerning everything and everybody, that no inconsiderable portion of the people that inhabit the earth, not only dispense with any sort of dwelling whatever, but have actually never imbibed, or at least evinced, the slightest desire to provide themselves with anything of the kind. Such a mode of life has, of course, obvious advantages; but it tends, without doubt, to render one's habits exceedingly primitive, and it is certainly desirable, not to say much more respectable, to provide oneself with a dwelling of some sort.

There are few cities in either hemisphere so liberally endowed with natural advantages as is Sydney, and the greater number of those that view them will regret, I think, that so rare a gathering of nature's favours should suffer from want of taste or architectural shortcomings upon the part of those who add their quota of residences to the ever growing city. Of course, in considering this question, reference is made more to middle and lower class dwellings, in which expense is a great consideration to the builders or occupiers of such property.

In and around Sydney, very often in most out-of-the way places, we come occasionally upon one of the much older houses, of what we might term the Macquarie epoch, standing amongst its more modern fellows, which suggests itself as an ideal dwelling for a semi-tropical climate. It is conspicuous by its high-pitched shingled roof, and cool, ample verandahs, shadowed by the spreading branches of the Norfolk Island pine, or that dark leaved, umbrageous evergreen, the Moreton Bay fig-tree. The lawn is trim, the garden well kept, in which the bright scarlet of the waratah, the graceful droop of the banana leaf, and the tall feathery bamboo are as novel as they are pleasing to the English eye.

Turn now to the production of to-day. Of course land has increased in value in giant strides, but look at the miserable plots which are offered in Sydney suburbs to the intending builder of a modest little house as "highly eligible sites." Sometimes the frontage will be only twenty feet or less, on which it is certainly a puzzle how to erect a presentable dwelling, and one, at the same time, suited to the requirements created by the climate. The "commodious detached villa residence," therefore (as advertised) is squeezed into a narrow strip of land, which the "land boom" of a few years back has rendered so dear, that the Sydney public are not expected, I suppose, to buy more than one meagre plot. A miserable, narrow nondescript building is the result, with the tiniest verandah conceivable, in which the "harmless, necessary cat" can scarcely sun itself. Of glaring stucco, it is tastefully relieved by highly ornate railings to the said verandah, brave in blue and gold, any shade tree that grew near has been ruthlessly sacrificed, and there stands the modern Sydney suburban villa, a sight to make the angels weep.

Then there is the weather-board, or, as it is termed in advertisements, the W. B. Cottage, which, save for the fire-place and foundations, is innocent of brick and mortar. It is, of necessity, hotter in summer and more chilly in the winter months than a building of brick or stone; and owing to its component parts acting as excellent conductors of sound, it is, unless detached, hardly as quiet as some would desire. Still, for anyone who is fond of company, and cannot afford to entertain, a weather board dwelling, in a terrace of the same, has its advantages. If the gentleman on the right practices on the flute, cornet, or the soothing trombone, his performances can be enjoyed to the full by the company-loving individual; and should the lady on the left be apt to lecture her husband, who, in his turn, comes home drunk and smashes the furniture, as a practical illustration of the benefit of such admonition, he can enjoy such conjugal amenities unseen and unnoticed.

Lastly, before coming to the question of rents, it seems a pity that, in building up new suburbs, the city or municipal architect should be without considerable power in the matter. Liberty of the subject is all very well, but it is not right that, in building on the frontage of public thoroughfares, either the professional builder, or the amateur, who for the nonce turns architect, should be allowed to set the canons of good taste at defiance. I believe that in America certain architects issue drawings, working plans, and specifications, of smaller dwellings, for town and country, charging a moderate fee for the same. Competition in this would lead, I am sure, to greater taste and comfort being displayed in smaller dwellings generally, and, in the case of Sydney, tend much to beautify the suburbs of so happily-situated a city.

Now to secure a house—terrace, semi-detached, or detached There are plenty of advertisements of houses to let in the daily papers. and there are numerous house and property agents who will be glad to supply our wants; and, on interviewing any one of them, it is more than probable that anyone coming from provincial or country England especially, will be startled at the rent demanded in Sydney and its suburbs.

Beginning with the least pretentious houses. say a small one-storied cottage with four living rooms besides the kitchen, which is not unfrequently built simply of galvanized iron apart from the house—the weekly rent will be 11s. or 12s., including rates and taxes; for a fair terrace or semi-detached house, 30s. or £2 weekly; for what might be termed a good detached house of two stories, £120 to £175 yearly; while a ten-roomed house, with grounds and stabling, would command £300 a year. As to furnished houses, there are few to be had under £3 10s. to £4 per week.

Many people would like a nice detached cottage; for these there is a great demand, and they are not to be had, say with six living rooms, under 25s. to 35s. weekly. As these prices may seem high to some people, I should, perhaps, state that I write with authority upon the subject, and I will mention two instances that came especially before my notice, to illustrate the value of property in Sydney One was a question of rent. The house was a very commodious one in Macquarie street, opposite the Sydney Hospital; the rent asked was £400 a year, with rates and taxes to about another £40. The other was a question of the value of some freehold property in a very aristocratic part of Sydney, with a water frontage: the house, detached, of course, contained ten rooms, had stabling, &c., and stood in about two and a-half acres of ground; the price asked was £10,000. I was confidently told that £9,000 would be taken.

The question may naturally be asked if salaries generally, apart from government "billets," are not high, how do people manage to pay such rents? That I cannot say, but the number of houses in and around Sydney, for which two and three pounds weekly are paid, must somewhat astonish a stranger. I have remarked elsewhere that a spare room is not unfrequently utilised for accommodating a boarder or two.

The butcher's bill is a far less formidable affair than "at home." The following prices were chalked on a board outside a butchers shop in a main thoroughfare through which I passed on one of my last strolls through Sydney streets:—

	PER LB.		PER LB.
Whole or half Sheep	1½d.	Beef	2d. to 3d.
Forequarter ,,	1½d.	Pork	5d.
Hindquarter ,,	2d.	Corned Beef	from 1½d.
Chops ,,	2½d.	Veal	3d. to 4d.

Beef and Mutton Sausages, 2½d. per lb.

Bargains may be struck on Saturday evenings. Poultry is, I think, cheaper than in England. Of game there is little, but wild fowl is abundant in the winter season. Hares and rabbits are little used as articles of food.

c

In the country mutton and beef run about 3d. to 4d. per lb.

That next important item, the grocer's bill, is much about the same as in England, the principal items will run *about* as follows:—

Tea.. ...1/6 and upwards per lb.	Sugar ....2d. to 2½d. per lb.
Coffee...1/- ,, ,,	(if other groceries are bought therewith)
Bread.. 3d. and 4d. per 2lb. loaf	
Bacon.. 9d. and upwards per lb.	Tinned Salmon .... ⎫
Butter...8d. ,, ,,	,, Lobster .... ⎬ 9d. to 10d. per tin.
Candles ....6d. to 7d. per lb.	,, Kippd. Herrings.. ⎪
Cheese...8d. and upwards per lb.	,, Findon Haddocks ⎭
Jams, Marmalade, &c, from 5d. per tin.	" Fresh Herrings, 7d. per tin
Pickles.. 7d. per pt and upwards	Eggs...9d. per dozen, and upwards
Sauce...small bottle 6d. and upwards	
	Salt............ .. fine, 1d. per lb.
Soap ....4½d. per bar	Flour ..13/- and 15/- per 100 lbs.

As to vegetables, we are, in England, frequently blamed for not making use of them more extensively than we do, and probably the people of New South Wales, considering their climate, are still more open to reproach upon the subject. But here, the question of expense steps in, and the housekeeper must look carefully at the large item which the free use of vegetables would imply. For the most part they are purchased from hawkers (generally the producers), who, as a rule, are Chinamen, and I deal with the subject as also with the fruits of the Colony in a separate chapter. Suffice it to say that the best potatoes come from the neighbourhood of Warnambool in Victoria, and from Tasmania, the price is about 6/- to 8/- the cwt. Good cabbages and cauliflowers are 6d. to 9d. each; onions 2d. per lb.; pumpkins and tomatoes are plentiful and cheap; carrots, turnips, &c., are sold in bunches at 6d. each and upwards. The price of other vegetables, peas, asparagus, indeed all that you buy, depends upon what you are able to pay, and the Chinaman's conscience, which latter is somewhat of an unknown quantity. Dealing with shops is not much of an improvement, as these are mostly in the hands of Italians.

To the fish of the Colony I have also devoted a special chapter, but for housekeeping purposes it will be sufficient, perhaps, to note that there is a deplorable absence, with one or two exceptions, of good fishmonger's shops in Sydney. Such sea-fish as are caught, are despatched in the evening to the wholesale fish market at Woolloomooloo, to be sold at a very early hour next morning— the sales actually commencing at 5.30 a.m., and in a couple of hours or so the day's business is over. The fish are sold in small lots. Hawkers attend the sales, and are soon on their respective "beats," and to make anything of a living they are of course obliged to ask a good deal in excess of wholesale prices. The Italians hold a number of fish and oyster bars, and are amongst the principal buyers at the wholesale market. It is hard to give an idea as to price. The Sydney Fresh Food and Ice Company, however, who are large retailers of milk, are also importers of fresh fish (frozen) from New Zealand, and deliver any fish ordered the day before, with the milk, at six to seven a.m.; their lowest price, I think, is 6d. per lb. The cost of milk generally in Sydney is now, I believe, raised to 4d. per quart.

Tea may be called the beverage of New South Wales. As a rule it is tea with every meal, and herein, no doubt,

lies the great secret of saving in household expenses.*
Setting aside the question of whether so much tea drinking is healthy or not, the habit of drinking it at all meals in place of beer or wine must save a large amount annually. British ales and stout in bottles are obtainable in quantities of not less than 1 dozen, at 7/- and 9/6 per dozen pints and quarts respectively, as the lowest figures. An immense quantity of ale is brewed in the Colony and retailed in Sydney at threepence per pint. Colonial wines are too well known in England to need description. Prices range from 1/- per quart upwards. Foreign wines are somewhat dear owing to the duty of 5/- per gallon imposed on still and 10/- on sparkling wines, which means, in the case of champagne, an addition of £1 per dozen to the shippers' price. Spirits are from 40/- per one dozen case upwards.

Household furniture is, perhaps, the especial "bogey" of the young married couple—or rather of those about to marry—and, no doubt, is a very necessary item. No one will, I think, deny that cheerful surroundings and a display of taste in the choice and disposition of household furniture are exceeding beneficial to anyone in that state of tension which mental exertion creates, or the lassitude which follows bodily toil, and it is equally patent to most people that lavish expenditure is not required to effect this. On the contrary, a room can be neatly and very cheaply furnished with a pleasing, I might term it soothing effect, which the most gorgeous efforts of the upholsterer might fail to convey.

* The estimated annual consumption of tea per head of the population in New South Wales exceeds 8 lbs.

COST OF FURNITURE.

In a climate such as that of Sydney, where the verandah is, at least during many months of the year, the favourite spot; where open windows are necessary, and dust is by no means unknown, the least "stuffy" feeling is apt to become in the summer months almost unbearable. Too much carpet, too many hangings, curtains, and too much over elaborate furniture are bad for health and pocket alike, forming cover as they do for a noisome collection of particles of all sorts known by the generic name of "dust" which, during that sage and scientific process dear to housewives under the name of "dusting," "tidying up" and such cognate terms, are set afloat, to fall by the never failing law of gravitation, so soon as the room has been triumphantly "set to rights."

Of course, in Sydney, there are furniture marts, and auctions of all sorts daily, the "time payment" system is also in vogue, and there are local factories, from the catalogue of one of which I take at hazard the following :—

	£	s.	d.
Walnut drawing-room suite, in tapestry and plush, 9 pieces	34	0	0
Dining-room suite, complete, comprising suite in cedar, of nine pieces, covered in real leather; 4ft. 6in. cedar sideboard, with bevelled plate glass back; 3ft. 6in. dinner waggon, and 6ft. extension dining table	45	0	0
Pine bedroom suite, comprising wardrobe, dressing table, washing stand, with towel rail, and two chairs	9	9	0
Half-tester bedstead, very strong	1	7	6
Austrian suite, consisting of settee, two arm and six small chairs	4	15	0

All bedsteads for use in Sydney should be, *at least, half-tester*, so that mosquito curtains may be used in the summer months.

Then there are crockery ware, kitchen requisites, &c., but I think I need not go further into details; freight by sailing vessel is very cheap—and there is plenty of competition among Sydney tradespeople, so that things that are not too bulky are little dearer, if any, than in England, household linen, &c., among the rest. Gas is about 4/- per 1,000 cubic feet. Coal is about 20/- per ton, and wood is greatly used for fires, being obtainable at fairly cheap rates. In the bush they use nothing else.

CHAPTER V.

CONSUMPTION OF MEAT—THE LIVE STOCK RESOURCES OF THE COLONY — THE SYDNEY MEAT SUPPLY—ITS IMPERFECTIONS—THE FROZEN MEAT TRADE.

I have stated in my introductory remarks that "I hope "rather to prove the means of exciting some curiosity or " desire upon the part of my readers to learn something of "the resources of the vast Continent of Australia than to "pose as an authority upon the subject" (of its industries), and this applies most especially to the present chapter, in which I will attempt to describe what may be developed into a gigantic and beneficial industry.

I am compelled to deal to some extent in figures, and they are taken from the Report of the Government Statistician for 1890, the Report of the Minister of Agriculture of the same year, and some from the "Year Book of New South Wales" for 1891, which is compiled from official sources ; and, as it will be understood that, with the exception of Western Australia, stock is continually on the move between the other Colonies, it is necessary to take Australia as a whole in calculating with respect to the live stock generally.

First, before entering into details, it might be of interest to give the amount of meat consumed in different countries, as estimated by Mulhall, the great statistical authority :—

In Australia each inhabitant uses annually	-	276 lbs.
The United States ,,	-	120 ,,
Great Britain ,,	-	105 ,,
France ,,	-	74 ,,
Holland and Belgium ,,	-	69 ,,
Germany ,,	-	69 ,,
Scandinavia ,,	-	67 ,,
Austria ,,	-	64 ,,
Spain ,,	-	49 ,,
Russia ,,	-	48 ,,
Italy ,,	-	23 ,,

Next let us see what the estimated live stock is in Australasia (that is including Tasmania and New Zealand), and, for the sake of comparison, the area of each Colony and its estimated population. The following are the figures up to the end of 1889 :—

NEW SOUTH WALES.

Horses	430,777	Estimated population
Cattle	1,741,592	(including Aborigines) 1,222,200
Sheep	50,106,768	Area of the Colony in
Pigs	237,276	square miles 309,175

QUEENSLAND.

Horses	352,364	Estimated population... 406,658
Cattle	4,872,416	Area of the Colony in
Sheep	14,470,095	square miles 668,224
Pigs	80,730	

SOUTH AUSTRALIA.

Horses	170,515	Estimated population... 324,484
Cattle	324,412	Area of the Colony in
Sheep	6,386,617	square miles............ 903,425
Pigs	106,856	

TASMANIA.

Horses	29,778	Estimated population .. 151,480
Cattle	150,004	Area of the Colony in
Sheep	1,551,429	square miles............ 26,375
Pigs	58,632	

VICTORIA.

Horses	329,335	Estimated population
Cattle	1,394,209	(including Aborigines) 1,118,028
Sheep	10,882,231	Area of the Colony in
Pigs	249,673	square miles............ 87,884

WEST AUSTRALIA.

Horses	42,806	Estimated population... 43,698
Cattle	119,571	Area of the Colony in
Sheep	2,366,681	square miles............ 975,920
Pigs	27,079	

NEW ZEALAND.

Horses	187,382	Estimated population... 620,279
Cattle	815,461	Area of the Colony in
Sheep	15,503,263	square miles............ 104,235
Pigs	369,992	

And for the sake of further comparison for those who have not such matters at their finger ends :—

The estimated area of Great Britain is	121,000	square miles.
,, India	1,400,000	,,
,, United States	3,000,000	,,
,, Australia	3,075,000	,,
,, Europe	3,900,000	,,

all of which, I trust, will not be considered out of place.

Now to see how live stock has increased in New South Wales in twenty years:

1869.		1889.	
Horses	280,811	Horses	430,777
Cattle	1,795,904	Cattle	1,741,592
Sheep	16,848,217	Sheep	50,106,768
Pigs	175,934	*Pigs	237,276

It will be seen, therefore, that the great increase has taken place in sheep only, possessing, as New South Wales does, half the entire stock of Australasia. For exports of beef, we must ask those that require them to go to Queensland, which, according to official estimates, should have, yearly, a surplus of 250,000 to 300,000 head of cattle over and above local demand. Sheep therefore being the speciality of our Colony, we will confine ourselves entirely to them.

The estimated stock is made up of †:—

Merino	48,959,341	Rams	778,313
Longwoolled Crossbreds (Lincoln, Leicester, &c.)...	452,574	Ewes	23,647,106
		Wethers	13,501,656
Crosses of above with Merinos	694,853	Lambs	12,179,693

And lastly, to show the occasional heavy losses caused by droughts and epidemics, I give the losses estimated during the past twenty years, over and above natural

* The breeding of swine, which might well deserve greater attention, has not made much progress, as in 1880 the stock was much greater than at the present time, being 308,205 head.

† Now, Feb. 1892, I believe the stock is estimated at no less than 60,000,000.

decrease (where they have exceeded three millions), in *Australia* only :—

In 1869 the losses from drought and epidemics were - 4,700,000 head
    1871 ,, ,, 5,420,000 ,,
    1876 ,, ,, 5,881,000 ,,
    1877 ,, ,, 11,284,000 ,,
    1881 ,, ,, 3,495,000 ,,
    1882 ,, ,, 3,911,000 ,,
    1883 ,, ,, 4,804,000 ,,
    1884 ,, ,, 15,425,000 ,,
    1886 ,, ,, 4,408,000 ,,
    1888 ,, ,, 7,983,000 ,,

Lastly, the official returns give to Australia, under ordinary circumstances, an *available surplus* of 3,996,000 sheep in an average year, without trenching at all upon local requirements ; and of this we may fairly estimate that New South Wales possesses, say 2,000,000, and there is, I think, little doubt but what the quantity could be very materially increased, if an export trade were started upon a sufficient scale. It may be found difficult, therefore, to give any reason why Sydney, in time, should not boast of possessing the largest meat trade of all the Australian Colonies. It may be added, though the matter is referred to later, that, although the occasional losses are discouraging, the founding of large meat-killing centres at the several railway termini, and at fixed points on the railway lines, might encourage a system of water conservation, which would largely minimise the effects of a continued drought.

We will now see in the first place how Sydney is fed. The humane treatment of beasts, attention to securing the best quality of meat, and the care generally taken to give consumers healthy, nourishing food, are distinctly marks of progress. We shall look for them, I fear, in vain.

Sydney, with her 375,000 inhabitants, or thereabouts, uses, weekly, about 1,500 head of cattle, and not less, so it is estimated, than 15,000 sheep, which are, with few exceptions, trucked from all parts of the Colony to Homebush, a station eight miles from the Sydney terminus. Here they are unloaded, yarded, lotted, sold, and removed some three miles to waiting paddocks, where they are kept some twenty hours, then driven to the abattoirs. At this stage, being in the hands of the "carcase" butcher, they are, as soon as slaughtered, delivered by means of specially constructed vans to the retail butcher, the fellmongers and others buying and taking delivery of the head, skin, loose fat and offal generally, to receive the usual treatment of boiling down, dressing, &c. All refuse not merchantable offers somewhat of a difficult problem to the authorities as to how it is to be satisfactorily dealt with.

Such is the ordinary programme, respecting which, lest it be thought I write too strongly or in exaggerated terms, I will proceed to give the exact words of the Official Report, estimating, in the first place, or giving rather the official estimate* that in the case of stock sent from Bourke to Sydney, beasts are on the average 7 days 5 hours "without any food whatever, and sometimes "without water," and "from this it will be seen that a "considerable portion of 1,500 head of cattle and 15,000

---

* See Report of Minister for Mines and Agriculture, Sydney, 5th May, 1890, appendix G, page 17.

ABUSE OF LIVE STOCK.

"sheep are, week after week, subjected to the terrible
"torture of five, six, and seven days starvation and some-
"times more, till the cattle are to be seen at the abattoirs
"with their heads hanging down, their bellies tucked
"up to their backs, and looking utterly miserable and
"wretched.

"Nor is this all, the poor animals in trucking are
"terrified, beaten, and bruised, and when in the truck
"they push and horn each other. The stopping and
"shunting often throw them down, and some of them
"are not unfrequently trampled to death. The losses of
"cattle on the train, and the bruses on the ribs, hips and
"rump (so noticeable on their bodies when killed), show
"conclusively the cruelty now inflicted on the animals
"under the live stock trade, and, with the terrible starva-
"tion which that system entails, cries aloud for a thorough
"change."

To the foregoing I have only to add, if anyone thinks
it needs supplementing, that much of the transport in
question takes place during great heat day and night,
which must terribly aggravate the suffering of the ill-starred
brutes. In addition to this both cattle and sheep are
naturally much more wild than we ever perhaps see them
in England. Was no notice taken of such a Report in
the New South Wales Parliament? one feels inclined to
ask. I am not aware that anything more serious than a
passing reference was evoked, if that.

Bushmen visiting Sydney and English visitors are inclined to disparage the quality of the meat consumed
there. They say it lacks flavour, firmness, and satisfying
qualities, and, as a rule, butchers and housekeepers find

that it is soon tainted. Is it to be wondered at? Why some of the meat can be barely wholesome!

Now, apart from humanitarianism, leaving out all thought of the question of cruelty inflicted upon the "beasts that perish," considering the matter solely from a monetary point of view, it has not even the merit of being business-like. The official report says, that during the longest journeys, by the worry, the knocking about, the long, weary fast, and maddening thirst, a bullock will lose one-eighth of its weight—the best of the meat.

The question then arises, What can be done to avoid this, to lessen the cruelty, to benefit owners of stock, and to provide better meat? The answer is:—

1.—Up country centres on the railways for killing.

2.—Refrigerating cars or trucks—of which more than one style has been successfully experimented with.

3.—Ample cold storage at the terminus.

And such a system would not only greatly facilitate the supply of meat for local requirements, involving, as it would, as little cruelty as possible, but give everyone greater value for their money, and better meat might mean a less consumption. Furthermore, which is of great importance, it would establish the means of working what might be a vast export trade on a proper basis, and here, I might as well add, that people will be inclined to own that such meat as is now placed upon the London market from New South Wales can hardly be accepted as a fair criterion, or as a standard by which New South Wales mutton should be rightly judged, and if some prejudice exists against it, it is not unreasonable to attribute a great portion thereof to circumstances not beyond control. Let it be distinctly understood that the idea of establishing up country centres is one which has been strongly recommended by the officials connected with the Department of Stock, in order to mitigate the evils connected with and arising from the Live Stock trade; also as a means of securing station owners a better return, giving the public better meat, and providing a suitable basis for an export trade, and not only will it develop the resources of and encourage production in New South Wales, but it might be reasonably expected to bring the *Cattle of Queensland* to the Northern, and *Victorian Stock* to the Southern termini.

First as to the centres in question. They will have to contain stock yards, and all appurtenances for slaughtering, and chilling the meat upon the latest principles. The carcases to be conveyed to Sydney by refrigerating cars, of which more than one pattern has already been successfully tried in the Colonies. At the Sydney terminus the carcases can be, in part, removed at once by the vans for delivery to the retailer, or placed with the meat required for export, in cold storage, until wanted for home consumption or shipment.

Such cars could take, it is estimated, the skins, offal, &c, for fellmongering and boiling down purposes, at, including the carcase, a less rate than the live bullock or sheep is now carried. No doubt, however, in time, such establishments would be transferred to the slaughtering centres.

The cars would also be adapted for taking return freight, which the live stock trucks are not, as a rule, and as the centres would, in addition to fellmongering and boiling down, very probably encourage tinning, salting, and tanning industries, the Railway Commissioners would be distinct gainers by the traffic the system would encourage.

It would remove many people from Sydney, thus serving to somewhat decentralize the Colony; in other words, spread the inhabitants a little more, for one-third of the entire population of the Colony is herded together in Sydney; such I respectfully think would be a great gain. It would also permit of experiments being made as to whether the plague of rabbits and hares could be turned to account; while the refrigerating cars would encourage such industries as that of pig and poultry farming at a greater distance from the city. In the butter producing districts also it would facilitate the export of the summer surplus, which should find a good market in England during the corresponding winter months, while milk could be better conveyed to the city or butter factories.

The locality for such centres should, of course, be chosen with an eye to the provision of good waiting paddocks, in which travelled stock would be able to recover condition. The selling of stock at such centres need, I think, be no obstacle, and the removal of the sale yards from Homebush, and the slaughtering generally, from Sydney, would, I am sure, free the neighbourhood from a terrible nuisance.

As to the conveying of meat to the English market, steamers come to Sydney to discharge cargo, provided with the most ample requirements for carrying chilled meat, but go to New Zealand to get a cargo thereof.

To show the part that Australia plays in the London meat market, I will instance the Board of Trade returns of the imports of foreign mutton for the first six months in 1891. They are:—

    From New Zealand .... 485,637 cwts.
         Australia .... 72,548 ,,

The estimated stock of sheep as already given is:—

    In New Zealand .... 15,503,263 sheep.
         Australia .... 85,769,821 ,,

Comment, I think, is unnecessary.

Taking Messrs. Nelson Brothers' report for 10th July, 1891, I find the following:—

"The market is well supplied with Queensland and Sydney sheep, and this class of mutton feels severely the competition of cheap supplies from New Zealand and the River Plate."

I think most people will be able to form an opinion from what I have written and quoted, whether New South Wales mutton has ever had a really fair trial in the London market. Another thing, spasmodic and intermittent supplies of such an article, as they are at present for the most part, must be fatal to its success, as I take it that the assurance of an adequate and regular supply of a thoroughly merchantable commodity, must inevitably be the precursor of a steady and increasing demand for the same.

CHAPTER VI.

VEGETABLES AND MILK SUPPLY IN NEW SOUTH WALES — FRUITS, THEIR COST — SUPERVISION OF DAIRIES.

The semi-tropical position of Sydney, the bright blue sky and powerful sun will, no doubt, raise expectations in the breast of the new arrival, who may be familiar with southern Europe, of a magnificent display and supply of the fruits of the earth, in which I fear he will be disappointed.

His imagination may lead him away to some market-place in Spain or Italy, or it may be in southernmost France, with its brightly-coloured awnings, under which he sees the life of the city in the delicious air of the new-born day. Here are gathered the early-uprising housewives of all degrees. Some with well-filled purses, others anxious as to how they may best spend the meagre sum they have, but all chattering and bargaining with the fullest measure of noise and laughter.

Here are, in their season, heaps of great melons, blood-red pomegranates, figs bursting with ripeness, luscious grapes, oranges with their dark-green coat fast changing to the golden livery the children of the north best know. But away with the picture. Our desire is not realized in sunny New South Wales. We might echo the complaint of the sluggard. We have been awakened too soon. The hour, we can plainly see, is an unearthly one for Sydney. English manners and customs prevail. The market is a very poor one. The streets present long vistas of shuttered windows, and are almost deserted. The housewives and people generally are evidently not early risers. We must wait a couple of hours and more, though it is 6 a.m., before the life of the city is warmed into action.

How, then, are the daily wants supplied? Well, in nine cases out of ten, by the peripatetic Chinaman. He may be the possessor of a horse and spring cart, or in a more humble way of business as a market gardener and retailer. If the latter, he is provided with a stout "slat" of bamboo, from both ends of which hang baskets containing his stock-in-trade. In the morning the weight he carries is something very great, but his burden lightens as his sales multiply. He gets along at a great pace, however, his mode of progression being an indescribable shuffle like that of a bear on its hind legs. He comes past our verandah, lowers his baskets, "unships" his bamboo:—

"Wanchee cabbage?"

"No cabbage, John. Any carrots?" you casually enquire

"Plenty ca-allot, belly fine ca-allot?"

(The Chinaman, as some may not know, pronounces v as b, he also substitutes l for r, thus "carrot" becomes "callot," "rice" he terms "lice," "very" becomes "belly," and so on. The habit is not pretty, I am willing to concede, but it is one for which I am, of course, in no way responsible.)

"How much?"

"Ni-i-ne-pencee," he drawls, holding out at the same time a tiny bunch, which is nothing more or less than the deadliest possible insult in vegetable form, at the price.

" I'll give you sixpence."

He gazes slightly upwards. Talk of the Sphynx with its marvellously contemptous look!

"Staring straight on, with calm eternal eyes."

It is an open book to his placid features.

" Seespencee, al-li-i-te," (allright) and the especial treasure of the vegetable world is yours.

Looking, however, into John's baskets, or even the cart of the more pretentious huckster, we find no great variety, and the prices are high. There are potatoes, cauliflowers, carrots, parsnips, peas, and asparagus in their season. Tomatoes are cheap enough. The banana is ever present; and when ripe, apples, peaches perhaps, and plums. Grapes are cheap enough during the brief time they are " in." I have known them sold as low as twopence or even one penny per lb. Oranges are sometimes very low in price as well. The loquat and passion fruit may be new to the English visitor—they are neither of them a great acquisition.

But, as to fruits generally, let it not be understood that I wish to give the productions of the tropics the place of honour, this it is far from my wish to do. The novelty of tropical scenery, its surroundings, and accompaniments, generally create a great impression upon the traveller who sees all for the first time, and he is nearly always prone—it seems, in fact, fashionable, to bestow endless praises upon tropical fruits.

But, setting aside the fact that you must, of necessity, be much more careful in the eating of fruit in the tropics than in more temperate zones, take two dishes, fill one with the fruits of the tropics, the other with those grown in less torrid lands. In the first, place the mango, the mangosteen, the custard apple, the shaddock, the banana, the alligator pear, the guava, the pommelo, and others. Fill the second with velvety peaches and golden apricots, satin-skinned nectarines, pears, apples (red, streaked, and russet), with the tribe of plums—their king, the luscious greengage, not being forgotten; add a cluster of grapes, some ripe cherries, strawberries, and other kindred dainties—and which takes the palm? I have omitted several, no doubt, having named them merely from memory, but they may suffice for the illustration.

As to the shops in the city, at which fruit and vegetables are offered for sale, they are, for the most part, in the hands of Italians; I might say completely, without exaggeration. The usual display is of a somewhat beggarly nature, and the staple article may be said to be the banana. It is almost wholly an imported fruit, and does not ripen except in the northern part of the Colony, though it flourishes in parts of Queensland, which is frequently termed, in the Colonies, Banana-land. The greatest supply and best quality comes from the Fiji Islands, and the steamers, which make the passage thence to Sydney in about five or six days, will bring as many as

20,000 bunches at a time. The usual retail price is a dozen or fourteen for sixpence, though they are sometimes hawked about, on the arrival of a big shipment, as low as four dozen for sixpence. Of fruits of the soil, apples are dear; no doubt the Italians combine to keep up prices. As an instance, during the autumn of 1891 (Feb.-April), at eighty or ninety miles distance, I was told it would not pay to send apples to Sydney, they being extremely plentiful. One particular kind, which was fairly abundant, I found retailed at twopence each in the city.

Magnificent oranges are grown at Parramatta, 14 miles from Sydney, and also around Hornsby, a very nice neighbourhood, 12 miles north of Sydney, but rather further by rail at present. Whether the Colony, having her own sugar plantations on the northern rivers, will ever even make her own marmalade, is a question which may be asked, but I fear only answered in the negative at present. There is, I might also add, fresh, dried, and candied fruit imported annually into the Colony, to the value of about a quarter of a million sterling, which is an eloquent, and fairly substantial proof that there is little desire to encourage home productions, as far as fruit is concerned.

As to the vegetable supply, the Chinaman is, to nearly all intents and purposes, the market gardener — not only of New South Wales, but of the whole of Australia. It is his life-work to a great extent, in such little as I have seen of the interior of his own country, and there is little doubt that as a gardener, and likewise as a hard worker, he is, perhaps, without an equal, though some of the ideas he carries out in the way of fertilization might be advantageously modified. In Sydney, therefore, it may be said that the people, for the most part, must eat such vegetables as he finds it pays him to grow, and pay such prices as he cares to accept.

On middle-class tables in the Colony, at the least, we might look in vain for such plants as the several artichokes, the egg plant, seakale and the toothsome salsify, the endive also might be grown and used in a land where a cool salad would be always grateful; indeed, I believe it is only of recent years that the tomato has come into general use. It is easy to find fault as a rule upon most subjects, but with respect to New South Wales on the score of expense, meat and vegetables stand reversed as regards price to what they do elsewhere. The cookery is therefore wanting in originality. Meat is abundant and is absolutely the cheapest form of food—meat roast or boiled, grilled or fried, is monotonous, but satisfying. Vegetables, in comparison, are dear, and to make a feature of them is apt to be characterized in most households as "a bother;" so the lover of vegetables in New South Wales, unless he has ample means, must wait, and hope, as they say in melodrama, that "a time may come."

A few words on the milk supply may not be out of place, as it is so important a matter in every community. Few people require to be told how valuable good milk is as an article of food, containing, as it does, every element necessary for nourishing the human body—at the same time, it may be equally well known how highly absorbent it is, thus, unfortunately, being often a fruitful means of disseminating disease.

I have told the housekeeper that, in addition to there being dairies in the outskirts of the city, the milk supply comes largely from the Illawarra district, and from the nearer stations on the Southern Line; the former sending perhaps the bulk of the cities requirements by means of what is termed the South Coast Line, at many stations on which supplies may be seen pouring in in astonishing quantities, to catch certain trains which are almost wholly laden with milk.

In a few words upon the public health, I have instanced an outbreak of typhoid, owing, as the Health Officer declared, to the use of an infected well upon the premises of a certain dairyman in a Sydney suburb. This might imply that there was an absence of proper supervision of dairies, but there is a Dairies' Supervision Act,* and I believe it is intended to supplement it with further regulations upon the subject. The provisions of the act apply to dairymen and milk vendors alike.

Those who have visited the Island of Malta, have many of them, no doubt, been in the well-kept and abundantly stocked market of Valetta, where some may have noticed a small ticket on each piece of meat offered for sale, examination of which will show that it is to certify that the meat has been passed by the inspecting official. Such may be considered unnecessary, because, in the case of meat or fish, the appearance might condemn it, apart from the sense of smell which most people possess.†

---

* An act to establish sanitary regulations in respect of the production and distribution of milk, 30th September, 1886.

† I have heard great stress laid upon what may or may not be a fact, viz., the good health that Jews generally enjoy owing to the careful examination of all beasts killed for their consumption, before the meat is certified and sealed as "Kosher," *i.e.*, fit for their food.

Herein is the necessity for careful, and what is most of all to the point, *skilled* supervision of dairies, for the glass of milk, to all taste and appearances sweet and sound, might contain the germs of a fatal disease.

Now the dairymen of New South Wales occasionally complained of too much supervision; at all events they were not, I have reason to know, generally satisfied with the existing state of the law. I can quite understand supervision being irksome, without being in an equal degree *useful.* That is to say, a policeman or ordinary official, might go over dairy premises day after day, and every day. It requires no extraordinary brilliancy of genius to note if everything is sweet, and clean, the utensils well scoured, &c., but how about infected water, or incipient diseases in the stock? Tuberculosis, for instance, could they detect it in its earliest stages? As a matter of fact, it is left to the dairyman to declare the presence of any contagious disease (as specified by the Act), whether amongst his employés or stock, it rests with him, and until he finds it out, and chooses to declare it, he continues to supply unwholesome milk. I need not shew how necessary most careful supervision of dairies is, but it must be more of a skilled nature, I respectfully think, to be thoroughly useful.

Chapter VII.

"THE HARVEST OF THE SEA"—SALT AND FRESH WATER FISHERIES — THE FISH MARKET IN SYDNEY—OYSTER CULTURE

The " Harvest of the Seas " it has, I believe, been said, is one that needs but the reaper, that costs nothing for the sowing, and needs no fostering care while it grows— poetical, no doubt, but like many matters crowned with the halo of poesy, neither strictly reasonable nor true. The beast that preys upon the weaker members of its kind, the hawk that would decimate the brood of plover or partridge, cannot reason about their food supply, whether it will wane or no. But man's intellect and reasoning power tells him, as no doubt has often been argued, that he must gather all nature's gifts "in due season," and that he should, by observation and deduction, learn how and when they most need his fostering care, and practise it.

From the tiny bird that flutters helplessly out of some grass-grown bank, and simulates a broken wing or weakened powers of flight to turn the passer-by from her eggs or callow brood, to the tigress with her fearful solicitude for her tawny, sprawling progeny, all birds of the air and beasts of the field are cared for in their early days, but alas! for the poor little fishes, like old Mother Hubbard's legendary little dog, they have none. From their first appearance upon the scene, as a more or less tiny insensate egg, they are left severely alone, a dainty morsel in many cases to their finny brethren, as the poacher well knows; to counterbalance this, no doubt, nature has given to fishes an enormous power of reproduction, but man should lend his aid to the growing of the " Harvest of the Seas."

A glance at the map of New South Wales will shew that her coast line is about, in proportion to her boundaries, as one side of a square is to the remaining three. Therefore a large number of her inhabitants are debarred from participating in such marine harvest as she may reap. Closer investigation shows that there are comparatively few important inlets or large estuaries, and soundings show that the Pacific has a fair depth of water right up to the foot of the many bold cliffs that line the coast. Submarine reefs of rock run out here and there, a splendid haunt for certain fish, but of shoals or banks, like the famous Doggerbank or those of Newfoundland, there appears to be none, though the adaptability of the coast for trawling has yet to be thoroughly ascertained; in fact, the art of culture, preservation, and taking of fish is in no high and flourishing state in the Colony at present.

As to the inland waters, a further brief glance will enable us to see that the dividing range gives to New South Wales two altogether different types of rivers—those running eastward into the Pacific being for the most part shorter, with a quicker fall, and towards the south feeling least of all the effects of drought;

those flowing westward, all of them eventually joining issues with the Murray, the father of Australian rivers, being more sluggish in their career. Of lakes there are comparatively few.

Now, as to Australian sea fishes, the English visitor who first sees an assortment of them will recognize but few, and if presented with an extensive bill of fare, say at a fish dinner, might be puzzled what to choose. "Schnapper" will have no associations for him, good or bad; "Trevally" may mystify him; "Trumpeter" sounds well, but that is all; "Flathead" may only suggest the opprobrious epithet of "fathead." Such names as salmon and whiting he will know; but the former is very, very far from being the peer of the king of fishes, while, on the other hand, the whiting of the Antipodes claims the very highest rank amongst Australian fishes for flavour and delicacy. The John Dory, mullet, and flounder, will be familiar. The bream, as far as the name is concerned, will be known, but it is not the bony, tasteless fish of our inland waters, being the black or red sea bream (or "brim" as it is generally termed), and an excellent fish it is. The blackfish, too, is capital while the garfish are surely the most delicate of the finny tribe. Then follow the king and Jew fishes, gropers, parrot-fish, Sergeant Bakers, yellow tails, tailors, leather jackets, and others, and that brilliant bit of colour is a "nanny gai," all of the deepest, brightest, vermilion—relieved alone by the jet blackness of two big eyes.

And how do they compare, on the whole, with the fish of English waters? Of course, all depends so much on individual tastes. Some place the salmon first, others the turbot, trout, or sole; while, as an "all-round" fish, I am inclined—perhaps in company with a few other benighted and degraded beings—to favour the oft despised herring, whether fresh from its home, 'long shore, innocent of salt, or in the guise of bloater or kipper, pickled, salted, or high-dried; or with the abstracted roe, devilled on toast, to spur the jaded appetite, the herring plays many parts—and, I venture to think, plays them well—and is not the "two-eyed steak," the poor man's cheap but appetising dainty?

On the whole, I do not think that the lover of fish will be disappointed by any means with the flavour of Australian fishes; and one great thing, such fish as come to the Sydney market are fresh, and have not been spoiled by contact with or packing of ice, so you get their true flavour. Take a grilse which is lying high and dry after its last "flurry," bright as the brightest of new shillings, with an ugly sea-louse or two fast holding to it. Let the thick blood well up from the rent the gaff has made—the fish is the daintier for it—and after detaching the "Jock Scott" or "Doctor" from its jaw, have a cutlet cooked as soon as you can, and compare it with the salmon of commerce, which has been goodness knows how many hours in ice, you will then know what I mean by fish being spoiled by ice.

But I have spoken of the freshwater fishes of Great Britain, and nothing as yet of those of the Colony. There are far and away less of them than their saltwater brethren, the principal being the Murray cod, the Murray perch, and the silver eel; and it is worthy of remark that the latter, while found in fair abundance in those rivers which empty themselves in the Pacific, is wanting, as far as I can ascertain, in the westerly flowing streams, while, on the other hand, the cod and perch aforesaid are found only in the latter rivers, and not eastward of the dividing range, though an attempt has been made to acclimatize them throughout the Colony.

The Murray cod is extremely like, in appearance, the codfish of northern seas, and like that toothsome fish, more remarkable for bulk than beauty. I have seen them up to 90 lbs. in weight; but a fish of 7 to 14 lbs. is best for the table, and from an edible point of view worthy of high praise. The Murray perch is very like our freshwater perch, which is so kind and liberal a patron of the youthful angler, but runs to a much greater size. These two excellent fish, of course, materially compensate any inland lover of fish for the absence of their saltwater brethren. The eels are well-flavoured, and I have caught both sharp and broad nosed silver eels in a tributary of the Nepean, of considerable size, the latter up to 10 lbs. in weight.

Lastly, we come to the oyster, familiar to and well-beloved by most of us, whether alone, or acting in pleasing conjunction with codfish or juicy steak. I have remarked in connection with restaurants, that it is cheap in New South Wales. The question is, How long will it remain so? A large quantity of oysters I should, however, remark, are taken at Stewart Island at the south end of the southern island of New Zealand, and retailed in Sydney.

I trust I may be pardoned for a few lines upon what I might term the "oyster at home," and the encouragement afforded him in obeying the divine injunction to increase and multipy, and I premise that it is generally admitted that the coast of New South Wales is exceedingly well adapted to the growth and cultivation of the oyster, it remains therefore for man to foster the gifts and provisions of nature.

First, as to the propagation of the oyster. It is, I believe, generally accepted, that it is effected by *ova fecundated* as in the case of fish, and though estimates differ widely as to the number of eggs each matured mollusc produces, the average may be fairly put down at half-a-million, as far as I can learn.

The spat, as the spawn is usually termed, on leaving the parent shell, floats about, tossed and drifted hither and thither by waves and currents. In the meantime, the tiny oyster (it takes about three weeks to grow to the size of a pin's head) is developing, by incrustation on its viscid surface, the protecting shells. On finding a rough, clean surface it adheres to it, and thus acquires a home for future development. Failing to meet with this, the increasing weight of the shell bears it in a few days to the bottom, where, if it lights on some surface as before described, its well-being is assured, roughly speaking : but, if it falls on mud or sand, it perishes. The season for spawning is in the hottest months of the year, and that is the reason why oysters in England are said to be unwholesome when there is no "r" in the month. It is very probable that a close season alone saved the oyster of the British Isles from absolute annihilation. For the rest the oyster feeds on minute animalculæ; and, having no apparatus for seizing the same, its gill-plates or "beard," possess an elaborate mechanism which, the shell being open at the time, works so as to cause a current, thus attracting food which it is likewise constructed to retain. Finally, I trust the foregoing will not be considered wearying ; I simply hope to show that oysters are like most living things, none the worse for being looked after in their young days.

Turning now to the consideration of how New South Wales is furthering the growth and cultivation of her fisheries, it must be borne in mind how exceedingly cheap meat is in Sydney, of the kind that is usually termed "butcher's meat," and, no doubt, it will be impossible to retail fish upon anything like equal terms in the near future at least. It is more in England that fish cultivation is to be advocated on the score of economy, and I fear it is also by no means in the "near future" that fish culture* shall afford a cheaper and more frequent meal, if only as a change, than beef or mutton, the price of which to anyone fresh from a term of years in Australia seems simply appalling, when a young and hungry family has to be fed.

To briefly explain how the supervision of the fisheries of New South Wales is conducted, I should state that it is a Government matter. There are four Commissioners (honorary), a secretary, who is also Chief Inspector of Fisheries, a small clerical staff, and twenty-two inspectors, assistant, and acting-assistant, a few boatmen, and others, so that, if all are capable men, the six hundred miles or so of coast should be fairly well understood as to its capabilites as a fishing ground.

* By fish culture, I mean the cultivation of certain of our freshwater fishes in great part as a staple article of food.

THE SYDNEY BILLINGSGATE. 65

Is this the case, however? There are no shoals upon which the fish may spawn away from the coast, as far as general knowledge of the subject goes, so they must seek the most secluded and least exposed inlets. What is known of the habits of the fish?

I fear very little is known even about, much less done to protect the gravid fish, the spawn, and young fry. I have been out "seining" with fishermen before now "taking notes," and seeing what mischief is done, most of all by hauling seines inshore.*

I have seen and heard great complaints made about the sale of the fish in Sydney, that justice is not done to the fisherman and so on. The process briefly, is, the fish are caught, basketed, sent down by train in the evening, arriving in Sydney early in the morning. Now occurs one drawback, they have to be carted a mile or so, but I believe a market at the railway terminius, is being built. When they reach the market, they are passed as to size and freshness, heaped into small lots on the floor of the market (very low, broad benches might be substituted with great advantage, at small cost), and they are sold by accredited salesmen, who are allowed to charge 5% for their trouble. All this is done on the fisherman's account, who thus gets his catch sold, and sold carefully, for a bare commission, to the general public, and yet he is not happy. I suppose the fish trade is not worth "ringing,' if so, the fisherman might have more cause to complain.

The oyster fisheries at present are, I fear, in a low way; to begin with, half the leasehold rents, amounting to

* Now and again certain waters are closed, but the fishermen, mostly Italian, are at work as soon as they are thrown open.

E

£2,000, were unpaid, according to the Report of the Commissioners for 1889. Altogether, no care whatever seems to be taken to really cultivate the bi-valve.*

To strip the bed as soon as possible, and as completely as can be done, is apparently all that the New South Wales fisherman, with the exceptions named, is capable of. The cleansing of the beds, the laying down of "cultch," as it is termed, for the spawn to adhere to, and proper attention to the spawning seasons, are complete exceptions to the general rule.

For the rest, efforts are being made to stock certain of the suitable rivers in the Colony with trout, and also with Californian salmon, and it would be interesting to see these efforts successful, but I think it would be more satisfactory to see the fisheries generally on a better footing than they are at present.

I have not mentioned sharks in my list of Australian fishes—as they are hardly a dainty—though, as a nuisance of a serious nature, they are much to the front, and render bathing in the open sea a dangerous, if not actually a hazardous, pastime.

* There are one or two honourable exceptions to this—Messrs. Woodward, the oyster dealers, of King Street, Sydney—I think, among the number.

Chapter VIII.

THE LIQUOR TRADE — ARE AUSTRALIANS TEMPERATE? — WHAT THEY DRINK — THE LICENSING LAWS.

It is only after most careful consideration that I venture upon a chapter under the above heading, and at the outset, I should state, that it is far from my wish to take up the cudgels on behalf of either the abstainer or consumer of malt, vinous, and spiritous liquors. Each party has its own conclusive (?) arguments, its *overwhelming* statistics, and though I am prepared to admit the truth of the trite saying that "figures cannot lie,"— as they are not sentient Christian beings—I do not, by the way, see how it can be reasonably expected that they should—they are nevertheless occasionally coerced into the support and fabrication of statements, which are the reverse of correct.

It has been by no means unfashionable, at one time and another, for Englishmen who have visited Australia, and recorded their impressions thereupon, to take its inhabitants to task more or less severely upon the score of manifold shortcomings, and the vice of intemperance has, at times, been laid to their charge.

I am prepared to admit that there is a fair amount of drinking done in the cities, and it is from a sojourn in them alone that I fear many travellers collect for the most part their ideas and form their impressions upon the country, and its inhabitants generally. But the Bushman who may claim, I think, to be considered more the typical Australian than the dweller in the cities—which, after all, are few and far between—is, I venture to assert, a temperate man in the real sense of the word, that is in eating and drinking alike. There are many who pride themselves upon their moderate indulgence in, or entire abstinence from strong liquors, who, in respect of the consumption of solids, are most emphatically the reverse of temperate. It must also be remembered by those who would condemn such drinking as goes on in Australian cities, that the summer heat in all of them is far greater, more exhausting, and continued, than anything we ever experience in the British Isles, and allowance should be made on behalf of men who pursue the ordinary business routine of an English city, in for the most part, a semi-tropical climate.

According to Mr. Coghlan, whose authority, as Government Statistician, I have elsewhere referred to, the following is annually consumed by each unit of the population of the Colony :—

Tea -	8lbs. 3oz.
Coffee	13oz.
Wine	0·72 gallons.
Beer	12·85 ,,
Spirits	1·20 ,,

Or classing the last three items as alcohol at proof, it is equal to 2·88 gallons, of that much abused article. The outlay on liquor by each unit of the population is averaged at £4 8s. annually, as against £2 19s. expended in the same time by each unit in the British Isles; but the average income per unit is greater in New South Wales, so much so, that the percentage on the average income is estimated as the same in both cases, viz.: a trifle over 8 per cent. Liquor, it must be borne in mind, is dearer in New South Wales than in England. The amount of tea certainly seems excessive, and it requires no arithmetical genius to work out what a family of six, including, say, three small children, will average in the twelve months. I have elsewhere remarked that in some districts cider and perry might be made and used, I think, with advantage.

As to the law of the Colony with respect to the sale of liquor, I do not know that, with the exception noticed later on, it is marked by any harsh or unreasonable features, or that there is much of what I think I may reasonably term, fanatical opposition.

There will, for years to come at all events, be many that will sell and consume drink, and I think that each side is before all things entitled to reasonable protection under the law—the seller from silly and vexatious enactments, the buyer from bad liquor. These I humbly conceive to be the main principles on which each side, the producer, dealer, and retailer, on the one, and the general public on the other, deserves. not as a class, but each individual one interested, by virtue of his citizenship, fair and sensible legislation.

I have made use of the term fanatical opposition, and most, if not all, who have taken any notice of opposition offered to the liquor trade will, I think, fully understand what I mean. Many must have known men, otherwise kindly, sensible, and clever, whose mental balance has been completely upset when they come to touch upon the drink question. Is it fair? Is it reasonable that such men should legislate upon, or deal from the magisterial bench with so important a question? Again, there is much of that selfishness often too openly displayed in such matters, which Macaulay so ably satirized when he declared that the Puritans put down bear baiting, not because of the pain it gave the bear, but on account of the pleasure it afforded to the people.

The Sunday Closing Act, compelling the closing of all licensed houses during the day in question, save to travellers who had come nine miles from where they had slept the preceding night, was in force certainly, until recently, throughout the Colony. I use the expression "in force" advisedly, for, as a matter of fact, the enactment was "more honoured in the breach than in the observance," certainly up to the early part of 1891, and I think that anyone who took trouble to notice how matters stood, will bear me out when I state that it would have been better for all concerned if licensed houses were allowed to open during reasonable hours on Sunday. Wholesale disregard of a law implies one of two things, either that the measure is rotten, and therefore tacitly ignored, or else that the Executive is painfully lax and unobservant.

From the Maine Liquor Law to the Sunday Closing Act in Australia, and northward again to the much vaunted Gothenburg system, I have seen each and everyone either dodged or openly defied, and I am sure that those who have travelled much, must have remarked upon the part of the aggressive northern races, and their offspring throughout the world, a desire to break an obnoxious liquor law, simply through what has been aptly termed "pure cussedness." I have no doubt prohibitionists have an imposing array of figures in their favour. I write simply of what I have seen.

The next fault I have to find is an universal one. It is one worn threadbare, I fear, as it concerns Great Britain in like measure. It is the crying necessity for prohibiting the payment of duty, final removal from bond, working, or blending in bond, of any spirit under a certain age. I do not wish to harass the publican, quite the reverse. If a law is passed which forbids his buying cheap stuff, he is no worse off than his competitors—at present, he must, to meet competition, buy in the cheapest market. Is there need for a great change in, or burden, upon customs or excise routine, in order to bring this about? I do not see that there can be. And the gain? Bad meat is injurious, *bad drink* is worse than poison! I fear it is not so much the "cursed drink" against which our teetotal brethren inveigh, as the "cursed *bad* drink" that does most of the mischief.

As to Sydney bars generally, they are, I think, well managed; and are divided into two classes, the private, and public bars. In the former the minimum price for all drinks is sixpence, an exception being sometimes made in favour of draught British beer, for half-a-pint of which threepence is charged. Ærated waters are included in the foregoing charge, if the customer cares to dilute his wine or spirits with them. In most of the bars, as in

America, if spirits are ordered, the decanter or bottle is handed to the customer that he may help himself. In a great number also, following another custom familiar to those who have travelled in America, a table is laid with materials for a "snack" or luncheon, for which no charge is made.

Scotch whisky and British beer are most in demand. "Square gin" or "Square face," as Hollands gin is usually termed, is much used; also "Schnapps" while in hot weather "shandy-gaff" and similar mixtures are in request. There are also places where Colonial wines only are retailed, and here a capital glass of native production of a claret, hock, or Burgundy type, may be had for threepence. At "bush" and country "pubs" all drinks are at least sixpence.

Then comes the public bar where all drinks are threepence. Here the "long-sleever" or pint glass of Colonial beer is much in demand, and so also are spirits, at threepence the "nobbler," occasionally snacks of bread, cheese, and meat, are provided, and in some houses the Boniface gives his customers a substantial piece of hot boiled beef at about the luncheon hour, which is served out free, in ample slices, and affords many a poor fellow who can get his mate to "shout"* a pint, a fair meal.

Barmaids are much in evidence in some of the private bars, and, as is the rule in most countries where they are employed, they come in for a fair share of uncharitable abuse at the hands of the "unco guid." As a class they are well paid, and, as the business needs no long apprenticeship, the ranks are often filled by girls who are com-

* The common term for "standing treat" throughout Australia.

pelled by domestic trouble and disaster, to earn their own livelihood.

As regards licenses, a public house for which one is required must contain certain accommodation in the way of bed-rooms and stabling. I believe that now, local option is a feature in the present Licensing Act in force in New South Wales, and the issuing of new licenses is regulated by the votes of the ratepayers, in each municipality that the voting shews eleven-twentieths of votes in the negative no new license is to be issued for three years, but hotels having considerable accommodation are exempted.

For the carrying out of the Licensing Acts there are different districts appointed, each presided over by a licensing court. Three convictions under the Licensing Act for offences against it, or the conviction of the holder for felony or serious misdemeanour, cancels a license. The cost of a publican's license in Sydney is £30, except under special circumstances. A brewer's or wine and spirit merchant's license is £30 in Sydney, and £20 in the country. A good many public-houses are more or less in the hands of brewers, as in England.

CHAPTER IX.

THE RAILWAYS, TRAMWAYS, AND ROADS OF NEW SOUTH WALES.

Leaving behind us the foreign concessions, French, English, and American, which form the European portion of Shanghai, and strolling by the side of the Shanghai River towards Woosung, where it joins the muddy swirling current of the widely spreading Yang-tse, one would have noticed some few years ago—for aught I know they may be there still—a varied assortment of sleepers, rusted rails, chairs, fish bolts, and such-like portions of railway plant, tossed here and there in picturesque confusion, where once was a railway. The explanation is, that the Chinese acquired it from the "foreign devils" who built it, and tore it up. John Chinaman does not believe in railways for his beloved flowery land, and he may be wise in his generation.

But, first, a few words as to Australia and her five Colonies, their political and physical aspect. I would, indeed, prefer refraining altogether from political matters, but the question of Free Trade and Protection is one which must be referred to in the matter of railways and railway traffic. As most people are aware, the several Colonies are not agreed upon an uniform policy, but vary from strict Protection in Victoria, to the levying of a customs duty on certain goods and produce only in New South Wales.*

As to its physical aspect, Australia differs widely, it must be borne in mind, from Europe and America. In the former, there were busy centres and capitals to be joined by railways; the latter has her eastern and western sea-boards, besides inland commercial centres and industries to be connected in the same way; and such a railway as the Canadian Pacific has furnished Great Britain with a speedy route through her own dominion, in troublous times, to her possessions and settlements in the east. The central portion of Australia is only partially explored. She has few, if any, inland centres of great importance. Her principal cities are all upon the coast, and steamship communication between them is not circuitous, but essentially the reverse.

Next, let us look at the effect railways have had upon some of the country they pass through. Suppose we take a point, say eighty miles from Sydney, and thence travel thirty or forty miles along the broad, well-kept road that leads to her Victorian rival. Hard by this, the first line of railway in the Colony was opened. So it may best serve to shew the benefits conferred by railways upon the territory they traverse. We may travel many miles without seeing an inhabited house; a solitary "swagman" plods along exchanging a "Good-day, boss—far to the next township?" and his face falls as you give him the distance, and so on, until the punishing sun suggests a

* The revised tariff of the Protectionist party at present in power is still a subject of fierce discussion.

halt, or, as it is universally termed in Australia, a "camp" for an hour or so, by the wayside.

It is an exceedingly pretty bit just here, ridge after ridge, wooded to the summit, rises around. A narrow, but deep and transparent creek, threads its devious way lazily through flats where the grass grows rich and green in rank luxuriance. Still reaches widen out here and there, and a grey heron flaps lazily away, as we take our horses to the water.

Before the "iron horse" ran close by, this clearing was a teamster's camping ground. Here, towards eventide, was all bustle and confusion; there were loaded drays and teamsters, and campfires and all the noises of a camp, with clanking of bright chains as the tired bullocks were unyoked. Those crumbling bits of masonry by the roadside are all that is now left of busy stores, of the saddler's, and of the blacksmith's forge, of the inn, and of all where there was once a market for the farmers' produce, among the teams that thronged along the road, but the railway has cleared all away. The township where we pass the night has now a railway station, but it was better off in the old days, so many will say. And finally, ask how much land has been taken out of cultivation, giving employment or a living to one tenth of what it did since the railway was in operation.

But has not the much vaunted "cheap and rapid transit" enabled the farmers on the lines of railway to find a market for their produce in Sydney? No; they cannot compete with importations from other Colonies. The intending farmer should look over the Sydney wharves, and see the produce daily landed from the Sister Colonies—Victoria and New Zealand especially, he may then wonder what chance there is for him or his calling in New South Wales. It is unfortunately for the Colony, perhaps, that her capital city is on the coast, for her to be fed by the foreigner. Her largest inland cities are mere villages compared with Sydney, so the local or up-country demand for agricultural produce is slight—there being no Birmingham, Manchester, or Leeds in the Colony, as yet.

Lastly, it will naturally be asked, if the railways have driven people off the soil, who made a living by the passing teams, have they developed the back country in a manner sufficient to counterbalance this drawback, and, at the same time, justify their creation or building? If New South Wales finds it her best policy to import her breadstuffs, fruit, and such produce, and go in for a pastoral industry solely, becoming, in fact, nothing more or less than a gigantic sheep run, is all being done to make such industry a success? this I am bold enough to question altogether in my remarks on the meat supply.

Having thus instanced from personal observations one or two points of view from which to look at the railways of the Colony, I will as briefly as possible describe their extent and principal features, as much British money has been expended upon them, in fact the British investor is looked upon in the Colonies as a right noble fellow, and I think it shameful that Antipodean wags should make irreverent gibes upon so free-handed a lender to foreign lands, going so far as to alledge, I regret to say, that England once lent money to a country that never existed, the heaven-born genius who organised the loan vanishing with the subscription list. There may have been also a little too much railway work put in hand for political purposes. If Codlin bribes his constituents with a promise to spend two millions sterling in railways, Codlin is undoubtedly the man, not Short.

Well, for the thirty millions or so sunk in railways, New South Wales has to show (see maps) :—

THE NORTHERN LINE.

Sydney to Tenterfield, with branches	479 miles.
Hornsby to St. Leonards	10 ,,
Werri's Creek to Narrabri	96 ,,

THE WESTERN LINE.

Sydney to Bourke, with branches	503 miles.
Blacktown to Richmond	16 ,,
Wallerawang to Mudgee	85 ,,
Orange to Molong	24 ,,

THE SUBURBAN LINE.

Sydney to Parramatta	14 miles.

THE SOUTHERN LINE.

Sydney to Albury, with branches	386 miles.
Goulburn to Cooma	130 ,,
Murrumburrah to Blayney	112 ,,
Cootamundra to Gundagai	34 ,,
Junee to Hay	167 ,,
Narrandera to Jerilderie	65 ,,

THE ILLAWARRA OR SOUTH COAST LINE.

Sydney to Kiama	70 miles.

In addition, there are two private lines, the Deniliquin and Moama (45 miles), and that from Silverton to Broken

Hill, the famous silver mine of Australia, which is in the extreme south-west corner of the Colony, the consequence is that all the traffic passes through, and all supplies are drawn from South Australia, an alien Colony, and South Australian railways no doubt owe very much to Broken Hill, where there was really an industry to develop. From the foregoing it will be seen that her railways radiate from Sydney, their centre, fairly well over the Colony, and I believe that Parliament has approved conditionally of a considerable mileage of new lines, some of which are in course of construction. The South Coast Line, I might remark, has done much to bring dairy produce to Sydney, and I hope an export trade in butter may be created on a sound basis. Here, there was an industry to develop, not to mention that the railway runs through a coal and iron district.

The lines are single, but some are in process of duplication, for which, in some cuttings, at all events, no provision was made, the consequence is, that the work must be carried on under some difficulties. The gauge is 4 feet $8\frac{1}{2}$ inches, and it is a pity the several Colonies could not agree upon this question, as, in going from Melbourne to Brisbane *viâ* Sydney, there are three breaks of gauge, viz., the Victorian, 5 feet 3 inches; New South Wales, 4 feet $8\frac{1}{2}$ inches; and Queensland, 3 feet 6 inches.

The Sydney terminus is at Redfern, about two miles from Circular Quay, and the railway is to be extended to the quay—*some day*. The appearance and general appointments of the railway station are not calculated to create a great impression upon the visitor. The refreshment rooms on the lines are good, and the tariffs reasonable.

The carriages are seated, in part, on the English plan, and there are sleeping berths to be had at 12/6 each. There are only two classes, first and second. The ordinary fare to places near Sydney is about one penny per mile; greater distances one penny three-eighths, second-class. The first-class fare is about fifty per cent. more. Then, there are excursion tickets at special, in some cases very low rates. As to speed, there is no "Flying Dutchman," "Scotchman," "Wild Irishman," or "Zulu," in the Colony. The distance from Sydney to Bourke, 503 miles, occupies from 21 to 22 hours, and the mail from Sydney to Melbourne requires 19 hours for its journey of 576 miles. For the convenience of commercial men principally, annual tickets are issued, by which the holder can travel for a year on one, two, or more lines, and their branches, as often as he thinks fit, for amounts up to £100, which sum enables one to travel over all the railways of New South Wales for one year.

For the construction of the lines tenders are publicly called for, certain portions of the line being separately tendered for. Nearly everything has to be imported from England, though there is a local factory which turns out railway coaches, trucks, &c., and has made refrigerating cars, which have been successfully tried. An attempt was made to start a locomotive works, but it fell through, at least, for a time.

The rates of carriage upon goods and produce depend upon district, distance, and nature of freight carried,

RAILWAY RATES.

which, with the exception of wool and live stock, is divided into six classes. By district, I mean the Riverina or south-western portion of New South Wales, for the trade of which, Victoria, with her railway to Echucha on the Murray, makes a big bid; it is necesssary, therefore, to adopt differential rates in this part.

As to distance, a fixed charge is made for every 50 miles—intermediate distances being charged in proportion, —thus, for every 100 miles, the rate is double that for 50, for 150 about one-third more, and then about one-fourth more for each 50 miles. Sheep and cattle (live) are carried at rates which vary per full truck, from £1 13s. 4d. for 50 miles, to £9 6s. 3d. for sheep, and £11 3s. 4d. for cattle for 500 miles. For wool, scoured, is charged about one-fifth more than greasy. From the furthest stations to Sydney the charges are:—

	Scoured, Undumped.	Greasy.
Hay (Riverina) ... 454 miles	£4 3 9	£3 4 9 per ton.
Bourke (West) ... 503 ,,	5 0 3	4 0 3 ,,
Tenterfield (North) 479 ,,	5 10 0	3 15 0 ,,

As to the general management of the railways, in order to remove them, and all concerning them, from the influence of political jobbery, a Chief Commissioner has been appointed in the person of an English official, who occupied a responsible position on a British railway. He receives £3,000 a year, and is aided in his duties by two Commissioners, who receive each £1,500 per annum. They are in a great measure independent; but, of course, subject, in proposing new lines, &c., to the Department of Public Works, which, in its turn, is subject to the Legislative Assembly. Under the Commissioners are the following departments : — Accountants, Traffic, Audit, Stores, Locomotive Engineer, Engineer for Existing Lines, Traffic, and Engineer-in-Chief, all with ample, well-paid staffs.

New South Wales claims, I believe, that her only public or national debt is about forty millions sterling, nearly all raised in the London market, and against this, I understand, it is urged that she possesses a sufficient asset in the public works upon which the whole of the money has been expended.

As to the thirty millions or so which have been sunk in railways, I believe I am correct in saying that as recently as 1889 and 1890, the profit made, in neither case reached, certainly did not exceed, $3\frac{1}{2}$ per cent.; and, as Mr. Coghlan, in his official work, makes the average interest payable on railway loans slightly over 4 per cent., the lines throughout the Colony, taken as a whole, can hardly be termed, as yet, even self-supporting. Whether they *indirectly* increase the revenue of the Colony is a matter I am not in a position to confirm or gainsay.

Now, although the wealth and total revenue of the Colony may be all that could be desired, I still imagine that most people interested in New South Wales loans would like to see a somewhat better return from the working of the railways. It may be said that the system of working by commissioners has hardly had a fair trial as yet, but surely there has been time to profit by the development of back country, and all the stereotyped advantages given in justification of railway extension? No business concern would be justified in borrowing money to lock it up in a department, which, after reasonable time, did not pay even the interest on the loan, while there remained only a bare asset equal to the debt.

A few words are due upon the steam tramway system in Sydney, another government property, which, though like many things, not without fault, provides a fairly cheap and quick means of transit from near Circular Quay to nearly all the Sydney suburbs. The motors are similar to those in use in Leeds, Bradford, and other cities, where they are used as a motive power for steam street trams, but instead of one car, two to five are used. The cars are much upon the same principle as English railway carriages, being divided into compartments, but they have more glass about them; the doors do not open in or outwards, but slide lengthways. They have no regulation, or if so, do not keep it, as to overcrowding the cars. They possess smoking compartments.

Some are "double-deckers," *i.e.*, having accommodation upon the top which is roofed over, forming a terribly cumbrous affair, and somewhat of an eyesore, when considering the general aspect of the thoroughfares they patronize. They do not stop to pick up or set down except at appointed places. They travel at a good speed, and are somewhat astonishing to the visitor, as they present the aspect of a train running through a crowded street. To suit business men they frequently have in the morning and evening "express trams," which do not stop between certain termini. By early trams workmen travel more cheaply, and school-children have special rates. The fare is regulated by sections, at twopence generally for the first, and one penny for each following, or part of a section. As a rule, there are waiting rooms where you can purchase tickets, little slips at one penny each, which are also obtainable at shops on the lines, if you pay in cash you have to pay about double, this is to avoid peculation. Accidents are not unfrequent, but at the principal crossings there are flagmen posted, to warn vehicles and foot passengers.

The roads of New South Wales are of six classes, and those of the first-class are well metalled, and thoroughly well kept. Roadwork is tendered for by contractors, as far as re-metalling or making is concerned; repairs to bridgework are done by men in Government employ, while a roadman is appointed to keep a certain length in order. Road superintendents, under the Head Office in Sydney, are dispersed throughout the Colony. The amount yearly expended by the Government on the roads runs from £50 per mile for the first-class, to £5 per mile on sixth class roads. Coaches are the general means of conveyance where railways are not, but a long journey during the summer heats, or after heavy rains, is only to be enjoyed by a person possessed of peculiar tastes and ideas as to what constitutes pleasure. The name of "Cobb" is a household word in Australian coach lore.

I may conclude with mentioning one item of interest with regard to railways in Australia, that is, the longest stretch of travelling which can be done upon them. It is from Charleville, in Queensland, to William Springs, in South Australia, a distance of 2,636 miles.

Chapter X.

AUSTRALIAN SCENERY—"THE BUSH"—BUSH TOWNSHIPS AND CITIES — SWAGMEN — SUNDOWNERS—"ON THE WALLABY."

The verdict on Australian scenery is not always of a kindly nature, and I have heard all sorts, from that form of condemnation which is termed "faint praise," to the occasionally severe decision that there is "absolutely no scenery" in Australia.

There is little doubt, I think, that it is the fashion, more or less, to admire the scenery of some countries, while it is equally the custom to disparage that of others. A few words from some great writer may make or mar a place in the eyes and minds of those that see it. A well-known remark, for instance, about the smells of Cologne has given that city an evil notoriety, which most people who describe it, keep up in a most amusing manner For my own part, I have visited Cologne at all seasons of the year, and have been in quite a score of Continental cities more full-flavoured; while in Asia, Africa, and tropical America, I can call to mind towns to which it is even as a "bank of violets." It is the old story of connecting a dog with an evil reputation, with a disagreeable, not to say disastrous, result to the dog.

Each, according to his nature, disposition and temperament, admires different kinds of scenery, just as his tastes vary, fortunately, in other matters, and so, though it may not please all, there may be many who would find much to admire in Australian scenery.

It is for the most part wholly unlike much that we see elsewhere. We have variety enough, and beauty sufficient, in the British Isles, from the lofty peak, wild moorland, and savage glen of Scottish Highlands, Wales, or westernmost Ireland, to the more peaceful lakesides of Westmoreland, the tangled sweetness of a Warwick or Devon lane, the bosky, breezy downs of Hants, or Surrey, or the brave autumnal tints by Thames or Isis riverside.

Further afield, we have Norwegian fells and fiords, and valleys so deep and narrow as to get but small share of sunshine in the longest summer day. Canadian pine forests, endless almost, the home of elk and caribou, with broad, rapid waterways rushing seawards. Alpine peaks and green valleys, and the climbers fascinating world of eternal snows, rifted glacier, and grim gaunt precipice. Even to tropical forests, where around and high above you is so bewildering a growth of tree-trunk, branch, and foliage, and every kind of creeper that twines or hangs, themselves in turn an abiding place for lesser parasites of the vegetable world, and, where in and out of all this maze of nature's weaving there dart such tiny gorgeous birds as would shame a diadem of richest gems—all this, and more, you may have seen, and yet find some wholly new features in Australian pictures.

Immensity, wildness, untouched, untutored, are perhaps the leading characteristics of Australian scenery. On the dividing range, ridge after ridge, woodclad, seemingly an illimitable forest, meets the view, without sign of human dwelling or artifice of man, and all around, under the cloudless sky and all-pervading flood of midday sunshine, there is the silence of the grave. Take any one of the ridges that rise like waves of the sea in endless succession, pick it to pieces, or produce its "counterfeit presentment" in picture or photograph, it has neither beauty nor grandeur—the trees that clothe it are scrubby, the foliage is without variety for the most part, and monotonously, nay, painfully scant, and grey rock, brown herbage, or sandy soil, shews here and there through it all, but how endless all is apparently, what massing of different shades in the interminable ridges, until the furthermost is only a degree darker than the sky itself.

Now and again the sun, more especially towards its hour of setting, warms up some rock face, some sheer precipice, that drops into an apparently unfathomable gully, and these deep Australian gullies have, I think, a character which is peculiarly their own.

The granite walls that spring from that greatest, perhaps, amongst the world's natural wonders, the Yosemite Valley, exceed in sheer height and abruptness the rock faces which hem in Australian gullies, if indeed they do not, on the whole, excel in sublimity any in the known world. From an angle at the summit of one of these cliffs, known as Glacier Point, there projects, or did some few years ago, a slab of rock, from the edge of which you can look, for it completely overhangs the valley beneath, through more than three thousand feet of space upon the tree tops and open glades, watered by the silver threading of the Merced River, or from the summit of the Half Dome, the eye can fathom with difficulty, craning, as one does, carefully over the edge of the fearful wall, the mile of perpendicular height which lies between the climber and the dwarfed sheet of water known as Mirror Lake.

But come cautiously to the edge of this rock face, towards which a little creek is running, more slowly it almost seems, and hesitatingly like ourselves, before it takes its leap, and falls in a glittering shower hundreds of feet below. We look down into the blue depths a thousand feet and more below us, and stretching away for miles. The bed of the gully shelves gradually upwards from its centre, to meet on each side, the vertical rock walls, but here, there are no open glades, no occasional clearings, which would suggest the existence, if nothing more, of mankind, nothing but billowy masses of never ending forest, and all around is the same.

To change the scene, come to one of the outlying spurs that almost overhang the Illawarra district, the dairy of New South Wales, and look down upon the low-lying strip of littoral. A white line of surf, here and there, shows where the rollers of the blue Pacific break inshore. The neatly cleared paddocks lie mapped out below, with here and there a township, and farms dot the landscape, each with its stock of red, roan, and brindled specks of cattle—beyond, is the burnished sheet of Lake Illawarra, while further south, is the turquoise-hued semicircle of Jervis Bay, and the estuary of the Shoalhaven river glitters in the sunlight. The day is perfect,

"Bridal of earth and sky."

Carefully descending, we plunge into frequent "corries" that seam the mountain sides, with vegetation as thick as in a tropical forest, and where a stream comes trickling down, are mosses, ferns, and the lovely tree-fern with its rough trunk of darkest brown, and a crown of fronds like filagree-work of daintiest, brightest green. From over our heads, a cockatoo darts out with harsh scream, and in a few moments of powerful flight looks like a fleck of white against the blue sky, and many coloured lories, and parrots, flutter about, red, green, and purple, and a bright-eyed, brown-furred wallaby hops away; and so on could I write about quiet, tree-fringed, billabongs, as back waters of river reaches are called, caves and waterfalls, and sun-browned arid plains stretching out under the fierce Australian sunshine, but I have written enough already, it may be, too much.

Australia generally, I fear, lacks "bits" of scenic beauty, there is, for instance, no Bettws-y-Coed, as far as I know on the Continent. Varied wealth and colour of foliage is, as a rule, lacking. Another thing, there is enough galvanized iron in New South Wales and Australia generally, to madden a far less sensitive person than Mr. Ruskin. Its nature is so severely uncompromising; it is eminently useful, no doubt, but it is equally unpicturesque. It can never look even respectable from an artistic point of view, and it has an appearance of perennial youth and freshness with its bravery of spangles, so the selector's hut, or framehouse, in which our ever present metallic friend mostly plays a conspicuous part, though it may be a substantial joy to its owner, is rarely a thing of beauty.

Then "The Bush"—what is "The Bush?" many are

tempted to ask—well, more or less, it is what the country is to the smoke-dried Londoner, the backwoods to the denizen of Canadian cities, or the mofussil to the Anglo-Indian dweller in Calcutta or Bombay, it is anywhere out of the city or town, in Australia.

The swagman or sundowner, who sets out "on the Wallaby," makes off to "the Bush," so let us follow him. What does "On the Wallaby" mean? Well, much about the same thing as going "on the tramp" in England. Its derivation I cannot give.

Sometimes we pass such scenes as I have attempted to describe upon an earlier page, but in many cases it is a dreary, monotonous tramp. We may skirt for miles the paddocks* of a station, fenced with stout posts and rails, or less substantial looking wire. A growth of saplings may flourish here and there, but the great trees have all been "ring-barked" by an unsparing hand, and stand up, gaunt, grey, sapless, and withered, or lie rotting on the ground, a dispiriting landscape. Now and again we pass over miles of scrub and forest, perhaps on a dusty road, guiltless, of course, of hedgerows. The pendent, scanty leaves of the trees generally give us little shade from the pitiless sun, or perchance the heavy rain. Here is apparent a sad monotony of foliage. Here are miles of white, bare, trunks, from which the bark hangs in tangled streamers, and endless fastnesses of the everlasting gum tree, enlivened occasionally by the bright steel-blue bloom of the leaves of the peppermint, shewing out against the gnarled and dark brown limbs of the parent

---

*The word paddock is used where we should say "field" in England.

tree. Anon, are great plains where water is an anxious matter; hunger is bad enough, and we may know what it is; however, the tightened belt will dull the gnawing pain, but thirst! of your charity sympathise a little with such of your unfortunate fellow-creatures of whom you may read the few pregnant words, " they suffered much for want of water."

In our travels we come, of course, to the "bush township," though it is sometimes, a long, long day between them. As we "open it out" at the end, perhaps, of a dusty stretch of road, it looks hazy, and seems to blink, almost, in the quivering sunshine, like some great, sleepy cat. Underneath the verandah of the " pub" are seated, most likely, two or three "travellers," swagmen, like ourselves, with for-the-time-discarded swags and "billies" at their feet.*,

The horses, of some guests within, have their bridles hooked to a convenient post, and edging towards the shade, switch with their tails, at that ever present pest, the black fly.

The clangour from the neighbouring forge, denotes that a couple of the township's worthies are at work. A few gossip here and there, about the stores; there is not much high-pressure here: A well-appointed trooper of police rides past, sleek and natty, on his well-groomed horse. Yonder pretentious house will be the local bank, of which, there will be another opposite, for the name of such branches is legion, and if the business is over for

---

*A swag consists of a blanket, shirt, &c., rolled up and strapped; in fact, it is "bush" for baggage, a "billy" is simply a small tin can, indispensable in bush life.

the day, the white-coated manager will perhaps be taking the air, and his leisure, in the verandah. The occasional rattle of wheels, or the clatter of hoofs, breaks the silence, and perhaps shouts of "Gee-back, Redman! Snowy!" and the swish of a long-handled, longer-lashed green-hide whip, heralds a swaying, straining, sleepy-eyed team of bullocks.

  Crook-knee'd and dew-lapped, like Thessalian bulls,

and so goes on, day by day, the life and business of a bush township.

Then, again, there is the inland city. Take Goulburn, it lies high above the sea level, surrounded by not unfertile plains; a great relief if you have been much in scrub or forest. It is somewhat straggling perhaps, but has fine, broad streets, and well-stocked shops and stores. A public garden, with well-tended shade trees, abuts upon the main street, which is as wide as that named Sackville, the pride of Dublin city. Here is centred most of the life of the city; and it is a busy scene on Saturdays, or Wednesdays, the sale day, when the capacious stockyards are filled almost to overflowing. Horsemen and buggies are flying about in all directions; bullock drays, and teams generally, toil more leisurely along. One of the many handsome banks graces a "corner lot," which, if you chance to gossip about with some old "identity," he will tell you he remembers being sold for a few gallons of rum. Fine churches shew that the people are not unmindful of their religious duties; and factories and flour mills, though few in number, prove that industries are not wholly neglected. Well-built hotels, with spacious verandahs, are suggestive that the wants of the more aristocratic traveller will be duly met; while the not unfrequent "pub" indicates that his more humble brother will be well cared for. But cities like this, it must be remembered, are not sown broadcast over the Colony. They are very much like plums in a cheap pudding, very few and far between.

As to the "swagmen" and "sundowners," they are, for the most part, a motley crew. Some of the former have a trade, some are labourers, some prospectors.* Some are nothing at all, or anything, whichever you please to term it—young fellows who have come out to find Australia very far from what their fancy painted it. The "sundowner" is more of a professional swagman. He is one of those honest, truthful men, who is not afraid to tell you that he hates work, and, for the matter of that, those, that profess to like it; he "knows the ropes," and rarely suffers from privation. If he approaches his goal somewhat early in the afternoon—a "station," for instance—he "camps" until sundown, resting during the hours allotted to vulgar toil, and bestirring himself as the hour for refreshment draws near. Hence his name.

Our "camp" sometimes may be a lonely one, miles from another human being. Perhaps, in pitiless rainfall, a friendly bridge may offer a shelter, unless the creek comes roaring down and promptly evicts us. Otherwise we lie where we can best get some shelter, wrapped in our blankets, awakened, perhaps, when dozing off, by the pitiable cries of the native bear, or by some startled "possum," that "misses his tip," as acrobats say, and

* A prospector is one who "prospects" or "fossicks" for gold, &c.

comes down with a "swish" on some friendly branch below. Perhaps the moon comes out, and casts weird shadows over all, and makes the forest look ghost-like and more lonesome than it did, under cover of the darkness; and the grey dawn, that sometimes seems so long in coming, is very welcome to enable us to get on our way, and stretch our cramped limbs.

Sometimes we come, toward sunset, to an old tumble-down house, such as I have described as an erstwhile haunt of teamsters, in days gone by. Such is often a favourite "camp," and here sometimes we meet of an evening a few "of all sorts," boiling their "billies." Some silent, some disposed to "pitch," from the "swell," querulous of his bad luck and weary tramps, to the grey-headed old "fossicker," full of yarns of luck on the gold fields. Failures all of them. I suppose the man of the world will say. If money be the be-all and end-all, the chief and most laudable aim of life, failures they must be, and their lives a mistake. Some may have never tried, or, having done so, fallen by the wayside discouraged. Others, there may be, who have a folded page among the leaves of their book of life, or one so desperately wrenched away that the remaining pages hang together anyhow; while there may be some, who have stood up, like men, to shoot their last shaft, so carefully, so anxiously, only to see it miss the mark at last. And this is being "on the Wallaby."

CHAPTER XI.

SHEEP RUNS — WHAT HAS TO BE DONE UPON THEM—A WOOLSHED IN WORKING ORDER—DROVING.

We hear in England a fair amount, as regards the mere mentioning of the name, about "stations" and sheep runs, which naturally form a great feature in New South Wales. I really do not know that so very much need be written upon the subject of station life, that would be of great interest. A farm devoted exclusively to the raising of sheep, though the acres and the "heads" of stock be numbered by tens, sometimes hundreds, of thousands, has nothing very romantic about it; in fact, there is less of variety and more of monotony about life and occupation upon a "station" than is at all times pleasant.

A good deal depends, of course, on the district. Some pastoral country will "carry a beast an acre," while on some runs, four or five acres, year in, year out, are wanted to feed a sheep. Some stations are large, others small. In some cases the banks may have a greater or less hold upon the ostensible proprietor, and expenses are cut down accordingly; while, at others, things are generally more flourishing, and greater liberality, and a better style of working the establishment prevails. The homestead, of course, depends much upon its own resources, shops are sometimes miles upon miles away, so there are stores of all kinds, the meat has to be killed for station use, the horses must be shod, there are the huts for the station hands, and the travellers, or swagmen, have their rendezvous as well.

The larger the station the more regularly divided is the work. The boundary riders and stockmen have their time exclusively devoted to their duties, that of the former being, as the name implies, riding around the boundary fences, patching up, temporarily, any breakdown, and reporting it to the overseer at the earliest opportunity, seeing if any stock has got away, &c. Then the stockmen have the care and mustering of stock, their treatment in disease, &c.

The station may also possess a "jackeroo" or two— a human being, not to be confounded with a kangaroo, in the shape of a young gentleman, who has come to acquire a knowledge of sheep farming in Australia. He pays a premium, and lives at the best table with the "boss," thus getting his Colonial experience in a less rough way, but he might do better by taking a couple of years at droving and station work generally, in more than one district, and have a nice "cheque" at the end of the time, instead of having to pay, and learn more, perhaps, in the end.

Now comes the shearing, the event of the year, and as a "shed" in full swing may be considered as playing an important part in the production of the staple article of the Colony, I will attempt to describe one.

The day before we start to " cut in "—which is the term for commencing to shear (when we have finished we are said to have " cut out ")—is a busy day. The shearers are riding in, each with his swag on his saddle before him, or on a led horse, in two's and three's, and the horse paddock, where each has free run for two horses while he is shearing, begins to make a good show of horse-flesh, in quantity at all events. The "roustabouts "* are turning up, and so is that all important person the cook, who is probably anathamatizing the individual who should have the " wood pile " ready, or anything else the station has to find him, swags are being unrolled, and each one is fitting up his bunk as comfortably as he can.

The station hands are busy mustering for the morning, and over the ridge there come horsemen and yelping collies, with a "mob" of some few thousand sheep in front of them. A thickly packed brown mass they look, the centre being apparently motionless, with the outsiders "ringing" ceaselessly round and round.

We will now take a look at the shed; that, we select, is not a very modern one, but the idea is the same. It is surrounded by numerous yards and enclosures, and here is the " race " for " drafting," or separating certain sheep from a mob. It is ingenious, and simple enough; a narrow passage formed by wood work breast high, down which only one sheep can pass at a time. Coming up to meet the centre of the race is a fence, and to this, is hung a gate, which swings easily on its hinges, and taking this

* The "roustabout" or "rouseabout" implies a general utility man or boy in a shearing shed, the term is used frequently to denote all hands besides the shearers.

G

in your hand you make an exit to the left or the right, as you wish, and thus your " drafting " is done.

Inside the commodious shed are ample pens, and moving to the far side, you will notice that they get smaller as you pass along. You now come to "the board," an open space, some ten feet in width, running down the entire length of the shed, having on the far side a series of small pens to receive the shorn sheep. Pens are usually balloted for, and a shearer who is taken on is said to have "got his pen." At the head of the board are the tables, on which the fleeces are rolled. They are strongly made, some six or seven feet long, four wide, and three or more in height; they have not a solid top, but are of laths, placed on edge, some half inch or so, apart.

But it is now early morning, and there is considerable bustle at the hut. Some of the hands are washing, some giving their shears a final touch, others are discussing pannikins of hot tea, and slices of "brownie," a generic name for seed, sweet, or currant cake; and as the hour draws nigh, a move is made toward the shed, each shearer with a couple of pair of shears,* a bottle of oil, and a whetstone, the roustabouts with their hands in their pockets, not a few have refilled their pannikins with tea, for refreshment at their work.

Time is nearly "up," the shearers stand at their appointed places, stripped to shirt and trousers, feeling the edges of their shears. The "pickers up" roll up their sleeves, the wool-rollers lounge at their tables. The overseer saunters towards the bell. The men look like sprinters waiting for the pistol crack. The bell tinkles. Into the

* Each man finds his own.

pens they rush. Out they come each with a struggling sheep, which is dumped into a sitting posture, and held firmly between the knees. And now, work begins in earnest, the "bellies" are off in a twinkling, and taken charge of by the roustabouts, to be placed in the bags allotted to them. Now the "ringer" of the shed, as the best man is called, has his fleece off, and as he darts into the pen for a fresh victim, first having deposited the shorn sheep in his pen, the "picker up" stands over the filmy looking rug which lies in a heap on the floor, gathers it up deftly, and bearing it to the table, flings it neatly out at full length, with the cut side downwards. Hardly has it settled down, when the wool-roller has caught the neck, and flung it inwards; in go the edges of the fleece, and each end is rolled tightly inwards, and tied in a peculiar way. It now looks like a solid and capacious lady's muff, and it is classed, and binned, or perhaps handed to the wool-pressers, who make it up for shipment.

Now the fleeces are coming off thick and fast. The "pickers up" are having a lively time of it. They are urged on by peremptory requests to "snap it up" or "wool away." Shouts for tar are now and again heard, as some unlucky sheep gets a cut from the shears—and the healing produce of the pine is applied to the quivering flesh; while "saw" is occasionally called for, to remove a portion of an ingrowing horn that threatens to bury itself in the flesh or eye of some ill-starred brute. Then there is the penning of fresh sheep, and the "speaking up" of the dogs employed over it—but under the shears, as the Scriptures tell us, even the deepest gashes, for shears *can* cut, evoke no sound from the sheep.

At eight the bell tinkles for breakfast, but the shearers mostly manage to get a sheep just before the time, so it is full twenty minutes before the last roustabout is out of the shed, for the board must be swept; then there are "pieces," "locks," and "clippings" to be sorted.

Breakfast is an ample meal. A profusion of mutton, roast and boiled, bread and potatoes, washed down by unlimited pannikins of tea. Back to work by 9 a.m. Smoke, oh! of fifteen minutes, at 10-30 a.m. Knock off for dinner at 12 noon, more mutton, potatoes, &c., and tea, back at 1 p.m. Smoke, oh! at 2-30 p.m., another fifteen minutes. Lunch is brought in by the cook at 4 p.m., and knock off for half-an-hour to enjoy it: the "snack" consists of tea and "brownie," both of which the famished workers consume in a fashion that would astonish the most capacious school boy. At 6 p.m., knock off for the day, and after a good wash, for it is dirty work in a woolshed, more mutton and potatoes follow, with the ever-present tea, so it will be seen there is no starving done. The style of meal served, of course, greatly depends on the cook, who above all should be a good baker. The evening is spent in various ways, songs, dancing, a game of euchre, and a little horse play, perhaps, and early to bed is the rule.

It will, no doubt, appear that a good deal of tea is consumed. The work, of course, is hard, and no alcoholic drinks are allowed, so half a score of pints a day is only a reasonable allowance. An ex-kerosene tin, with two holes bored in the sides, and a piece of fencing wire for a handle, is the usual tea-pot and tea-kettle in one—elegance, simplicity, and capacity combined. When the water boils, take a double handful of tea, throw it in with a couple of fistfuls of sugar, and there you are! When you think it has stood long enough, help yourself. The etiquette of the shearer's hut does not forbid your doing so.

As to the number of sheep a man can shear in one day. In "Tom Brown at Oxford," the rustic hero, Harry Winburn, can, it is said of him, "shear twenty sheep in a day." Harry would not make much of a cheque in Australia. I doubt if he would "get a pen," though a Southdown is a different customer to a Merino. I have *seen* a man shear just over the hundred sheep— a big, very rough, lot of wethers, in nine hours, catching, and penning his shorn sheep; and have, of course, heard of very much bigger "tallies," especially when ewes and lambs are being sheared. Then, of course, they are more particular at some sheds than in others about the "clippings." On the whole, he is a good man who will shear his average of ninety a day; the tallies, I might add, are taken at intervals during the smoke oh! and knocking off times. It must always be remembered that a man who *follows* shearing can get work nearly all the year round, hence he is in splendid practice. I refer fully to the question of wages, &c., in a special chapter upon the subject.

A good shearer is born, as one may say; that is, some learners "shape" better than many a man who has had some practice. A great deal lies in holding the sheep so that he shall not kick, which hinders the shearer and tears the fleece. A good, clean "blow" should also be given with the shears, so as not to "chop" with them, as this cuts into the fleece and shortens it. As to the rules, I hardly know what will be in force when the labour troubles are settled, whenever that may be.

Machinery, as a good many people are aware, is sometimes used for shearing. The instrument is somewhat after the style of a horse clip, and is worked by compressed air mostly, the shearer having only to hold and guide the instrument. It is used on some of the largest "runs" in the Colony, so its utility should be beyond question.

Finally, I wonder whether those who handle wool in this country, imported from Australia, think that more care might be taken with it, with advantage to all concerned—that is, in the "skirting," "dagging," and general treatment of the wool. In some cases it might be.

Droving, or "overlanding," is another great feature in pastoral work, as it must give employment to a very large number of men, and it means a fair "cheque." It is, in the case of sheep, to which I shall principally refer, not hard work, except in wet weather and floods, and a steady young fellow in two or three years would be able to make a bit of money, see the country, and come into contact, if he laid himself out to do so, with many practical men. Of wages I give full particulars under a separate heading.

Cattle, especially from out-of-the-way stations in Queensland, are very different to deal with to a mob of sheep, as they have an awkward habit of making "rushes" when scared, or nearing water after a long march, they then require "steadying," which is not child's play.

We will suppose that we are at a station, and receive

an early call from a gentleman, who holds the requisite authority for obtaining from us 10,000 wethers, which he has undertaken to deliver for the purchaser, at a place two hundred miles away. With him are his men, mounted of course, each with his dog, and followed by a light waggon or cart, which contains the "swags" of the "boss" and the men, provisions and tents for the journey.

All preliminaries are soon settled, the sheep are mustered and yarded, or penned rather—the former term being applied to cattle—and as the buyer has the right of rejection of say five per cent., we count in 10,500, which are run through the "race" before described. The exact number is then counted out, and the customary receipt given. The sheep are counted as they pass through an aperture between hurdles or rails, those that count stand near them, and as each hundredth sheep passes through, call out "hundred," another then adds one to his "tally," and calls out "seven hundred" or the number passed through in hundreds as the case may be; all this cuts into a day, even if we start early. So the mob cannot leave until the morning.

All travelling stock must be reported to any station over which it has to pass, not less than twelve, and not more than forty-eight hours before it will be at the boundaries, so that the overseer or a station hand may see them over and off the premises, to detect if any of his own stock have joined issues with the travelling mob, as sheep are apt to get out of sight in a gully, and "wing on" to stock passing through. While we are counting out, therefore, the "reporter" goes over the next day's march, and duly reports to such as may be concerned that 10,000 sheep with a certain brand, property of Robinson Brothers, Mr. John Smith in charge, intend to pass through to-morrow. A day's march for sheep, weather permitting, must be at least six miles. In addition to fulfilling the requirements of the law, the "reporter" also selects a camping ground for the next evening, and returns to make himself generally useful.

The next morning they are away, and we see them across our boundary, the cook and reporter will pass us on the way, for sheep move slowly, the latter taking the hero of pots and pans under his wing, to the camping ground he selected the day before; there he leaves him, and rides on to do the needful reporting for the next day, and select the next camping ground, which, being done, he rides back, gives the cook a hand with the tents, &c., and perhaps cuts down a few saplings, to make a "break" for the sheep, and when the drovers come in, takes their horses, off-saddles, and hobbles them.

As to the drovers, a mob of 10,000 sheep will be split up into several smaller mobs of 1,500 or 2,000 each for greater convenience, each with, at least, one man in charge. They have all sorts of times, easy, and the reverse, especially when rains are heavy, and the creeks swollen; but a good dog is everything in driving sheep, and greatly helps his master to get a job. Towards the hotter part of the day, the sheep will lie down for a long "camp," and certain men must watch them, while the remainder rest, and explore their "tucker" bags. In the afternoon they finish the march to the camp, where the sheep are looked after in "watches," until a start is made, in the morning, the hour for which depends on the personal habits of the "boss."

Such, briefly, is the routine of droving; and of chief drovers, they may be divided into owners, men in the fixed employment of large dealers at a yearly salary, and others who take charge of stock at so much per head delivered. For the rest, I would refer the reader to the chapter on "Wages in Town and Country."

CHAPTER XII.

ART IN NEW SOUTH WALES—THE NATIONAL GALLERY—NATIVE ARTISTS AND LOCAL EXHIBITIONS—MUSIC—THE THEATRE—LITERATURE.

I have referred in a previous chapter to the building that contains the art treasures of New South Wales, as an "architectural gem," and, as the remark applied, in addition to the Art Gallery of the Colony, to a severely classical structure of galvanised corrugated iron, I trust it it will be understood that I aimed at being, if possible, sarcastic in so describing it. The façade, to descend to commonplace explanation, is nothing more or less than a plain brick wall, relieved by two sheet iron doors of Spartan-like simplicity of design, and were it not for the fact that National Art Gallery is inscribed thereupon, you would be pardoned for mistaking the building for the back premises of a general warehousing establishment.

Art, native born, and product of the soil, especially music and painting, has, no doubt, somewhat of a struggle for existence in a new country, owing, as I think is patent to most people, to the slavish deference paid to those who rightly or wrongly judge upon native talent generally, and set themselves up as art critics in the especial "set"

ART PATRONS.

or circle of which they are so great an ornament. Humbug, a "dictionary" word, I believe, so I will not apologise for using it, is fairly universal, but nowhere more, I presume to think, than amongst those, who set themselves up as authorities upon one or all of the many branches, the parent tree of which, is art.

There are also in any new country, many newly-enriched among those who can afford to pay for luxuries. It may be by patient toil, successful speculation, or "money grubbing generally," as the unsuccessful man is wont to term it, and with such, there exists some bewilderment as to what they should buy, for they are, as a rule, wanting in self-reliance, as far as their own tastes are concerned. "Success to the mayor," said one of the crowd, at the memorable Eatanswill election, "and may he never forget the nail and sarspan business, as he got his money by." That is the trouble; there are not a few examples to the contrary, but many of those who have built up their own fortunes, can rarely get away from the "nails and sarspans." They seem to weigh down the would-be Pegasus who aspires to fly to new and artistic surroundings, and keep him down to the weary plough, and the self-same narrowed furrow, in which a life of toil has been spent. So native art in a new country is prone to languish.

Let us now enter the very unpretentious building we have referred to somewhat disrespectfully. Inside it is commodious enough, but there is certainly little to distract our attention from the works of art it contains. The strong lights of sunny New South Wales are judiciously tempered; entrance is free, and I am glad to say that it is open on Sunday afternoons.

De Neuville's well-known vigorous painting of the "Defence of Rorke's Drift," is the first that greets us, hanging upon the opposite side of the spacious entrance hall, from whence extend, right and left, the several galleries dedicated to the reception of oil and water-colour paintings, and engravings, and here and there are choice bits of statuary, and, it must be particularly stated, that while many of the finest specimens of the English and other schools have been purchased by the trustees of the National Art Collection, not a few are the outcome of private munificence. It is not necessary to detail or attempt to give an account of the pictures, many of which will be old friends to the English visitor, who will be, perhaps, more tempted to examine with greater interest "a 'billabong' (a backwater) on the Murray." "Rounding up a 'straggler,'" an incident in cattle driving. "George street, Sydney, on a wet evening" (dreadfully like Manchester under the same rollicking conditions), " Off the track," a terribly realistic illustration of what being "bushed" means. Piguenit's illustrations of Tasmania. "A pass in New Zealand;" and other local scenes by local men. Finally, to give a better idea as to the value of the collection, I might add that it is estimated as being worth about £80,000, and it is to be regretted that some of Sydney's wealthiest citizens do not see fit to combine, and give such valuable artistic treasures a better home.

On alternate years there is opened in Sydney, Melbourne, and Adelaide, the Exhibition of the Royal Anglo-Australian Society of Artists, each city being in turn favoured therewith; while in Sydney, the Art Society of New South Wales also makes an annual display. I shall no doubt err, through ignorance, in making such a suggestion, but I think some might not be displeased if some space were reserved at Burlington House for good work from the Colonies. Why should not the Royal Academicians give their Colonial brethren a lift in this way? Space on their walls is precious, I know, and the army of "the rejected" is not a particularly small one, but it is possible that the general public would like to see on the inner walls of Burlington House more pictures and fewer portraits. The "counterfeit presentment" for instance, of some worthy alderman or city magnate, though he be an ornament to his own circle, lacks, I think, general interest.

As to music, there are, of course, few of the old world celebrities, who have not already added, or intend to add, Australia to the scene of their triumphs, and I do not suppose that many have been disappointed at the financial success of their enterprise; but I fear that the support accorded to local musical societies is not of a lavish nature. Matters may have assumed a different aspect since I left the Colony, so I will not particularize, lest I be in error, but certainly, I think, I am right in saying that one society, and one meritorious orchestra, was in 1890, languishing for want of funds. Perhaps the most prosperous is the Sydney Liedertafel, with about 1,000 subscribers, of whom more than a 100 are acting members, vocal and instrumental. They give a certain number of concerts annually, and occasionally serenade distinguished personages.

Resembling, as the climate of New South Wales does, in many respects, that of the land of Italy, so prolific in sweet songsters, one might, perhaps, expect that it would be favourable to the development of singing powers, but I am not aware that such is the case. Certainly among the men, if voices of a superior quality are found, they seem generally of a lighter order, and I doubt very much if there is anything like the proportion of bass voices to be found in New South Wales that one meets, say in Wales and Yorkshire. As to being musical, a widely-abused term by the way, I have no doubt that Sydney folks have an excellent and indisputable claim to be considered so, judging by the numbers of pianos in constant employment; for go where you will about Sydney suburbs, it is rarely you can get out of earshot of a piano, more or less in tune, played more or less out of time. Of course, that Australia has contributed to the operatic stage and concert platform, is well known.

The climate, during the summer months especially, is suggestive of open-air musical entertainments. Walking through Hyde Park, say on a hot evening, when theatres and such like places of amusement are well-nigh unbearable, it is the first thing that is likely to suggest itself, I think, to the visitor. Two afternoons during the week, as I have mentioned, in describing the public parks, there is an hour or so of music, but it is more the monotony of the evenings, that need relief; and it must be remembered, that in Sydney you have not the long light summer evenings as in England, for on the longest day the sun says goodbye at 7·15 p.m. and darkness soon comes. In this matter, I think, however, that it is not the fault of Sydney folks, but larrikinism, that forbids such mode of entertainment. Of this curse upon Australia I have written elsewhere.

I should, indeed, be too remiss were I to omit to notice the actor's art, to which lofty pinnacle of fashion and greatness very little local talent aspires. The companies which play at Australian theatres consist, for the most part, of imported talent, and "stars" of all magnitudes pour into the Colonies, rarely failing in securing a welcome, for I never had the pleasure of sitting in a more friendly audience than one meets in a Sydney theatre.

As to theatres, the principal are the "Royal," "Her Majesty's," the "Criterion;" and the "Garrick" is the latest addition, and besides these, there are minor theatres and places of amusement. The prices of admission are very reasonable, and with the general management, both stage, and in "front of the house," as well as with the accommodation provided, there is little fault to be found. In Sydney, however, there is, alas ! a "poverty point," where those sons of Thespis, who are "taking a well-earned rest," discuss the topics of the day, and comment upon the talents of their more successful brethren, in that spirit of due acknowledgment, and hearty appreciation thereof, which is so loveable a feature of *the* profession.

An excellent free library, well stocked and thoroughly well appointed, with a staff, whose civility might be copied with advantage by officials generally, a technological museum, and a school of art, with a reading-room and lending library, available by payment of a very small subscription, are leading and pleasant features of Sydney.

Finally, as to native literature, it has not made giant strides. As far as I could see, a not too pretentious magazine, to encourage contributions from local writers, should possess interest not only in Australia, but in

England. Australians complain that there is nothing, or next to nothing, said about them and their country in the English newspapers; they might find a remedy by sending us a readable magazine. As to books, many may be familiar with the almost ghastly realism of "His Natural Life," by the late Marcus Clark, as well as with the more pleasant reading given us by the gentleman who writes under the name of "Rolf Boldrewood," while the poems of the late Henry Kendall and Adam Lindsay Gordon do not stand in need of eulogy from me.

CHAPTER XIII.

WAGES IN TOWN AND COUNTRY—THE PROSPECTS OF PROFESSIONAL, CLERICAL, AND WORKING-MEN, AND ALSO OF WOMEN, IN THE COLONY.

Early in 1891, a labourer, "on the Wallaby," was passing through a township about eighty miles from Sydney, near which I happened, at the time, to be, and in response, I suppose to the usual enquiry—" Know of a job hereabouts, Boss?" was invited to do some work which lasted three days, during which he was, of course, lodged and fed, and at the end was presented with six or seven shillings, which he indignantly refused, and "took the law of" his " Boss," but his claim for more, like that of Oliver Twist, was not entertained, his temporary employer bringing overwhelming evidence to show that 15/- per week, with board and lodging, was ample wages for the district; for my own part I should say 12/- was nearer the mark. This was on the line of railway, and in, for New South Wales, a thickly populated district.

Now anyone will admit that the list of wages paid for labour, skilled and otherwise (by otherwise, I mean *hard* manual labour, not pastoral) is very tempting, seeing that the majority of the trades and callings are based upon the eight hour system. I proceed to give a few of *about the average* of rates paid in the city and neighbourhood :—

Carriage builders - 11/- per day	General labourers 7/- to 8/- per day
,, painters - 10/- ,,	
Wheelwrights - - 10/- ,,	Wharf labourers - 1/- per hour
Stonemasons - - 11/- ,,	,, (night) - 1/6 ,,
Plasterers - - - 11/- ,,	Saddlers - abt. 50/- per week
Bricklayers - - - 11/- ,,	Shoemakers ,, 55/- ,,
Carpenters, Joiners,	Tailors - ,, 55/- ,,
and Painters - - 10/- ,,	Shipsmiths ,, 11/- per day
Slaters - - - - 12/- ,,	Iron turners and
Shipwrights - - - 12/- ,,	blacksmiths - 12/- ,,
Coal lumpers - - 1/3 per hour	Boilermakers - - 11/- ,,

Which I have taken every care to have as correct as possible; and they all, no doubt, look very well on paper, but I think that any member of any one of the above trades, who has been in the Colonies, will be tempted to say :—Yes, but how many weeks wages during the year does the working-man get? At present, I think I am well within the mark in saying that, in Sydney especially, for every job, there are two or more men eager for the same, and capable of doing it; I might further add, badly in want of it.

To turn from the town to the country and the special callings exercised there, for most of the rates already quoted are laid down by the unions, and apply throughout the Colony, the following are about the figures :—

		Per annum.
Married couple on stations, including food and lodging		£65 to £80
Boundary riders, stockmen, &c.	,,	52 to 65
Shepherds, farm labourers	,,	35 to 45
Boys on stations*	,,	£20 and upwards
Drovers, all found, while droving		20/- to 25/- weekly

* Often made to do a man's work.

During harvesting time, labourers will get 5/- or 6/- daily, board not included; bullock drivers, and similar classes of labour, about the same. Of course, with such, the eight hours system is not, it is very often sixteen. Labourers on the road, under Government, are paid 7/- per day of eight hours, and navvies, of whom there are at present a great number employed in the Colony, get 7/6 daily, for forty-eight hours a week.

Now, a few words about navvies and railway work generally in the Colony. We mostly find imported labour employed upon it. It is said that young Australia does not relish hard work. In this, as I may have elsewhere remarked, I do not consider that he is singular, and it may further be said, I think with truth, that, unless he goes on a droving or "overlanding" trip, he does not care about leaving his district very much, but does what he can in one way and another, perhaps getting a decent cheque at shearing time, taking a job at fencing or so, cutting billets, or supplying fuel, a turn at any or all of which, very often greatly helps the small selector who may leave his wife to milk the cows, and do the dairy work. This, of course, all tends to make farm and "bush" work not particularly remunerative; on the other hand, it may be said, with truth, that the young bushman's physique is not always equal to navvying, though just before I left the Colony, more than one "ganger" upon a certain line told me that a large number of young fellows from the district had started to work under them.

Railway work has, of course, to be carried on, very frequently, where there is no sleeping accommodation; but a capital tent is to be had for about £1, so, consequently, quite a canvas city soon springs up. The navvy's swag contains his blankets, clothes, &c. So, after the first outlay, his lodging costs him nothing. Then comes the question of "tucker," and to meet this all-important want, boarding-houses soon spring up, where he can be very well fed at about 2/- daily; but, if he elects to "batch"* himself, I have heard many declare that they can live well for 7/- weekly, and thus be 30/- a week or so in pocket, which, in a few months, amounts to a fair sum. If he can save up and buy a horse and tip-dray, he is nearly always certain of being taken on at any railway work going. He will be paid about 12/- per day for the horse and dray, and 7/6 for his own labour; he must provide a boy to lead the horse, feed the boy, the horse, and himself; but he can save £3 to £3 10/- weekly, and he can also make small contracts.

The trouble of it all is, very often, that the terrible monotony of pick and shovel work—and I do not think it is possible for anyone to form an adequate idea as to what it is like, unless they have had actual experience of it—tells, like that of a sea voyage or bush life, after a period of months, and though our friend, the navvy, may have religiously fought shy of the legitimate beer-shop, or "shanty" not unknown in railway work, where strong drink is retailed upon that principle, or want of principle, termed "the sly," and only drinks "soft stuff,"* with

* A common expression for finding yourself in food, derived, perhaps, from the word "batchelor."

* "Soft stuff" is a generic name for teetotal drinks; they range according to the taste of the consumer, from ginger beer to Warner's Safe Cure.

the most pressing of his mates, he succumbs at last, only too frequently, and he starts to "knock down" his cheque, with startling rapidity. How it is gone he rarely knows; that it has gone, is generally all he does know.

How many months to the Melbourne Cup? was the question often put to me by a certain brawny Irish navvy, and a calculation would follow as to what he would be worth by that eventful week. Now this man had, in a a few years of navvying, made over and over again, "cheques" representing a substantial sum, by the hardest of hard work, to vanish in a few days of senseless debauchery. When I saw him last he was saving up for a horse and dray. I sincerely hope he has bought it.

Now the stupid idea of throwing money away, is not confined to navvies and shearers, it is not only the result of monotonous toil, but monotonous life as well, and the squatter, in the most remote of the "back blocks," when he gets on the "burst," "tangle," or "jamboree," will knock his cheque down with any man I know, but he doesn't "knock down" his station with it. He goes back in reality, as the French say, "to his muttons," and drinks nothing but tea for another twelve months, till the time for the annual "burst" comes round. The poor navvy "knocks down" the lot, and has to start work, when he is almost or completely unfit for it. If he would try a couple of pints of beer a day, I think he would save money in the long run. The shearer cannot have liquor on the stations, so he is more liable to its effects. I do not pretend to lay down, as a rule, that a man is physically better for a certain amount of malt liquor daily, but if it prevents him from going upon a senseless "spree," and wasting his money, then I think it is better for him, if he took it regularly, in moderation. A good many "yarns" are extant as to how bush publicans take advantage of men with "cheques," but I should like to have proof of a good many; my experience of bush publicans has been a favourable one upon the whole, they have many calls upon them, and their business is not all profit.

As to shearer's wages, I do not know how the present troubles may be settled between them and the squatter; it may be estimated that £1 per hundred sheep shorn is about the standard, so a sum approaching half a million sterling is paid yearly in wages to shearers alone, in New South Wales. Of course, a great many Victorian shearers come over their border, most of all, to the sheds in the Riverina; on the other hand, Queensland is open to New South Wales men, who can, by starting in April or so, work to the western sheds of New South Wales, thence eastwards through the Colony, and finish up with New Zealand, if they are so minded.

I have, in writing of shearing, given the "tallies" usually done; say a shearer does 500 in the week, that means £5, but if wet weather comes, there is an end to shearing: a heavy shower will, of course, make a stoppage necessary. Then, again, there is the time lost in moving from shed to shed; so it is impossible to estimate what an average man may make, but with anything like luck, it will be seen that a good shearer will make, in six or seven months, a substantial sum. They mess together, and his week's "tucker" bill, including cook, should not average more than 11/- or 12/- weekly; he smokes a good deal, otherwise, excepting new shears, &c., he is at little expense. Roustabouts, "pickers-up," and wool-rollers, get from 15/- to 30/- per week, all found.

At droving, a fair cheque is to be made, the wages being 25/- to 30/- weekly, with everything found: a trip may last several months.

The wages of domestic servants will next require attention; and, as far as the city and suburbs are concerned, they are about as follows—full board, but no extras, such as beer, &c. :—

Cooks for private houses -	£45 per annum and upwards.	
Laundresses - - -	40 ,,	,,
House and parlour maids -	30 ,,	,,
General servants - -	35 ,,	,,
Nursemaids - - -	20 ,,	,,

Which, as may be seen, compare very well with the wages paid to men, who are not engaged in a trade or severe manual labour. In fact, I think that women, as a rule, do very well in the Colonies. They seem to pay governesses very well indeed; but I would not advise any young lady to go out, unless she has a situation of some sort (the respectability and good faith of which she is assured of) in view. If any such, on landing, is in doubt where to go, there is a Governesses' Home in Wynyard square, Sydney, where I have no doubt advice, and accommodation if necessary, could be had.

As to male domestic servants, grooms, coachmen, &c., their wages may be reckoned, for grooms, £35 or £40, and coachmen, £50, with board. Waiters in hotels and restaurants are not overpaid, and I have encountered good men, whom I have remembered in England, who were not pleased with the change. There are a large number of Cingalese in Sydney who engage as waiters at £1 per week or so, and keep, and are capital servants while Chinese cooks are plentiful at £1 to 25/- weekly, with full board.

There are numerous registries or labour offices, as they are called, in Pitt and Castlereagh streets, Sydney, where on payment of a small fee, situations in town and country may be heard of. Reference to any newspaper will furnish the several addresses. To any man, married or single, who wants to get on a station, I would say, take a few lessons in butchering, as an addition to his other accomplishments, killing and cutting up sheep especially; also, if he can shoe a horse, so much the better—"groom, garden, kill," is a very common description of what is wanted of a man for station work.

I now come to clerical employment of which there is a varied field, and an elastic scale of remuneration, which, perhaps, is not by any means remarkable for its magnificence. The clerical market in Australia is *completely overstocked*, and the upshot does not need description. There are scores of applicants for a miserably paid "billet," and the result of my own observation, and it has been over and over again confirmed by others who have had experience, is, that any commercial man receiving £5 or £6 weekly, is to be congratulated; even for very responsible work, £4 weekly is considered very fair pay. Of shop assistants there is no lack; but in certain lines, a young fellow with good recommendations, and first-class provincial, or still better, London experience, might do fairly well.

The many banks, with their multitudinous branches, give

employment, of course, to very many men at fair salaries; but there are naturally many with local influence who are desirous of placing their sons in these institutions. Still, an English bank clerk, who for health or other reasons, wished to make a change, might get along satisfactorily with really suitable letters of introduction.

Of Government officials, there are not a few in New South Wales; they enjoy, for the most part, I may say throughout, very comfortable salaries, and as a rule, I think there is no alarming percentage of sufferers from overwork among them. They enter the service, for the most part, young, qualifying by competitive examination, and interest is useful. Not a few of the best positions are filled by imported talent. I have given some averages of the salaries enjoyed by the Parliamentary staff.* The pay of Government clerks, including surveyors of the land department, road superintendents, clerks, and foremen of works, &c., will run from £180 to £450, while heads of departments, and more important officials, will receive from £500 and £600 up to £1000. The payment of military and police, I have dealt with in a chapter, which includes a few facts with respect to legal, naval, and military matters.

As to the opening that the professional man may find, that, of course, depends upon a variety of circumstances, not the least of which are his own capabilities. The law appears to me, to be the most crowded of any, and it seems to be, as far as many positions go, somewhat monopolized by certain families, one name being especially noticeable for its frequent occurrence. Medi-

* See chapter "On Government," &c.

cine is well represented, but doctors seem to do well, and should any young medico feel inclined to try his luck in Australia, he can very often gain a good insight into the country and city as well, by acting, if he can secure the position, as medical officer to one of the many insurance companies, who have agents continually travelling for them throughout the Continent. The life, for a while, is by no means a bad one; he rides or drives with the agent, and " passes " his victims, when, like Mrs. Glasse's hare, there are caught. His remuneration varies. A few good letters to a director, or anyone having influence with life insurance companies, would be useful.

Tutorships on stations are often obtainable, and any young fellow who would like to have a year of station life for health or other reasons, might try to secure one; the pay is about £50 per annum and full board. In addition to the usual routine, music is generally required, sometimes French.

CHAPTER XIV.

SPORT IN THE COLONY — SPORTING PROCLIVITIES AND SPORTSMEN — HORSERACING AND RACECOURSES — THE TOTALISATOR — "SWEEPS" — GAMES AND PASTIMES.

The intelligent foreigner, who studies our English journals with the object of informing himself concerning the manners and customs of the people, will not unfrequently find in the papers devoted exclusively to sport, some such paragraph as the following:—

Bill Scroggins, of Battersea, alias "Buster," having heard so much talk of Ikey Davis, of Whitechapel, alias "The Conkey One," he will run him 120 yards level, or give him 5 to make a match. Man and money both ready at the "Pin and Periwinkle," Little Whelk street, S.E.

And to shew that there is to be no frivolity at the hostelry in question, Mr. Scroggins adds the stern injunction:—

N.B.—Business only meant.

He, the intelligent foreigner, will also see numerous requests of a similar nature, worded in the same artistic strain, having reference to "knurr and spell" and "coddam," the singing of small birds in friendly rivalry, or the matching of pigeons; in fact, all and every kind of sport.

We might search the daily journals supplied to the

community in New South Wales without meeting with such varied testimony to the sporting proclivities of a nation, and it is extremely improbable that we should find, throughout the Colony, any individual so enthralled by his devotion to sport, as was the Lancashire gentleman, who received the news that his bulldog was worrying his revered parent, with the gleeful assertion that it would be the "makkin o' th' pup." Nevertheless, it would be incorrect were I to describe the people of New South Wales as other than a sporting community.

Between sportsmen and sportingmen there is, no doubt, a wide difference. Many who would be much offended were they not classed with the former, may not be practised horsemen, and quite unfamiliar with the use of rod or gun. The cricketer, the footballer, the player of golf and lawn tennis, will certainly claim that their pasttime be considered a sport, and themselves sportsmen, while the sportingman may be defined, perhaps, as standing more by the turf, the ring, and the running ground— from that somewhat "rare bird," the irreproachable owner of racehorses, to the "spieler," who attends the race-meeting in the general utility line, as it were, prepared, in the touching language of the fraternity, to "work the broads," or "lay a stiff 'un," as opportunity may offer.

Horseracing, however, may be termed without fear of contradiction, *the* sport of New South Wales (and Australia generally), from a "bush" meeting, or a gallop between a couple of "bushmen" for a few plugs of tobacco, or a "note," to the A.J.C.* fixtures at Randwick

* Australian Jockey Club

or a match between two equine cracks, for a few hundreds; and, as, I think, it may be said, that in any public conveyance you may be safe to hear every third man or boy talking "racing," it may reasonably be inferred that the pastime is of all-absorbing interest to a vast majority of the population of the Colony.

Without being too personal, I think I may state that a great many ladies and gentlemen attend our open race meetings in England, whose opinion you would hardly seek, say upon a delicate point of drawing-room etiquette, and whose language and general behaviour might be improved upon. In Sydney there are, as I have written elsewhere, no slums, so the crowd is vastly different to what the English racegoer is accustomed. All look very respectable as far as clothing goes, down to the humblest "spieler." In the city itself, too, about the racing clubs, the "hangers on" are quite swellish, have less of that taciturnity common to "horsey gents" in England. Their heads do not seem to bulge out with wonderful stable secrets, which they are for ever whispering most carefully into each others ears. As a rule, the Sydney "hanger on" is by no means ill-looking, and if he has any distinctive feature, it seems to be simply a languid contempt for those who work for a living.

By a process of reasoning, therefore, neither difficult nor unfair, it may be assumed that there is a certain amount of wagering, or as prejudiced people term it, gambling, upon horseracing, which is certainly a fact, and I have heard it said that Australians bet largely, and generally, because they like to make money easily. Now, of the desire to make money easily, I humbly regard it as being intensely human, but as to backing horses as a means of making money easily, or any how, I do not pretend to be an authority on the subject.

The "totalisator," or, as it is generally termed, the "tote," by which far less cumbrous diminutive we will henceforth term it, is similar, I believe, to what is called in France, the "pari-mutuel," and its use is a favourite way of backing one's fancy.

Now, the "tote" is illegal in New South Wales, like Sunday drinking. In New Zealand and South Australia it is legalized, and during the principal meeting at Adelaide, in April, 1891, Adelaide, the "City of Churches," £11,000, I was informed, passed through the "tote" in three days, $7\frac{1}{2}$ per cent. of which goes to the "tote," and $2\frac{1}{2}$ per cent. to charity.*

Being illegal in Sydney, and a heavy fine being the penalty, we will go with someone we know, who, in his turn, is known to the gentleman with whom we are to negociate. We pass along one of the best known Sydney streets, and here, standing off on the edge of the sidewalk, is our man. A few words, an exchange of money and vouchers therefor, and perhaps we are introduced as an honest sportsman, and no myrmidon of the police, in order to faciliate business in the future. We notice that the home of the "tote" is a tobacconist's shop, and here we could, no doubt, be accommodated

* According to the *"Daily Telegraph,"* 7th January, 1892, the French charities benefited by the 2 per cent. they receive on money passing through the "pari-mutuel," to the tune of £80,000, from 2nd June to 31st December, 1891. This means an investment of £4,000,000 in six months on racing. What about France and "le sport?"

with the current odds, if we wanted to back anything 'straight out," or get the market price for a "double event," a very usual form of betting in Australia.

I have said that the penalty is heavy for running a "tote;" lately they seem to have done something in the matter, but at one time it was carried on so openly, that anyone, new to Sydney, would wonder how so flagrant a breach of the law could, with decency, be permitted.

We now come to another form of speculation in, and concerning, horse racing, which—and here again, charming little inter-Colonial differences of opinion come in—is sternly put down in Victoria, but flourishes exceedingly in New South Wales. I allude to the famous Tattersall's sweep, or "consultation," which is annually held over the Melbourne Cup. The head-quarters are in Sydney, and, I have no doubt, it is patronised by many who would not care to see their names in print. There are smaller and supplementary "sweeps," but *the* " sweep " is a £50,000 affair, what a a Yankee would call " a large order." Of this sum 10 per cent. is deducted for agency and working expenses. The tickets are £1 each; the first prize is £22,500, and even a non-starter gets the lucky drawer, a substantial sum. I believe that the basis on which the whole business is worked, has never been questioned as to fairness. The big prize of 1890 was won by ten Javanese, residing at Thursday Island, in the extreme north of Australia, who had each "weighed in" two shillings towards a ticket. This shows, better than anything in the way of description, how widely spread the interest in Tattersall's sweep must be. Then there are, as I have said, other smaller "sweeps," so the amount yearly invested in Sydney in them alone, must come to a fairly large sum.

As to bookmakers, there are plenty of the fraternity in New South Wales. They obtain a yearly license from the Australian Jockey Club, and have to prove their solvency, and, I believe, give a certain guarantee (suppose business houses had to start the New Year on these all lines!); so, if anyone bets with an unlicensed bookmaker, he must take the consequences. A good many New Zealand "bookies" came over to Australia, as the legalizing of the "tote" somewhat spoiled their business. As to the amount of gambling that goes on in Australia, though it must be very general, I do not know that it is reckless. There is a good deal, I am afraid, written and said about betting, which those who have really followed racing, say an experienced sporting writer, would not confirm, and, I think sometimes, when I read the orthodox defence, "the petitioner attributed his bankruptcy to turf transactions, and losses on the Stock Exchange," that it is a respectable way of getting rid of money, and a safe excuse, but is it always true? Such channels for losing money without a voucher, are, as the Irish term it, "convaynient," and being the "yaller dogs" of society, whose colour is enough to hang them, they are splendid "scapegoats."

To conclude my remarks, such as they are, upon racing, I have merely to add that there are four racecourses available to the Sydney race-goer. The chief is the Randwick Racecourse, four miles from the General Post Office; the Sydney Driving Park, where trotting, driving, and racing events are held weekly, is nearer by a mile. Further afield are Rosehill and Warwick Park.

All these are enclosed, well-appointed, and provided with excellent accommodation at moderate prices. Racing is extremely fashionable, and much patronized by the fair sex. So the report of a big day, is an amusing collaboration between the sporting writer and "lady" reporter, a mixture of furlongs and flounces, "the odds," and the fashions. For the rest, one misses, with some sense of relief, the fulsome adulation, at one time, at all events, accorded to jockeydom in England. Antipodean jockeys are good riders, but, I believe, lack the skill in finishing, that their English brethren possess.

In the matter of sculling, it is almost needless to say that the rival "stables" have developed scullers, and brought sculling in New South Wales generally, to a pitch second to none anywhere; and the same may be said of boxing, for, I think, I am within the mark in saying, that at all weights, from heavy to feather, the Colony, perhaps, can shew the best all-round lot that is going at the present day. There is more than one gymnasium in Sydney, and a promising boxer, who can "keep his head," will, I think, be sure to find fair play, plenty of support, and very likely his match, in the Harbour City.

There is no doubt that cricket is the national game of New South Wales, just as, I think, football may really be termed the national game of England just now. In Victoria, also, the people are "football mad," and the youths wear the colours of their favourite club, in a profusion which is apt to mystify the new arrival; these are the "barrackers," the verb "to barrack," meaning to audibly encourage their own favourites, and comment disparagingly upon the performances of their opponents, a proceeding which frequently leads to an interchange of compliments between the "barrackers" themselves. Cricket does not evoke anything like such enthusiasm; but, where you see small children, in England, "shinning" each other over a half brick or old hat, or any such extemporized football, they play cricket, somehow, in New South Wales. Football is not taking, as yet, much hold upon the Colony.

"Our harbour" offers a splendid opportunity, which I have elsewhere referred to, for yachting and boat sailing, and also for rowing, though the water is sometimes terribly " lumpy " for out-rigged craft. Swimming is naturally a good deal practised, and there are spacious baths in Woolloomooloo Bay, carefully palisaded round to keep away the sharks, which materially interfere with one's comfort in open waters, on the Australian coast generally.

As to hunting, there is a pack of hounds near Sydney, while angling is confined, at present, almost exclusively to sea-fishing. As regards shooting, there are hares in great abundance; and hare, wallaby, and kangaroo drives are the principal form of sport. Some writers, who are more used to the pen than the gun, are very fond of the word butchery in connection with English sport, and I often long to see such an one attempt to "butcher" a driven grouse coming down wind, or a "rocketing" pheasant. In kangaroo "drives," however, I think the charge may be more reasonably made, as the victims have but little chance of escape. Coursing is practised, but does not seem to flourish.

Sea-fishing, as a sport, is carried on to a fair extent, and the enthusiast, who gets a good day with the schapper, should thoroughly enjoy the sport. They are taken as deep as fifty fathoms on a rocky bottom, and run up to 40 or 50 lbs. in weight. Beach lining is a favourite form of fishing, and in this way I have assisted to land that peculiar fish, the Port Jackson shark. There are two or more sea-fishing clubs in Sydney, who organize periodical sea trips. Information about them may be obtained at any fishing tackle shop.

CHAPTER XV.

TRADES UNIONISM IN NEW SOUTH WALES —THE GREAT STRIKE—THE SHEARERS' GRIEVANCE—LABOUR TROUBLES.

I think that for the guidance of those who have any idea of trying their luck in Australia, I should say a little upon trades unionism there, though I fear that the public must regard the subject generally, including that of "strikes," with a sensation of weariness, if not actually of disgust.

Royal Commissions have sat upon trades unionism. Many flowers of oratory, of rhetoric, and boundless argument have been expended upon it. Much labour of pen has resulted in endless leaders, magazine articles, and pamphlets upon the subject, while "one who knows," and "constant reader," air their ideas, and give each their own particular remedy, in the open columns of the daily papers.

First, a word or two upon the "great Australian strike," as it was termed. It may be comparatively fresh in the minds of many. It was an effort on the part of a very complete organization of labour to preserve intact the principles of trades unionism, rather than a question of

OBEDIENCE TO THE UNION. 133

higher wages, and was a trial of strength against shipowner, squatter, and employer of labour generally. They had funds, as they thought, amply sufficient. Their system was complete. Their particular oracles, or mouthpieces, gave the word that the integrity of unionism was threatened, and, like the Fiery Cross of old in the Scottish Highlands, the unquestionable edict went forth. Is it non-union wool, shorn, that is, and handled by "scabs," to be brought from a distant station? Then no union man must handle it. Wool is "taboo," and so is all kinds of merchandize. The shearer must lay down his shears, the driver of dray and trolly must leave his horse in stable or paddock, and smoke the pipe of peace in idleness. The wharf labourer must drop his hold of bale or case, as if it were red-hot. Is the steamer loaded, and ready for sea? Then, if she has a union crew, the officer must step down from the bridge, the "A.B." has to throw his kit over the side and follow it, the cook deserts the galley, the steward his pantry, the fireman tosses his shovel into a corner. The sequence is as formidable as in the remarkable history of the famous House that Jack Built, and so every branch of industry must stop until such time as the shipowner, squatter and employer, or "bloated capitalist" generally, choose to "kow-tow" to the union, or the reverse, as was the case with the "great Australian strike."

I watched the procession of strikers forming on Circular Quay, Sydney, one Saturday afternoon, during the first few days of the strike. I could not but help being greatly struck by the superior and highly intelligent appearance of the men generally. They did not look the kind of men that any glib wire-puller could cajole, and were very different to the large leavening of the enlightened constituencies, who, some while ago, followed that Brummagem will o' the wisp, the phantasmal "three acres" and allegorical "cow." The bystanders generally, who watched the scene, did not seem to express much sympathy, if any, with the proceedings, and I remarked upon the same to an elderly man, in whom I thought the fires of youth might have given place to the wise counsels of riper years—" It touches their pockets, this strike does; the public don't like anything as touches their pockets," was the reply.

So, in time, the great Australian strike neared its inglorious end. Free labour came in abundance. The Union might have been too conservative, but of this anon. Men who, at first, when strike pay was good, were pleased to jeer at the somewhat clumsy efforts of amateur wharf labourers, and exult in their occasional injuries, were in no mood for joking. The members of the council, the wirepullers, delegates, and platform friends of the working-man, were, no doubt, all right. Such gentry have a knack of taking care of themselves, but many and many a poor fellow who had left, perhaps, good, constant work, and fair wages, must have suffered bitterly, seeing his home broken up, his savings gone, and his little ones starving; and this is no fancy picture. Such a man felt, no doubt, though he remained true to Unionism, as sometimes must the dying soldier, who, as the tide of battle sweeps onward, strains his fast glazing eyes, and nerves his numbing arm, to give a last loyal salute to king or kaiser, who follows with his gorgeous staff, in its wake. He has lost his life, but he has been true to king and country. So, like war, must Trades Unionism claim its victims.

It is, however, far from my intention in this little book to argue on behalf either of Unionism or free labour, or foolishly embark upon the troubled sea of the eight hours question. Each and every one that seeks to make a home in the Colony will, I think, be quite capable of judging for himself upon the subject. There is a goodly show of the trades and callings upon the public holiday, known as Eight Hours' Day, which enjoy the eight hours' system ; on the other hand, there are not a few that do not.

I cannot help thinking that the great strike was initiated at a bad time for the cause of Trades Unionism, as coasting steamers were just then being run on a very low scale of rates for freight and passage. The strike thus brought owners together, and, in forming a steamship union, the occasion enabled them to bring about a satisfactory re-adjustment, which was, no doubt, very welcome. In the long run it is, therefore, a question whether steamship owners did really lose much by the delays at first caused by the strike. Again, the entrance fees asked for admission into some unions were, prior to the strike, in some cases far too high, if not actually prohibitive. For the privilege of working as a wharf labourer in Sydney, the sum of £5 or £5 5/- had to be paid, and a non-union man might starve before he got work on the wharves. Such a sum was preposterous, and, as a natural consequence, there was any amount of free labour forthcoming, when the union men went out on strike. Now, however, this is changed, as far as entrance fees are concerned.

English people get very little Australian news in their papers, which may account for the small interest they, as a rule, take in the country, and the slight knowledge they generally possess about it. So, perhaps, the disturbances caused by the shearers, during 1891, may not be widely known, or the motive understood. Briefly, the union men formed camps outside the runs in Queensland, where the shearing first begins, and endeavoured to win over to the union ranks, dissuade, or, deter all free labourers from working in the woolsheds. The question at issue, and the cause of all this trouble, was the "freedom of contract" to which the squatters, who had an experience during the great strike, expressed their determination to adhere, the somewhat ambiguous phrase, meaning, that they would not regard unionism, but do as they pleased, and employ non-union men, if they chose. The question was not one of hours, nor wages.

The serious nature of the situation may not, at first, be apparent, especially when one does not understand how scattered population is, in the "back blocks," and how isolated, many stations are—but imagine 200 or more mounted, and, perhaps, armed men, camping before a run. Lawlessness, perhaps incendiarism, might go on, certainly for a while, altogether unchecked, for the police are so scattered that some time must elapse before they can muster in sufficient force to be useful. Then there is loss of market to the squatter, and worse still almost, if the shearing is much beyond the appointed time, the grass seeds and burrs have developed, which do an incredible amount of harm to the fleeces.

Still, there is much to be said for the men. Put yourself in the place of a union man for a while. Your union has done much in the way of keeping up wages, and shortening hours of labour, thus giving more chance for the greater number to earn a fair wage. How would you like to see a man come in, and enjoy all these benefits, when he not only has done nothing towards procuring them, but may openly affect to despise the principle? How would you like to shear next to a "scab" (as a free shearer is delicately termed, so as not to hurt his feelings), or work "mates" with a "blackleg?"

The man who spends his hours of labour in monotonous toil deserves more consideration, I think, than he gets, as a rule, at least, in certain quarters. It is said that he has no anxiety, no responsibility; but surely the well-being of his health and limbs—his capital—is, I think, of paramount anxiety to him? He is as liable to illness, and far more so to accident, which may seriously incapacitate him, for the rest of his life, than the clerk, city, or professional man.

The city gentleman very often airs his opinions, as to the easy time the working-man enjoys, as he complains of his own arduous duties at the office. Let him take a day's holiday, and set-to to dig and pick a good sized piece of hard ground. Let his "missus" take up her position at the window, see that he turns to at eight o'clock promptly, and, though the duty may be, as it no doubt is, a wholly new and painful departure from wifely obedience, as enjoined by the marriage vow, let her "boss" him severely, be "down upon" him if he takes "a spell," and see that no subsidized olive branch, or "slavey" brings him surreptitious "sherries" or malt liquors. He will be glad to knock off for dinner, and more so, when his eight hours are done—he may then think more of manual labour.

Lastly, I am inclined to think that the emigrant to New South Wales may find a good deal of free labour there just now, for the most part brought about by ill-judged measures, and bad generalship, which must have greatly weakened the cause of trades unionism, for the while, at all events, throughout Australia. Anyhow, he will not find it a prohibitive or expensive matter joining issue with the cause, if he is minded to do so ; whichever he elects to do, I wish him success in his venture.

CHAPTER XVI.

BY STEAMSHIP TO AUSTRALIA—THE SUEZ, CAPE, AND AMERICAN ROUTES—PORTS OF CALL, AND WHAT THEY ARE LIKE—ORIENTAL TRADERS — LIFE ON BOARD SHIP.

It was with "the old Great Britain," as she was familiarly termed by her many admirers—with that bluff, breezy, Shetlander, John Gray, as her skipper—that my association with Australian steamships first commenced. As good and staunch a ship as ever battled with a gale, worsted at last by the elements she fought, for nearly fifty years, she is now, I believe, as a coaling hulk in the Falkland Islands, still serving out munitions of war against her old time foes, the wind and weather.

Then, as the sun was setting upon the Second Empire of France in a blood-red sky, came the Suez Canal, making the route to Australia more easy and less expensive. Soon afterwards there came upon the scene the White Star Line of Atlantic steamers; the "Oceanic," "Baltic," and others, small, compared with the "greyhounds" of the present day, but capital sea boats, and comfortable withal as any. With them the old order changed, and gave place to the new, as far as ocean steamers were concerned—so the traveller by sea should always be grateful to them. They inaugurated 'midship saloons, and smoking rooms, meals were served at civilized hours to suit the passengers, not the "watches"—to them we owe much that has been done to solve, at sea at least, the troublesome problem as to whether "life is worth living." So, on the heels of this sweeping reform, came the splendid vessels which now compete for the Australian passenger trade, as near perfection, one would think, as can be well achieved.

I have written so fully about steamship routes* that comparatively little has to be said, but in writing for the benefit of intending steerage passengers, I did not refer to the British India Line, or the Messageries Maritimes. The steamers of the former terminate their voyage at Brisbane, going "north about," viz. through Torres Straits. The passage is, as a rule, smooth, but somewhat hot throughout. After leaving Colombo, the steamer calls at Batavia, in Java, passing through the Arafura Sea, to North Queensland ports, ending her voyage, as I have said, at Brisbane, whence Sydney can be reached by rail, or by steamer, the latter taking about two days.

The Messageries Maritimes steamers afford a very excellent route to the indifferent sailor. The overland journey from London to Marseilles is delightfully easy, and passengers by the Company's Australian steamers have reduced fares conceded them. The accommodation, living, &c., on these boats, is of the highest order, and

* The question of routes and the relative accommodation offered, is discussed in Chapter XIX, headed "In the Steerage."

the fares include table wines. They call at Port Said, Aden, Mahé, in the Seychelles, where they connect with steamers, to Mauritius and Reunion; the time spent at sea between Marseilles and Adelaide will be not more than twenty-eight days. The calling ports of the Peninsular and Oriental are, Gibraltar, Malta, Brindisi, Port Said, Aden, and Colombo; of the "Orient," Naples, Port Said, Aden, and Colombo—the latter port, at one time, they called occasionally only, but now, I believe, they do so regularly. The German-Lloyd stop at Genoa, Port Said, Aden, and Colombo. I suppose in all cases, I ought to add Suez as a port of call.

The "P and O" steamers make but a brief stay at Gibraltar, and a drive out to the "lines," is all that can be comfortably done, or to Europa point, whichever may be preferred. From the lines, you have a splendid view of the grandly precipitous north front of the Rock, which alone is well worth a long drive. At Malta, there is usually a longer stay, and on first acquaintance, the visitor is sure to be pleased with it. Brindisi has nothing worthy of particular notice. Genoa, where the North German-Lloyd steamers call, is extremely convenient for "over-landers," who wish to miss "the Bay," and the first nine days of the sea voyage. It is an exceedingly interesting city, and its cemetery is well worth a visit; from the sea it presents a splendid appearance. Naples, I am sure, does not need any comment.

Continuing their voyage, both the Orient and German-Lloyd steamers pass through the Straits of Messina, and, if daylight and fine weather are enjoyed, the sight is a magnificent one.

Of Port Said, a great coaling and calling port, which came into existence with the Canal, the less said the better. When Mr. Snawley brought his two little stepsons to that worthy pedagogue, Mr. Wackford Squeers, it may be remembered, he was anxious about their morals. "You've come to the right shop for morals," was the reply of the master of Dotheboy's Hall. Even its warmest admirers cannot, I fear, say the same of Port Said.

Aden is barrenness personified. On the jagged peaks that rise, around, and about it, there is nothing green, and the atmospheric surroundings of the place are highly suggestive of a baker's oven in active service. The houses, we see from the ship, constitute Steamer Point; the town itself lies about five miles inland, and is well worth a visit; the magnificent tanks are often spoken of.

Colombo is by far the most interesting place of call on the voyage. I envy anyone who sees it for the first time during the proper season, *i.e.*, the N.E. monsoon, and whose first experience it is, of tropical scenery, vegetation, and life generally. A fair stay is generally made. Here, a break in the voyage could be made with great enjoyment in the cool season, of course, and excursions made to Kandy, Nourilya, &c. Hotel accommodation is dearer than in Indian hotels; I think, upon the whole, 10/- to 12/- a day seems to be about the charge. The Grand Oriental, I believe, asks a higher rate. Outside the town there is a quiet, nice hotel, the Galle Face, and still further, the Mount Lavinia. The magnificent breakwater has changed Colombo from a roadstead into a splendid harbour, and "killed" Point de Galle. Approaching the land the out-rigged canoes will interest and amuse the visitor, and, before the steamer is moored, there will be a crowd of urchins, whose wardrobe does not worry them much, diving and swimming around, as merry, and as amphibious, as the Aden boys, of whom I beg to make honourable mention. Then there crowd on board, washermen, or dhobe-wallahs, tailors, and pedlars. Huge coal-laden barges are pushed alongside by a crew of sinewy, glistening, coal-lumpers, upon whose skin the "black diamonds" sparkle as they hoist up bag after bag in the vertical rays of sunshine. But I must not indulge in rhapsodies over a place which, I am sure, will fairly bewilder the new arrival.

At all these places, there are special commodities for sale. At Malta, Genoa, and Naples, lace, filigree work of gold and silver, and at the two latter places, coral, as they are the headquarters of the Mediterranean coral fishery. At either of these places, or Port Said, any small stores required, can be readily purchased, as well as any toilet requisites or small articles of clothing, that may have been forgotten in starting. At Aden, ostrich feathers are to be had, and some fine leopard skins, as well as shells, rough coral, &c. Colombo is a great place for dealing in fruits, rings, jewels, walking sticks, and toy elephants, of all sorts and sizes, while moonstones and sapphires are the principle articles of what Mrs. Malaprop terms "bigotry," and need care in buying. Here, you will find a money-changer on board very likely, and it will pay you to get a little Indian money, otherwise they may, on shore, take your florins, as rupees, or try to reckon them so. The rupee, though nominally worth two shillings, is really worth about eighteen pence, so, for a sovereign, you should get about thirteen rupees and eight annas—twenty-four of the latter go to a rupee.

It will amuse, I am sure, and indeed interest, those who watch these eastern traders, to see how they enter into the selling of their goods, with their whole soul. If concentration of one's powers is needful to success, surely they possess, and exercise it. Go into a shop at Colombo, and look at the salesman, and his victim, how he eyes him, for one relaxing muscle to denote, that he is giving in. His lustrous-eyed olive branches are wrapped up, in the transaction—with what self-contained pleasure, they note the bargain. Their eyes dilate with all-absorbing interest, as they watch each glittering piece, pass into the dusky paternal hand. Selling and buying is in the blood, and bone, of these eastern races, and, as salesmen, they leave us westerners, far behind. Their offspring imbibe the science of dealing, with their mother's milk.

As to the Cape route, what I have elsewhere written about it, there is little necessity for repeating; it is only necessary to add that a poor sailor (I do not mean an impecunious mariner, but a lady or gentleman, liable to sea-sickness), might enjoy, it somewhat, less than the smoother weather, generally met with, in the Mediterranean and Indian Ocean. And the changes are also severe, if the southern hemisphere is traversed in the winter months, May-August. I believe that some companies insist upon their commanders taking a route, not south of the 44th or 45th parallel of south latitude, but, of course, circumstances might arise, which would justify the captain of a steamer in shaping a more southerly course. I have run south of Kerguelen land in the winter time, thus exchanging the sweltering heat of the tropics for frost and sleet, within a very short period. This, however, was under exceptional circumstances. In October-February, the weather will be fairly mild, but troubled seas, between the Cape and Australia, are met with at all seasons.

As to the ports of call on the Cape route, the first stoppage is usually at one of the Canary Islands, five or six days from Plymouth, Las Palmas, or Santa Cruz, being usually chosen. The latter is on the Island of Teneriffe, the views of which, as one approaches it, are magnificent, that of the well-known Peak especially, and it is from even a great distance, the weather of course permitting, that its great height and vast bulk are best appreciated. Santa Cruz is the port for Orotava, a health resort of notoriety, which is situated about 15 miles away, on the opposite or western shore of the Island. There is a very well-appointed hotel, close to the pier of Santa Cruz, and though the shops are not of overpowering splendour, anything in the way of necessaries for the voyage, that may have been forgotten, can be purchased. Spanish is the language spoken, and those familiar with it, may notice that the Islanders "clip" the pure Castilian a good deal. Good fruits may be had here.

From the Canaries, some of the liners steam to Adelaide without a break, a long, monotonous, trip. Both the New Zealand lines call, and make a brief stay, at Cape Town. Here, the visitor who makes his first acquaintance with Table Bay, will be struck with the unique appearance of the Lion and Table Mountains and the Devil's Peak, Cape Town lying on the slopes which run down to the bay, from the foot of the precipices of Table Moun-

K

tain. A trip to Wynberg by rail should be managed, if possible, while Cape Town itself may be rather apt to disappoint, if too great expectations have been formed about it. It is about thirteen or fourteen days steaming from Santa Cruz to Cape Town, and this is, as a rule, the pleasantest part of the trip. From Santa Cruz a course is shaped towards Cape Verde, sometimes sighting the African coast. Hereabouts, the heat, for a few days, makes itself somewhat severely felt, and provision for the same, in the shape of a little of the lightest possible clothing, should be made, though much less is required on this, as compared with the Suez route. Leaving the African coast, the S.E. trades are soon encountered, and temper the tropical heat. Neither Ascension, nor St. Helena, are touched at by the Antipodean steamers.

Leaving Cape Town, we enter upon a somewhat long stretch of steaming towards Hobart, the final port of call for Australian passengers. The sea birds, of which I have fully written in describing the sailing vessel route, keep us company in numbers, and we may see, very probably, barring sea and sky, little else but them—for shipping is widely scattered hereabouts—during the eighteen days or so of voyaging that lies before us. In fine weather some skippers, with kindly intent, pass close to the Crozets in search of shipwrecked crews, otherwise the Tasmanian "land fall" is eagerly looked for. A bright little city is Hobart, very homelike after all the long voyage, save for the frequent verandahs that line the streets. It is beautifully situated, and if you voyage up the Derwent in the day time, you will be charmed with the surrounding scenery, over which Mount Wellington rises grandly

—not unlike our lately visited friend, Table Mountain— more than four thousand feet above the streets of Hobart. Here, if you arrive during the summer, it is more than probable that you may be tempted to remain a while, but as it is a great resort for Australians during the hot months of the year, when Melbourne and Sydney Streets are far from enjoyable, lodgings are well filled and prices rise accordingly. Here, you take leave of your ocean steamer, and are provided with passes to your destination. First and second-class passengers can go overland to Launceston, thence across Bass's Straits to Melbourne or Sydney, or by direct steamer.

Coming from England by the Canal route, we usually make our first Australian land slightly northwards of Cape Leuwin, a neighbourhood which bears a somewhat bad name for "weather." A few hours after rounding "the Leuwin" we enter, by a somewhat intricate passage, the fine landlocked harbour of King George's sound, on which is situated Albany, the second town in point of size, in Western Australia, of which I would say, please do not expect too much, and you will not be disappointed with it. Steaming out of the sound, we head for the Gulf of St. Vincent, one thousand miles away across the Great Australian Bight, where, also, bad weather is not unfrequently encountered. About three days bring us in sight of Kangaroo Island, leaving which on the right, we come to an anchor within a mile or so of Largs pier—the shore being tame and flat for some miles inland, beyond which, blue and misty in the heat, rise the Mount Lofty ranges. Our mails and passengers are landed at Largs pier, whence they are conveyed by rail to Adelaide, nine miles away, thence the Melbourne, Sydney, and other portions of mails, together with such passengers as elect to finish their journey by rail, are despatched to their destinations. Railway tickets, at reduced rates, are issued to passengers who have a certificate from the purser to the effect that they are ocean passengers.

As soon as all transfers are made, we leave again for a 36 or 40 hours run to Melbourne, passing between Kangaroo Island and the mainland, through what is termed the Backstairs passage. We keep the sandy dunes of the South Australian coast in sight during a good part of the trip, and at last enter Port Philip, between the Heads, and through the ever-troubled waters of "the rip." Queen's Cliff, with its fortifications, is on the left, and Sorrento, a sea-side resort of the Melbourne folks, on the right. We have now sixty miles before we reach Hobson's Bay, which is the extreme northern portion of Port Philip, and leaving Portarlington and Geelong far away on the left, at length tie up alongside Williamstown pier, half-an-hour by rail from Spencer street station, Melbourne city (third class fare sixpence). Here, if we care to finish our journey by rail, a voucher that we are bonâ-fide passengers, secures us a ticket to Sydney for £2 14s., first; £2 0s. 6d., second-class; sleeping berth, about 12s. extra. If we, on the other hand, choose to remain by the ship, we shall be boarded during our stay. At length, after a couple of days or so, we cast off for the last length of our trip, and once more through "the rip," round Wilson's promontory, and past Gabo, forty to forty-eight hours in all, brings us to Circular Quay, and the end of our voyage.

As to sight-seeing at the various ports of call, what I have to say, applies mostly to those who have to limit their outlay. The best way at Naples, Genoa, and Colombo is to take a guide, go in a party of about four, and share expenses. In Colombo, do as much sight-seeing as you can in the early morning, avoiding the afternoon sun. In all cases, do not be in a hurry for the shore, and do not overdo your shore-going costume, as you feel heat and exercise very much after lolling about on a steamer. At all ports between England and Melbourne, the going ashore is effected by boats. At Albany and Adelaide, by steam launches, for which one shilling each way is charged, unless it is your final landing place, or port of embarkation. At some of the other places, the charge is more moderate, but always have an arrangement before starting. At Gibraltar, if the weather looks threatening, take a ticket on board, and go by the boats carrying the "P and O" flag, for Spanish boatmen know how to charge, if there is a "capful" of wind on the bay.

My list as to routes would be incomplete were I to omit the American, *viâ* San Francisco, which, if the journey has to be commenced say, in May, June, or July, has its advantages. The railway trip across the Continent can be broken at places of interest, and, if you elect to go through, I believe it is now done in four days and-a-half. From San Francisco, the average run to Auckland, New Zealand, is about twenty days, calling at Honolulu, Sandwich Islands, and Tutuila, in the Samoan group. From Auckland to Sydney about four to four and-a-half days are required. The heat is comparatively temperate in the tropics of the Pacific Ocean, and fairly fine weather is experienced, as a rule. The steamers, though comfortable, are hardly up to the standard of "P and O," Orient, or Messageries liners. Through rates are quoted from Liverpool to Sydney at between £60 and £70; but a trip *viâ* America is apt to become expensive. I wish I was able to chronicle a direct service to Australia from Vancouver, in connection with the magnificent Canadian Pacific Railway.

Now, as to the class by which we shall travel, I have written in what some might think very high praise of the second saloon accommodation provided on the "Jubilee" boats* of the "P and O" Company. Such is simply the outcome of my experience, and I am in no way recompensed for expressing it. I wish to point out, indeed, to praise, second-class accommodation on Australian steamers generally, for the benefit of those who might like to visit the Colonies for the purpose of health, business, or pleasure, but are deterred by first-class fares, and have misgivings as to the accommodation afforded by the second.

There are, of course, many unfortunate people who have "a position to keep up, don't you know;" but I think that any person who is merely afflicted with an imperfectly developed, or rudimentary position, so to speak, would be very comfortable in the second-class, and if money is any object to him, as far as economizing it goes, the difference between the second and first-classes will enable him to see the sights of the voyage

* The Britannia, Arcadia, Oceana, and Victoria are the Jubilee steamers.

very comfortably, buy a few curios, defray a good-sized wine and cigar bill, with perhaps a pound or so to spare, say, in a dinner to "the position" to compensate it for any indignities it has suffered in the second saloon. It is unnecessary for me to point out, I think, that a six or seven weeks' voyage can hardly be made without certain pecuniary extras being incurred, which materially increase the prime cost of the passage.

One somewhat important matter, when you are deciding upon a cabin, especially if it is an outer one, is to take one on the *port or left hand side*, you thus miss the afternoon sun, which greatly heats the starboard cabins; this applies to the voyage *towards* Australia.

As to dress, so long as it is neat, the dinner costume in the "second" permits of considerable latitude, flannels and white drills, clean, of course, are not "taboo," and are cool and loose for dining in. In the chief saloon, some affect evening dress, ladies especially; there is some sense in "low" dresses, in the Indian Ocean, and it adds a gay and festive appearance to the important ceremony of dinner. Washing is very often done by the quartermasters, and at Colombo you can always have this important item attended to, well and cheaply. A fancy dress ball or two, as well as impromptu dances, are part of the voyage nowadays, and if you have a suitable dress, it is well to include it in your baggage. Concerts, smoking and otherwise, are of frequent occurrence, and many steamers carry a good band.

If I can ever afford to start in business as a philanthropist, I should certainly try and establish a sort of school on board ships making a long voyage. I am in earnest. I do not intend to perpetrate what the late Artemus Ward was wont to term a "goak." I am fond of children, but on board ship they are, too frequently, an annoyance to people generally, and a source of constant anxiety to their parents. I have heard mothers complain that a long voyage completely upsets their children, and gets them "out of hand," for months afterwards. They seem also to be always eating, and destroy all recognized theories as to the capacity of the human stomach. If they were taken in hand, say for a reading class, during a couple of hours, twice a day, I think it would be a great thing for all concerned. I imagine that there are, by each steamer, passengers who would be glad to undertake such a duty, for a consideration. Children also, by annoying people generally, are a prolific source of trouble between the parents, and those less interested in the youngsters.

Of the pastime of card-playing, and of visits to the steamer's bar, I need say nothing, let each do as he is disposed, or what was the use of Magna Charta? I have only to remark, that anyone who is sent on a voyage, without supervision, to recover from the effects of inordinate conviviality, is translated, metaphorically of course, from the frying-pan into the hottest of fires. The captain, or doctor, may "stop the grog" of any transgressor, but it is one thing to issue the official edict, and an entirely different matter to carry it out effectually; for such a one, a passenger steamer is the worst possible place.

Before leaving the ship, our table and bedroom stewards, and, in a less degree, the bathman, will expect a "tip." Some people give stewards ten times the trouble that others do, and never compensate them. I am afraid that ships' stewards, generally, must see a good deal of the mean side of mankind. "Tips" depend much on what you can afford to give, and, if you must give trouble, I think you should make it up to the steward; I cannot lay down any rule upon the subject. I can only say, as another much-abused public servant — cabby — says sometimes—" Leave it to you, sir."

Chapter XVII.

THE SAILING VESSEL ROUTE—THE "ROARING FORTIES," "TRADES," AND "DOLDRUMS"—THE MONSOONS—BIRD LIFE AT SEA—HINTS UPON THE VOYAGE.

Sailing ships to Australia are apt to suggest to those whose memory serves them, not so far back after all, but say to the earlier "sixties," names of the old-time "flyers"—the "Redjacket," the "Marco Polo," the broad-beamed "Donald M'Kay," and the famous "Lightning," with her sharp, yacht-like "forefoot." Where be they now, those once famous caravels? Well, they have had their day, and now, for the most part, the waterway through the land of the Pharoahs, bears the giants of "P and O," Orient, Messageries, and German-Lloyd, and many another liner, "ocean tramp," and "canal-wallah," to Australian sea-ports.

Yet, I think, that no one can be said to know what infinite pleasure fair winds and fine weather at sea can afford, unless they have at some time made a longish trip in a sailing vessel, and though adverse winds and foul weather are a source of much unpleasantness, still a well-found sailing ship makes, as experts say, "better weather," than do the heavily-engined, fast-driven steamers of the present day.

What can be more delightful than a day "in the trades," with the wind well on the quarter, and all plain sail drawing. The broad expanse of well-scrubbed deck—more or less inclined to leeward, as the ship acknowledges the ten-knot breeze behind her—is free from "clinkers," coal dust, and "blacks" innumerable, which, to the detriment of our choice flannels, or spruce white drill, befoul the steamer's decks. There is no clanking machinery, no heavily revolving shaft, or "racing" screw to disturb the over-sensitive. No heat from the furnaces, and we miss, right thankfully, that indescribable "whiff" from the engine-room. The hot sun is tempered by the healthful breeze, and what a lazy, careless, appetizing life it is, and how reviving to the sick and wearied. Shoals of flying fish, like great dragon flies of silver and ultramarine, rise from either side of us, with swift albacore and dolphin in quick pursuit. And at night, to walk forward and look up at the bellying "white wings" ever so high above us, looking ghostly in the moonlight, which softens the outline of taper spar, and filmy tracery of rigging. The sound of a concertina, or, perhaps, of a jovial chorus, comes from the fo'k's'le. The sidelights reflect red and green rays upon the white foam. The look-out is at his post. We glance aft along the sweep of trim deck, where sheets and halyards are neatly coiled and " flemished" down, to where the light glows warmly through red-curtained cabin windows, suggestive of brightness and creature comforts within.

But, as with most things that are bright and pleasant, there is the reverse of this picture. We are now in a vast wilderness and waste of waters, "running down our easting" in the Southern Ocean, hove to, perhaps, in an adverse gale, rolling and plunging heavily, and shipping water over our already dripping and sloppy decks; everything is wet and miserable. The "landlubbers" are, as the old song says, "lying down below," the best place in such weather; some are trying to read, some may be sea-sick, all are holding on to something. The "Mark Tapley" of the crowd is trying to infuse some little jollity into the proceedings, but it is miserable work being at sea in bad weather.

Or, perhaps, we are running before the "brave west winds," which, for some time, have been blowing a strong gale behind us. A few may venture on deck, but, standing by something to hold on, if need be. The officer of the watch, and the skipper, have anxious eyes upon the wheel, lest the ship broach-to. What hills and valleys of water there seem to be! Can anyone describe them? With great foaming, curly, crests, that tower high above you, as they race along, threatening to poop your labouring ship, and sweep all before them: when, suddenly, you fly heavenwards, and, with a mighty swish, they rush by you, and away. And, at times, there rises like some watery Matterhorn, a cross sea, that comes inboard in tons of green water, and your maindeck is a raging surf, with capstan heads and harness casks, shewing, like rocks in a troubled sea. And, if you must shorten sail in all this tumult, you feel, perhaps, for those poor fellows, lying out upon the yard, which threatens every minute to jerk them into Eternity, from their hold upon the slippery footrope; and, as fast as they gather up fold after fold of the tough, wet canvas, the wind tears it from their numbed and stiffened fingers, and, as you watch them, very likely, a stave or two of those jovial sea songs, descriptive of a "Home on the Rolling Deep," or "A Sailor's Life for Me," may occur to you, as being a trifle misleading, occasionally.

But, having thus endeavoured to give two slight sketches of life in a sailing ship, and before I go into further details, I will take the liberty of explaining, as briefly as possible, the meaning of "trade winds," "doldrums," and "monsoons," which must necessarily figure when describing a voyage to the Antipodes, and, as it is as well to have some idea as to their meaning, I trust I shall be excused in doing so.

The oceans through which we pass on our voyage to Australia by way of the Cape of Good Hope, are the North and South Atlantic and the Southern Indian Ocean; in the two former, we encounter the trade winds and "doldrums;" it is in the Northern Indian Ocean, when using the Suez Canal route, that we have to consider the monsoons.

In the ninety degrees of latitude over which the North Atlantic stretches, that is, from the equator to the North Pole, there are four zones, or belts, each possessing distinct attributes in the shape of weather, viz. :—

1. The zone of calms, which extends for 6° to 8° or so northward of the equator, say about 500 English miles or more, distinguished by dead calms, light, variable "airs," heavy showers, and thunderstorms, generally called the "doldrums."

2. The zone of "the trades," extending from the "doldrums" up to 35° or 38° north latitude, where the

winds blow steadily, with greater or less force, from the north-east, throughout the year.

3. The zone of "the variables," or unsettled weather, extending over the "forties," or degrees of latitude from 40° to 50°, and occasionally further north, hence they are generally termed the "roaring forties."

4. The zone of steady winds from the pole, which blow southwards, but by the motion and shape of the earth, have a more or less westerly bias imparted to them.

The south Atlantic has exactly the same zones or belts, but owing to the peculiarities of the land and water, her "trades," which are from the south-east, extend to, and sometimes blow over, the equatorial line, and as the more extensive ice-fields of the Antarctic polar regions cause a more powerful current of southerly winds, which, for the reason above given, become south-westerly and westerly, the variable zone, for the same reason, is nearer the equator, somewhat, than in the North Atlantic.

As to the causes of the above, a few words may not be out of place. Winds are caused, as most people know, by inequalities in temperature. The heated air at the equator rises and flows in currents north and south. The scene of this uprising is the region already described as the "doldrums," and with the air goes a quantity of vapour in response to the vertical rays of tropical sunshine, which comes down frequently in sheets of rain, and being the battle-ground also of hot and cold currents of air, it is likewise the region of thunderstorms, of which we know little, in point of severity and frequency, in more temperate climes. Towards this uprising there rushes, from north and south, a continuous colder current; these currents form the "trades." Then, when the upper warm current from the equator has reached the "forties," it has cooled down, and it is about on a par, as regards temperature, with the current which comes from the poles. Hence the "forties" becomes the scene of frequent combats for supremacy, which have given them the name of "roaring," and thus is produced that absence of uniformity in point of weather, which is not unknown in Great Britain, for, though the British Isles lie northward of the "forties," it is through them, the said "forties," that we Britishers are blessed with that meteorological kaleidoscope known as the English climate.

Next, and lastly, as to monsoons. The word is Arabic for season, and it therefore explains that the north-east and south-west monsoons are really seasons during which the wind blows from the quarter indicated. The Northern Indian Ocean, though traversed by the equator, has no "doldrums" and no "trades." It lies between two continents, Asia and Africa. The former, lying to the north-east, has its hot season during the English summer, or rather those months which, in deference to accepted definitions, are termed the summer months. So the attraction, or uprising, caused by the summer heats in India, demands that a current shall rush in to fill the vacuum abhorred by nature; thus, from May to October, is the south-west monsoon in the Indian Ocean, during which time the wind blows from the south-west, and, generally speaking, it is not a favourable season for ocean travel, in what surgeons would term, the parts affected. During the "burst" of the monsoon, or change of season, especially from north-east to south-west, the weather is anything but agreeable, rough sea, terrific thunderstorms, and literally "torrents" of rain, are the leading features thereof. During the winter of the northern hemisphere, the direction of the current is reversed; from October to April, Africa is the goal of the cooler current, and the north-east monsoon, or season of the north-east wind, is the best season for travel in the Indian Ocean, and, of course in India, Burmah, Ceylon, &c. The "burst" of the monsoon in May, indicates the commencement of the "rains," or Indian rainy season. The tropics, it may be worth explaining, are derived from a Greek word, signifying a turning, and stand for the turning points of the sun. They extend $23\frac{1}{2}°$, or 1,410 geographical miles, on each side of the Equator.

We must now make a start upon our voyage; and the first thing to consider is the best time for leaving, and this, I think, is August or September, not too late in the latter month, so as to leave the dreaded equinoctials behind us. We may count it about ninety days on an average from London or Liverpool to Sydney, and this will bring us there in November or December, but, as I have pointed out in writing on the climate of New South Wales, we can pass our time very pleasantly in the cooler air of the mountains, until the summer heat is modified. By choosing the time I have given, we traverse the huge tract of the Southern Ocean during the early summer, which is a great desideratum, and a feature in the sailing ship route, which I beg to impress upon those who intend making the voyage, most especially if they are not robust.

Then follows another important matter, viz.: — The

choice of a ship, and in this we must consider our passengers, and their object in making the trip, whether from motives of benefitting their health, or with the idea of economizing. Let us hope that in the former case our invalids have not left it too late, that they have still a share of strength, and as soon as they have got over the first few days, and acquired those useful members, unacknowledged by comparative anatomy, known as "sea legs," that they will be able to get about and enjoy the voyage to the full.

Those who, unfortunately, are not in the best of health, will be safer, and, no doubt, more easy in their own minds, on board a regular passenger ship, where they can have medical attention, if necessary, fresh food, and frequently fresh milk; in short, be better off than if they went by "outsiders," even at a less fare, who only take passengers, to use a favourite phrase in shipping circles, when sufficient inducement offers. Messrs. J. Green & Co., 13, Fenchurch avenue, E.C., and one or two other firms load the regular passenger ships, which sail from London only. On ordinary trading vessels, a passage *may* be secured at a reduced rate, by introduction to the captain, owner, or loading broker—and such is entirely a matter for arrangement—payment, at the rate of £8 per month, would be about a "fair thing" for the ordinary sea-going fare; you must trust to luck for freedom from illness or accident.

As to clothes, you want a fair supply of all sorts, eschew linen shirts, giving preference to flannel, and have both thick and the lightest underwear in your "Wanted on the Voyage" portmanteaux. Blue serge, for state occasions, and tweeds, will serve best, not forgetting a warm, rough overcoat (an old one will do very well), and a good mackintosh. "Flannels" are best for the tropics, and a few white drill coats, buttoned to the throat,* so as to enable the wearer to conceal the absence of shirt front and collar, will be found almost indispensable. Of head-gear, you should have a good supply, as a good deal "blows overboard." Something that will "stick on" should be taken, and a light broad brimmed hat, or pith "topee," for the tropics. As to boots, canvas shoes are best for fine weather, and a pair of goloshes are very useful in wet and rough weather, as they give a good hold on slippery decks. Do not take what are known as sea-boots. Hold-alls of stout linen or fine canvas, with pockets for brushes, razors, &c., will be found very useful for your cabin, as well as a bag for soiled linen. As to books, you know your own taste best; light reading is most relished at sea, and cheap editions should be taken, as there are frequent borrowings and exchanges. Shakespeare is a delightful companion for a long voyage. For the rest, a pair of dumbells will do you good, if used, and they frequently encourage your fellow-passengers to take a little healthful exercise. Washing you can get done by one of the crew, as a rule, unless you like to try your hand at it.

Try to benefit by the voyage to the fullest extent, for you can do much to supplement the sea-air. Let your motto be "on deck," and practice it whenever you possibly can. The difference between those who have done this, and those who have been "mewed up" in cabin or

---

* Made like a military "patrol" jacket.

smoking room, is more marked, at the end of a voyage, than many would credit.

Let us make a start at last. The invalid, or, indeed, the sound man, is a gainer by joining his ship at Plymouth, if she calls there. The ship's company have settled down in their places, and the fuss, and bother incidental to a first start, is avoided, not to mention the chance of bad weather. Let us hope for fine weather, down channel, and across the "Bay." Off Lisbon, we may get an easterly "slant," the forerunner of the trades, and, by the time we pass Madeira, which we may "sight," we are fairly in them. This is the pick of the voyage, and every day should add new life to the sick man.

But one morning we wake to find the ship almost motionless; we soon become used to the movements of our ocean home, and get so much in touch with her, that she seems a sentient thing, and it is no mere poetic fancy that inspired the well known line :—

"She walks the waters like a thing of life."

We go on deck. We are becalmed in the "doldrums," rolling lazily, with sails flapping, blocks and running gear swinging about, and creaking monotonously. There are not a few sail in sight, some, like ourselves, just out of the northern trades, others beating up, somehow, in the hopes of getting them. One is enjoying a "catspaw" of wind, which fills her sails for a few moments, while another is blurred, almost hidden, by a squall of rain, which falls in buckets-full on her decks. The sea is like oil, the pitch bubbles in the seams, and the sky seems to glow like a vault of brass. What a place for an armed cruiser, you think; what prizes she could pick up in a few hours.

But a homeward bound ship has her flags up to signal us, and the officer dives below for the code book; flags are "routed" out. They represent the consonants of the alphabet, and endless combinations of three or four letters, duly given in the book, signify names of ships, port of registry, and dozens of useful sentences, and their answers.

"What ship is that?" ask two flags, B and D.

"The 'Swiftsure,' of London, 1,500 tons; London to Sydney; 26 days out," we reply.

"Where did you lose the trades?" comes next, perhaps.

"In 10° north latitude," is the answer.

"Where did you lose the trades?" we may ask, after hoisting our name, destination, &c.

"In 1° north latitude," and so on; or, perhaps, a "Pacific steam" or "Lamport and Holt" steamer comes in sight, for we are in the track of south American steamers. We shape our course towards her, and hoisting our official number, beg to be reported. Up goes the answering flag, and the request is duly "logged," to be reported in the proper quarter, with the comment—"Wished to be reported."

But how is the temperature all this time? It is an mportant matter to our invalids. Of course, it has been more than warm for some days; but the breeze and the quick travelling make it less noticeable. Now it is some_ what of an annoyance; but I have been becalmed for days in the doldrums, and never saw the heat exceed 88° Fahrenheit in the cabin, without any awning, whereas, on a steamer going to the Cape of Good Hope, I have seen it as high in the coolest deck-house, for the steamers hug the African coast; whereas, here, you are out in the open. Still, it is apt to be trying, and those whose lungs are weakly, will do best, perhaps, to avoid hot soups, &c., for a cold meat diet, and take ice in their beef-tea if it is procurable. Iced drinks, except as medicine, are altogether a mistake in such weather, and strict moderation in food, as well as liquor, will be found most comfortable.

We soon pick up the South East trades, and the weather cools rapidly. Do not expect to see anything of Ascension, or St. Helena, such a course would be dead "in the eye" of the wind; being square rigged, though sailing "close-hauled" upon it, we cannot steer much, if any, within eight "points" of it. We have in our general course stretched towards Pernambuco, on the South American Coast, crossing "the line," in 25° or 28° west longitude, so as to make the most of the north-east trades. We now shape a course to pass the desolate islet of Trinidad, and the Martin Vaz rocks (Trinidad must not be confounded with the West Indian Island of the same name), and probably bring up in sight of Tristran d' Acunha, a lonely island, with some 100 of Her Majesty's subjects dwelling thereupon, lying in about 38° south latitude, and 12° west longitude. It is an awkward island to approach, unless the weather is promising, but stores of beef, poultry, and vegetables can be obtained, the islanders having a whale-boat, supplied them by the English Government for boarding ships, and it is a charity to look them up. Hence we start to "run down" the tremendous stretch of "easting" which lies between us and Sydney Heads, no less than 160° of longitude.

The weather is now cool, but I thiuk it will be found bracing beyond comparison. I might remark that we have had the best of the voyage, and if a good sailing ship calling at Cape Town, or going to Cape Colony, can be secured, I think it would be the pleasantest and most healthful voyage obtainable, the duration would be fifty or sixty days.

And now, anyone who notices bird-life, of which one sees little or nothing in the tropical mid-ocean, will begin to find plenty worthy of his notice. Petrels of all sorts, Mother Cary's chickens, Cape pigeons, the sooty, and black-eye-browed albatross, or mollymauk,* on some days myriads of them, but one, more especially, will rivet his attention. It glides quietly, yet swiftly along, sometimes hidden in the trough of the seas, now, topping the crest thereof—a great bird, with surely the mightiest wings one ever saw. It rarely flaps them, but heeling over, as it were, now to the right, and anon to the left, rises without apparent effort on its lengthy pinions, and sweeps in graceful circles, like some deft skater, upwards and downwards, around, about, and above us. We are "spinning" through the water, but with all its circling motion, and easy flight, we cannot leave it astern. How untiring it is, and what a pace to maintain. There is no mistaking it, it is the famous albatross, and surely, if the eagle be the king of birds ashore, it is the monarch of those that people the waters.†

* Both these birds, though six or seven feet across the wings, are much smaller than the wandering albatross, which is twelve to fifteen feet from tip to tip of its pinions.

† The wandering albatross (Diomeda Exulans).

CATCHING AN ALBATROSS.

Now, fond as I am of anything in the way of sport, especially with rod or gun, I must say that I think it is cruel, beyond contempt, to shoot at birds from shipboard. No end is served. The victims are neither vermin, for the destruction of which there is some excuse, nor can they be recovered, so that their plumage may be used—and as often as not, they are merely winged, and left to perish miserably. But if you really want an albatross, I will tell you how to catch one, presuming that you wish to preserve the skin, and I would forewarn you that the birds fairly reek with the strongest fat and oil, so be prepared to deal with them accordingly.

Take say 150 yards of very stout, strong line, of the thickest used for sea fishing (and arm yourself with a duplicate) and plenty of strong hooks, four inches or so in the shank, and one to one-and-a-half across the bend. Splice them firmly to short lengths, and add them to your line, three or four, each 18 inches apart, like a strong paternoster, with a piece of cork to float them, and bait with some pieces of salt pork. Then go aft, make one end of your line secure, and coil it carefully, so that it may run out without a tangle. Having baited your hooks stand clear of the line, and having something, a rail for instance, to "brace" yourself against, drop the bait overboard. The Cape pigeons are the first to espy it usually, they attract the sooty albatross, who in turn gives way to the bold, handsome mollymauk, which, as I have said, is about seven feet across the wings—with a magnificent eagle-like head. The albatross now swoops down, and all stand clear, and keep respectfully distant, the mollymauk seeming half inclined to dispute precedence with the "big 'un." The quarry is painfully slow in his movements, he does not fold his wings at once, but holds them uplifted in a graceful curve, and seems to overshadow with them the little group of his subjects. He "bites" at last, and being hooked, spreads his wings, and "backs all," setting his great webbed feet in front of him like an obstinate "drunk" being carted to the lock-up; so you have a long pull before he is under the counter of your ship. With a spread of thirteen or fourteen feet of wing, you will be somewhat astonished at his dimensions. Make a slip-knot of stout cord, pass it over your line, let it fall over the bird's head, then heave away, and when inboard, 'ware fingers, securing his beak, with what sailors term a "mousing," in other words, tie some string around it, and then, if you must kill the ill-fated bird, despatch him quickly.

Of legitimate fishing, there is hardly any to be got in the open sea. Bonitos may be caught at the bows with your albatross tackle, and are sometimes speared. Sharks are sometimes taken with a proper shark hook, you may not see one, however, the whole voyage, until you get under the Australian coast. You might see a rorqual, the largest of known whales, which run to a tremendous size in the southern ocean.

Cape pigeons, with their black and white plumage, are exceedingly pretty, and are most easily caught by light lines, with hooks of small size. They are really of the petrel tribe,* but, barring their webbed feet, are very like the tame pigeon in appearance.

* The pintado or painted petrel.

Well, eastward ho! from Tristran d' Acunha is our course, each skipper has his own parallel, his favourite route, mostly in the "forties," for the days of the "great circle" route to Australia are for the most part over, and sailing vessels, as a rule, do not run south of Kerguelen Land. Of the uninhabited islands besides Kerguelen Land—the Crozets and Prince Edward Islands — you will not often see anything. It is as well to keep clear of them. The hoarse croak of the penguin on a calm night may be all that reminds you of their vicinity, save, perhaps, long tresses of sea-weed. The islands of St. Paul and Amsterdam are north of the route.

Although we hope to be favoured with fairly good weather, still, in so terribly long a stretch of "the forties," we must expect a little of the ups and downs of sea life; but at the time of year, say October and November, I think that the least robust even, will find, though the weather may be cool, that it is not unpleasantly so, and very bracing, seldom much below 45° Fahrenheit as an extreme. Few sails are seen on this vast ocean. I have twice traversed six thousand miles of it without sighting one, and was once seven weeks without seeing a single sail. In time we near the land, and decide upon going "south about," that is, south of Tasmania, instead of through Bass's Straits, and our skipper has decided to "make a fall" at Gabo Island, off Cape Howe, just where the boundary lies between Victoria and New South Wales. All eyes are watching the dimly seen shore, which soon resolves itself into a low-lying island, lighthouse, and signal station, with a background of thickly-wooded, wild-looking, mountainous country. Our "number" flutters from the peak, and the news is flashed to Sydney that we are "off Gabo." Excitement now reigns on board. Everyone is packing up, and more or less pre-occupied with what he or she is to do on shore. The tug comes alongside, perhaps, in the morning. The hawser is passed on board. Sydney Heads at last, and our voyage is ended.

CHAPTER XVIII.

THE CLIMATE OF NEW SOUTH WALES—THE COAST, THE TABLELAND, AND PLAINS—HEAT AND RAINFALL—HEALTH RESORTS AND COST OF LIVING—WHAT TO WEAR.

The climate of New South Wales is necessarily a question of more or less vital importance to all who intend to visit the Colony, and, while I attempt, in this chapter, a description thereof, I give, as much as possible, such details as may prove of service to the very many who are ordered, in addition to ocean travel, a complete change of life for the time being, thus involving residence, for a greater or less period, in a foreign country.

As I have remarked in my preface, I fear that cases of impending and premature breakdown of mental and physical powers alike, are yearly becoming of more frequent occurrence, which, in addition to pulmonary troubles, either hereditary, or brought about by the harmful nature of certain employments, or other causes, call for immediate treatment, in nearly all cases involving complete change, and the temporary abandonment of all business occupations.

Many circumstances, no doubt, combine to bring about disregard of the physician's timely warning. The enfeebled mind is prone to greatly magnify the difficulties which the absence from business involves, and the weakened bodily powers shrink from the idea of foreign travel. The question of expense is very frequently of paramount importance, and little more than a general knowledge of more distant lands may be possessed by the sufferer. He hesitates, therefore, to bow to the inevitable, and seeks in vain to put off the evil day until it is forced upon him; and those who have travelled much to southern seas must have seen many instances of what I write, cases in which it does not require the trained eye of the medical man to prompt the fatal but too common verdict—"This should have been long ago; it is too late now." And what, some months ago, was a man, weakened in good sooth, but strong enough to get about, and with health renewed by the voyage, able to enjoy and benefit by the change, even soon fitted, perhaps, for light employment if need be, is now a helpless invalid, compelled to lie, for the most part, in the vitiated air of a close cabin, so wretched that he even loses that marvellous hope which buoys up the doomed consumptive, so strongly, that medical science has distinguished it by a special name, and fit only for careful nursing, if he reaches his distination alive. This is, perhaps, a gloomy, but it is no imaginary picture, and it is my humble and sincere hope that I may contribute my mite of information to a useful end.

Of the several routes to Australia, I deal in other chapters, and I have only to add, or rather emphasize, as far as I can, what I am certain must often have been advised, viz. :—That a speedy renewal, in great measure, of health and strength, should not be regarded, as it not unfrequently is, as a complete cure; it is too often, in fact, the case, that " home sickness," or other causes, prompts a too early and wholly inadvisable return.

Now, first, when we speak of the climate of New South Wales, we are slightly in error; we should rather say climates, for the Colony possesses three distinct districts or regions, in each of which the atmospheric conditions are widely different. They are as follows :—

(*a.*) THE LITTORAL, or low-lying land between the sea and the dividing range.

(*b.*) THE DIVIDING RANGE, which runs from north to south of the Colony, and is a table land, in some parts thickly wooded or covered with scrub, and broken up by wild deep gullies. Opposite Sydney, and commencing about 40 miles to the westward of the city, it has a breadth of some 200 miles, 1,000 to 3,000 feet above the sea.

(*c.*) THE PLAINS, which lie to the westward of the dividing range, at an elevation of say 100 to 300 feet above the sea level.

The characteristics of the foregoing regions, as regards climate, may be briefly described as :—

1. That of the littoral—Hot in the summer, humid, liable to occasional sudden changes, and considerable rainfall.

2. That of the table land—Hot during the day time in the summer months, but cool in the evening and early mornings; sudden changes of temperature occur in a very short space of time, and at certain points there is a heavy rainfall.

3. That of the plains—Very hot in the summer, but very dry, and the rainfall is less than in the littoral or tableland districts.

As the number of rainy days is a matter of some importance to those who may have a choice of residence, I have taken the following cities and townships in the southern half of the Colony (South, that is of the thirty-second parallel of latitude, as I think it includes the "pick" of localities suitable for enjoyable residence), viz. :—four in each region, at points covering the entire extent of each, and the following details are taken from the official reports of the meteorological department. I should premise that rainy days are understood to mean those on which any rain falls; it by no means follows that they signify many hours of that dull, dispiriting, drizzle, so frequent in England :—

THE LITTORAL.

Newcastle to Eden, about 300 miles, N.N.E. to S.S.W.

City or Township.	Height above sea.	Number of rainy days, July 1, 1889, to June 30, 1890	*Mean number of rainy days	Mean annual rainfall in inches.
Newcastle	—	176	113	46·98
Sydney	—	215	157	49·23
Kiama	—	181	141	47·86
Eden	—	164	118	35·01

THE TABLE LAND.

Mount Victoria to Cooma, about 200 miles, N.N.E. to S.S.W.

Mount Victoria	3422	155	95	35·36
Moss Vale	2205	181	115	39·22
† Goulburn	2071	104	84	26·13
Cooma	2659	96	89	19·04

* The mean number of rainy days is from observations taken over an average of 17 years to each station.

† For 11 months only in 1889-90.

THE PLAINS.

Junee to Wentworth, about 300 miles, due west.

Junee	-	-	985	-	71	-	51	-	21·96
Hay -	-	-	305	-	68	-	70	-	25·11
Balranald -	-	-	—	-	51	-	36	-	12·44
† Wentworth	-	-	—	-	62	-	75	-	11·99

The foregoing will shew that, in some places, the rainfall was exceedingly heavy during 1889-90, that is, much above the average: in Sydney especially, if I remember rightly, for the first eight months of 1889, it was not less than seventy inches.

I have said that the littoral and tableland are liable to sudden changes of temperature, I will describe them. They are, of course, the results of the not unfrequent sharp conflicts between the hot summer blasts from the interior, and the winds that sweep up, cold and refreshing, from the Antarctic Ocean.

It is a November or December morning, and a hot wind is blowing. A breeze is generally cooling, but this is the reverse. It is like catching a whiff from a furnace, and you avoid it as much as possible. The thermometer even now, at ten o'clock, is high enough; in three or four hours it will be, perhaps, 96° or 100° in the shade. A dust storm may also come to vary the dreadful monotony. But towards three or four of the afternoon, as you pass the verandah of the General Post Office, you notice a crowd around the board, which gives the weather reports, with the so frequently desired "raining" written in red ink. You see that it is raining down the South Coast. A southerly "buster" is rapidly travelling up. It will rain in Sydney, very shortly, and the thermometer will drop in three or four hours, perhaps some 30,° still 65° or 70° is not too cold.

On the dividing range there are like changes. And I have in, the same hour, experienced great heat, and been wetted through, by a perfect imitation of a chill and dense Scotch mist. Still, this can be fairly well foreseen, and those who have to guard against the consequences, should take the advice of the weather-wise, and make provision accordingly.

Next comes the important point of temperature, and I might first draw the attention of those who have not travelled beyond the limit of temperate climes to the vast difference between a dry and moist heat. Thus 95° in the shade (Fahrenheit as throughout this chapter), in the plains of New South Wales, would be quite bearable; in fact, if you had not too hard work to do, not unpleasant. You could, and thousands of people do, work and ride about all day in it with perfect impunity, by observing temperance in food and drink, and, if practicable, avoiding being over fatigued. In the more humid, and proportionately less exhilarating atmosphere of Sydney, or the Illawarra district, it would be trying: while in Singapore or Calcutta, it would be little better than bearable. It must always be remembered that persons new to a hot climate suffer somewhat from the richness of their blood, but their greater strength enables them to bear what the thin-blooded, but more languid resident, is apt to feel more severely, hence, new arrivals generally bear their first Sydney summer better than those more acclimatized.

As to the recorded degrees of temperature, they are given each day in the daily journals, from a very large number of stations, but in some cases, I think, the shade temperature is open to question. In Sydney, according to the official returns taken at the observatory, 146 feet above the sea level, the following will shew the mean and extremes of *shade* temperature, from October, 1889, to September, 1890:—

TEMPERATURE IN SHADE.

Month.	Mean.	Extremes.	
		Maximum.	Minimum.
October, 1889	63·4	88·0	48·8
November ,,	67·2	82·3	56·2
December ,,	72·2	99·5	61·3
January, 1890	71·6	86·0	61·5
February ,,	71·2	84·8	63·4
March ,,	69·5	77·6	57·6
April ,,	63·7	75·6	49·8
May ,,	59·0	68·1	49.4
June ,,	57·2	69 2	45·4
July ,,	51·1	63·5	35·9
August ,,	54·2	75.6	42·6
September ,,	59·6	74·6	43 6

The average, or mean *shade* temperature in Sydney for 32 years is 63°

In the plains, or "back blocks," a shade temperature of 100° is very common, and a good many degrees over the "century" are frequently recorded, but in many cases they are, as I have said, open to question, that is, as representing a *bonâ-fide* shade temperature. Generally, when high temperatures are introduced as a topic of conversation in Australia, they are like snakes, bears, and tigers in the respective countries where such laudable institutions flourish, apt to develop any latent ability for fiction a man may possess. The palm for heat and "mugginess" combined, as far as Australia is concerned, is usually awarded to Rockhampton, in Queensland, which is poetically described as the abode of "sin, sweat, and sorrow."

Sydney, during the summer months, as will be seen from the figures given, is decidedly hot and somewhat trying; but eight months of the year—March to October inclusive—are delightful, and the peculiarly exhilarating air, and bright, beautiful mornings, really make life worth living there, and seeing that the Colony possesses so wide a range of climate, surely the seeker after health can always find somewhere well-suited to him?

No doubt Sydney will be the first sojourning place, temporarily, at all events, of the new arrival in search of recuperation, who, I trust, will have received material benefit from the voyage, and not be led to mortgage his newly-acquired stock of health by trusting too much thereto, or imagine that he has worked a speedy and certain cure, as before mentioned, and meditate an immediate return. His wisest plan, and, no doubt, the one he will follow, will be to take counsel with a local medical man, to ascertain what progress and improvement has taken place.

As he very probably will have left England at a time which enabled him to escape the cold of the latter part of the autumn and early winter, he will reach Sydney about the hottest time of the year, and may naturally feel somewhat disgusted with the climate. At such a season it is very improbable that he will be ordered either to the coast or the plains. The mountains will be cool at night and bracing, therefore let him lose as little time as possible in leaving Sydney, unless, of course, he is advised to remain there.

Seventy miles or so on the Western Line will take him to the most fashionable resorts of Springwood, 1,216 feet;* Lawson, 2,399 feet; Katoomba, 3,349 feet; Blackheath, 3,494 feet, or Wentworth, 2,856 feet; amongst fine scenery, and with plenty of amusements in the way of excursions, riding or driving, lawn tennis, picnics, &c. There is plenty of good accommodation in boarding-houses at from 30/- to £2 2/- weekly, and excellent hotels, in which, for the most part, a daily charge of 7/- or 8/- is made, and special terms can be made for a lengthy stay. Or, if the visitor is disposed to try the Southern Line, he can make for Bowral or Moss Vale, 80 and 86 miles from Sydney, and 2,000 feet above the sea. Thence he can visit such peaceful little townships as Berrima, which has a smack of the Old World about it, Sutton Forrest and Robertson, the latter situated in a very beautiful country, not far from the edge of the dividing range, which falls abruptly into the beautiful Illawarra district.† This neighbourhood, though by no means unfashionable, as the present summer residence of the Governor overlooks Sutton Forrest, is quieter than the summer resorts on the Western Line, and much better for the man who wishes to practice economy. The standard tariff at the "bush" inns is 1/- for a bed, 1/- for each meal, all drinks being 6d. each. In more pretentious hotels, they charge 8/- per day, but nearly always have a second table at the 1/- tariff. Travelling on horse-

* Above sea level.
† See Chapter on "Australian Scenery."

back means a serious item, the charge being 1/6 for a feed of corn, and 1/- or 1/6 for stabling per night. It would doubtless be better to obtain board in a private house, of which there are frequent advertisements in the local papers, and I should imagine that it could be had at, say 25/- or less. Still, it would not be expensive work to look about, leaving Sydney as soon as possible for some such centre as indicated, and suit one's taste and pocket. There will be plenty of riding to be had, shooting of a kind, while fishing is almost at a discount. The bush people are very kindly, and are always very glad of a "pitch," as a talk is called, with a stranger, and elsewhere I have taken the opportunity of bearing very cheerful testimony to kindnesses I have experienced in the Australian bush. The life may be a bit monotonous at first; but some occupation will soon suggest itself, and a temperate, open-air life will be fraught with best results to health and pocket. As a rule, there is generally a "leetle" too much of billiards, and late hours, even at health resorts, to make hotel life desirable for the invalid. Finally, a few quiet months can be thus spent enjoyably, and at very small expense compared with what a similar stay would cost in the South of France, Canary Islands, or Algeria, or, indeed, any Continental health resorts, with which I am acquainted; and, at the same time, amongst one's own race. One small matter more; I would advise no one to be "bluffed" from going into the bush, by Sydney stay-at-homes.

Should Sydney be reached in July and August, the westerly winds may feel somewhat too fresh and cool. If the coast be recommended, Manly Beach, 6 miles from

Sydney, is very mild, and so is Watson's Bay, a pretty little spot. Gosford, 50 miles north from Sydney, and two hours by rail, on one of the backwaters of Broken Bay, is beautifully situated, and boating can be enjoyed; while southwards, at Clifton, Bulli, Wollongong, and down to Shoalhaven, there is beautiful scenery, and some sea fishing might be had as an amusement; all are easy of access by the South Coast Line.

Lastly, if the plains are recommended, the Riverina district would, perhaps, be best, and it would be as well to make at once for Hay, an important township 494 miles from Sydney, and the centre of the district. It would be very pleasant to get on a "station" for a while, and this might be done by advertisement or personal application. An introduction to an influential bank, or wool shipping firm, would be useful.

Wishing the wanderer all possible good luck, wherever he may feel inclined to settle for the time being, I would remind those that travel from Sydney, north, south, or west, that, leaving in the evening, they pass the night 2,000 feet, and upwards, above the sea, and if a sleeping berth is not obtainable, *plenty* of *wraps* should be taken, or a severe, and, perhaps, dangerous chill, might be the consequence. Another thing that the invalid must always remember is, that even townships are sometimes, if unimportant, miles from a doctor, and in considering a place of residence, it is as well to bear this in mind.

I have included clothing in this chapter, because it is a matter that depends so much upon climate, though some might say fashion swayed it more; but it is a great question, when anyone is desirous of providing for residence for a while, at least, in a new and distant country. Briefly, having taken some trouble to get a good idea upon the subject, I think that clothes made in Sydney are about 15 or 20 per cent. dearer all round, than in England, and, perhaps, on the whole, not *quite* so well cut. Good ready-made clothing is as cheap as in London, or any of the large provincial cities in Great Britain; so also are shirts, underwear, hosiery, &c., as well as boots and shoes. As to the texture of garments, if the visitor intends remaining in Sydney, something very light, and not calculated to show the dust, is necessary for the summer months, while such a material as blue serge, or medium tweeds, is suitable for the cooler weather. Black or dark clothing is worn by business men, but not to the extent that is fashionable in London — altogether, a fair amount of latitude is allowed in matters of dress. During the winter months in Sydney, those who are not robust will do well to be provided with a light, but well-lined "covert," or other form of overcoat, for use about sundown especially. For the bush, or, indeed, out of Sydney, no elaborate toilet is needful, though neatness need never be lost sight of. For the mountains, fairly warm clothing is always useful—homespuns and woollen shirts, and the Norfolk jacket is a very good pattern, as it allows of a waistcoat being dispensed with. Good riding trousers, in preference to breeches, may be taken with advantage, leggings (New South Wales cavalry pattern), being generally worn in preference to riding boots. Cricketing shirts of well-shrunk flannel are indispensable, and so is a good mackintosh with cape. If one has a saddle, he may take it with him, as also a twelve bore breech-loading double, and a light rifle. As to clothing for the voyage, I have referred to it elsewhere.

With respect to assortment, cost, &c., of the, to me, Eleusinian mysteries of dress stuffs, mantles, bonnets, &c.—
> With other articles of ladies fair,
> To keep them beautiful, or leave them neat,

I regret I have to plead ignorance and inexperience, but, I think, none need be apprehensive of any but the slightest difference, if any, between the choice and prices in Sydney, and even the leading English shops. Riding, in the city, is not a favourite pastime with ladies—if it is to be pursued, a tailor-made habit might be ordered "at home;" of course, in the "bush," riding is frequently a necessity, if not altogether so, with both sexes.

CHAPTER XIX.

THE STEERAGE; HOW TO MAKE IT COMFORTABLE — THE SEVERAL CLASSES COMPARED — SPECIAL INFORMATION FOR STEERAGE PASSENGERS BY SUEZ AND CAPE ROUTES.

Cheap excursions, and the facilities offered now-a-days to dwellers inland, for seeing the wonders of our great sea-ports, have rendered very many, more or less familiar with the internal economy, and equipment generally, of ocean-going steamers, than was the case some twenty years ago. Nevertheless, looking over a vessel in dock, or lying snugly at anchor, gives one a very different idea to the picture she presents, say in tolerably bad weather at sea, and more or less crowded with passengers. So at the risk of being accused of making too much of the sea voyage, I devote a chapter from personal experience thereof, to the passage in the third class or steerage: describing what it is like, and what is wanted to make it as comfortable as circumstances will permit, the more so as those that travel by it, as a rule, have most need of advice. It must be borne in mind, that compared with Atlantic trips now-a-days, the steamer voyage to Australia, is a matter of weeks, instead of the few days required to reach the land of the Bird of Freedom ; hence the choice of the class by which to travel is well-worth serious consideration.

In bad weather there is, indeed, little comfort in the steerage, that is, when the deck is not available; but when fine, the deck will be pleasant, and most certainly, even if you do have all sorts and conditions in the steerage, you can not only be much amused, but also learn much in so mixed a company. Here, again, I advise all to keep on deck as much as possible, and, if it is not contrary to regulations, to eat their meals, or a portion thereof, there also. Fine weather means everything to the steerage passenger, and if it continues, it is a jolly, gipsy, sort of life ; while for a young fellow who is going to make his way in Australia, it is a good, useful, beginning. But in the case of gently nurtured women, and young girls especially, it must be remembered, and, at the same time, regretted, that they cannot shut their ears to much occasional "language," and they are compelled, at times, to hear much that is deplorable, especially if anything like a "ruction" takes place below.

Now, what I have principally to say about the steerage, compared with the other classes, is, that the comfort and accommodation provided is not proportionate to that afforded in the first and second saloons. Travelling by rail in England—such companies as the London and North-Western or Great Western Railways, offer three classes, the cost of the first is about double that of the third ; the second is a half-way house, as it were, in point of expense. The accommodation throughout, on long-distance trains especially, is perhaps without fault. A third-class carriage is by no means immeasurably below the first class as regards comfort and general appointments, the reverse, in fact.

But take the steamship fares to Australia. The second saloon is *about* half the cost of a first class passage, the steerage is from one-half to one-third less than the second saloon, the cost of the passage is, therefore, proportionate. but the accommodation is not. The difference between the third, and the first and second-classes, is very great. I do not complain about it, or suggest a change, but I want it to be understood that such is the case.

Between the first and second-class saloons, the difference is only in small matters and minor details comparatively. Every reasonable comfort, not to say luxury, is afforded. I take, as an example, the accommodation offered to second-class passengers by the Peninsular and Oriental Company on what are termed their Jubilee boats, and contend that the most fastidious person cannot, with any show of reason, find fault with the sleeping quarters, food, service, and appointments generally, placed at their service. I certainly think it is quite as good as some of their chief saloon accommodation not very many years ago.* At the same time, it is only common fairness to state that we, no doubt, owe this high standard of excellence, to such competition, as the Orient Line has principally been the cause of bringing about; while their steamers are more uniform in their magnificence, and in the equally high-class accommodation they afford, than are

* I am in no way subsidized by the "P & O," or any other company.

those, which their powerful rival employs in the Australian trade.

The second class passenger has :—

1. The best cabin accommodation in point of furniture, bedding, washing utensils, and good bath-rooms.
2. A luxuriously furnished, well-lighted, comfortable saloon. Should the weather be wet and uncomfortable, it is hardly any drawback.
3. A smoking-room for those who wish to use it, and in some cases, a special sitting-room for ladies.
4. Excellent and abundant meals, well served, and sometimes, punkahs (a great luxury), for hot weather.

Does the steerage passenger get half of the above for his money? No. Therefore if you can *afford* the difference between third and second class, you will receive ample value for your money.

Now, as to the season for leaving England by steamer, whether by the Cape or Suez Canal, try to leave between September and March, but, if you must leave during the early summer, the Suez Canal route, if you think you can stand the heat well, may suit you best; going from the Cape to Australia, in May, June and July, is cold, miserable work, the nights being very long, as it is then mid-winter in the Southern hemisphere. You enter the Red Sea fifteen or sixteen days after leaving England, and, if possible, but, especially, if you are of what is termed "full habit" of body, avoid getting there during the months of August and September. A good deal of unnecessary fuss is made *sometimes* about Red Sea heat, but it is always worth consideration, and a little abstinence in food and drink, for a few days prior to entering it, that is, at the hottest season of the year, will do you no harm. The passage of the Red Sea occupies about four days, and your hot weather by the Suez route will last you until you arrive within three or four days of first sighting Australia, in all, including stoppages, about three weeks of much hotter, and more trying weather, than you have ever been used to, if born and bred in the British Isles. If afraid of, or liable to sea-sickness, the Suez route is the better, if the heat is not an objection. But, anyone wishing to avoid the heat, and not fearing sea-sickness, would be better suited by the Cape route. These remarks, as well as the season I have indicated for leaving, apply principally in the case of anyone that is delicate, and it would be well to obtain medical advice, as to whether protracted heat should be avoided or not.

As to steamers *viâ* Suez, there is no need for me to give an elaborate list of them and their fares, as they are so constantly advertised. The Peninsular and Oriental take first and second-class passengers only. Then comes the Orient Line, taking all classes. The Norddeutscher Lloyd, or North German-Lloyd, I have also had the experience of, and can speak very highly of them; the food is exceedingly good, the third-class, generally, is very well looked after, and the fares are low. There is also the Deutsches Australisches Line, while there are other steamers. Few will care, I think, to go steerage by sailing vessels; I certainly do not recommend them, if they have option of steamer.

For the Cape route, there are available the steamers of the New Zealand Shipping Co. and the Shaw, Savill, and Albion Line, transhipping passengers at Hobart,

Tasmania; the Milburn Line, and the Aberdeen White Star Line, the Gulf Line, and, occasionally, others.

When enquiring about passage money, &c., be always sure to ask if the amount includes bedding and mess utensils, as, if it does not, you should add about £1 for cost of same. It means, also, that you have to wash up your breakfast or dinner service after each meal, which is not a positive luxury.

As to clothes for the voyage, remember, if you go by the Suez route, that, after the first few days, even if you leave England in the winter, you will not require any really warm clothing until you come within a few days of Australia: so both sexes urgently require a stock of very light clothing, which, bear in mind, will always be useful to you in Australia, so it is not as if you had to go to any expense for the voyage only. I do not ask you to be slovenly, quite the reverse, but people can always be neat, without display, or great expense. Blue serge is very useful, so is dungaree, and of whatever light material coats or dresses are made, for children especially, it should be coloured. Steamers' decks soon soil and spoil good clothes, so take none of your best for use on the voyage. These remarks apply to the Suez route. If going by way of the Cape, you will require more warm, and less light clothing, though, while passing though the tropics, a small stock of the latter will be most useful.

If you like to take a little medicine with you, aperient and cooling mixtures are the best, and most wanted. "Prickly heat" is a very common ailment during the hot weather, especially with young children, sometimes causing very unsightly eruptions. It disappears with the hot weather. "Toilet vinegar" is said to be a useful antidote. I am no authority on the subject of babies, but I might respectfully suggest that, as a rule, they might do with lighter costumes, being often wrapped up in several layers of clothing, which with the thermometer at ninety, cannot be agreeable to their feelings.

A basket-hamper, with a small stock of enamelled iron pannikins and plates, a few knives, forks, and spoons, a small stock of tea, sugar, condensed milk, and a few tins of potted meats, is very useful, as a "snack" can thus be often enjoyed by a person who cannot face the regular meals. For a supply of hot water, it will be necessary to make friends with the steerage cook or his mates. They are, indeed, great men, but like many other great men—warriors, statesmen, and the like—a ship's cook is not always adamant as regards the witchery and allurements of Beauty, neither is he, as a rule, averse to alcoholic beverages in moderation. Furthermore, like all men not wholly bad, he rarely turns a deaf ear to the pleadings of a little child; so, if you have neither, beauty, wealth, nor children, charter a youngster for a return trip to the galley.

Now, as to your boxes to contain your worldly goods. The ship's agents will tell you how many cubic feet you are allowed, and it is well to see that you have no excess, the charge for which is sometimes high, and it comes heavily upon anyone who may be under the impression that his boxes are all right. If you do not know how cubic feet are reckoned, I would explain, that a box 3 feet long, 2 feet broad, 2 feet deep, contains 12 cubic feet. Sometimes 15 feet are allowed; this could be made up as follows :—1 box 3 feet long, 2 feet wide, 1 foot 8 inches deep equals 10 cubic feet; and 1 box 2 feet 6 inches long, 1 foot 6 inches wide, 1 foot 4 inches deep equals 5 cubic feet. Small packages you can have at hand. Your bigger box—marked, "wanted on the voyage"—will, perhaps, have to go into the baggage-room, where you can have access to it on a certain day each week. All baggage marked "not wanted on the voyage" is placed in the hold; and it is well, if the expense is not too great, to have boxes tin-lined inside, the lid of tin being soldered down when packed. When measuring, be careful to go outside of all cording, laths, or similar projections.

There is, not unfrequently, a good deal of grumbling on board ship about all manner of things, and especially the food, however good it may be. Generally, it would seem, that a certain personage bears out to the full, on shipboard, the anxiety accorded to him by Dr. Watts, to find employment for idle hands. If you think there is, in anything brought up amongst the passengers, a sufficient ground for complaint, join in by all means, and aid in seeing it coherently reported in the proper quarter; if not, "sit upon" the grumblers all you can, as unreasonable growling tends to make everything and everybody uncomfortable, and officials, who are, in all probability, doing their best, get disheartened, and you are worse off than ever.

The doctor is not unfrequently the subject of complaints amongst the third-class passengers, sometimes there is cause for it. The otherwise aspiring soul of the young "medico," on his first voyage, is not by any means " above buttons," on the contrary, his "brass-bound suit" is usually much to his liking, and he naturally prefers to air it, in harmless flirtation on the first saloon deck, being but human, to wasting its sweetness on the desert air of the steerage. Here, of course, if you have cause for complaint, make it to the captain. On the other hand, many people having a real live doctor at call, and nothing to pay, are always discovering endless ailments, and worry accordingly. The most civil and attentive ship's doctor I ever met with, was on a North German-Lloyd steamer.

If your cooks and stewards have done all they can to make you comfortable, a round-robin, taking the form of a small coin each, may find plenty of supporters, though the collection thereof, amongst all classes, is a thankless task, especially if you have many people on board, who are possessed of those strictly Christian principles, which do not encourage generosity, or recognition of services rendered.

I describe the places called at, and other matters in another chapter.* I have only to suggest to those that travel by sea, that they might, with advantage, pack up in their "not wanted" boxes, any such trifles as narrow-mindedness, "strong views" upon certain subjects, and uncharitableness generally; indeed, if they are accidentally left behind, or lost altogether, it will be none the worse for them.

Any sum of money taken on board should at once be placed in charge of the purser. Do not take Bank of England notes to Australia, because you will be charged $2\frac{1}{2}$ per cent. when cashing them.

* By steamship to Australia.

Chapter XX.

ANIMAL LIFE IN THE COLONY—THE MARSUPIALS — WILL THEY SOON BECOME EXTINCT? — BIRDS, REPTILES AND INSECTS.

It is but a gossiping chapter I have to offer on the above. I give no Latin names, and have copied nothing out of technical works, to which I must refer my reader who wishes for the fullest information on Australian fauna. What I have to say about them might incite him to do so, and, at the same time, create a laudable desire to protect the marsupials of Australia from threatened extinction. The North American bison, or buffalo, as he is usually termed, once so plentiful, is now almost a thing of the past, and not a few noble animals on the American Continent, such as the elk and wapiti, are sharing a like fate. The outcry in all these cases comes too late, the mischief has been done.

The kangaroo proper comes at the head of the marsupial* family, and its skin is now a valuable article of commerce, the consequence is, that shooting them as a business is very common in districts where it can be made to pay in any way. The grey is the most common kangaroo; then there are the blue and red varieties, the latter being found mostly, I believe, in the Riverina district. In height, a big "old man" will measure six or seven feet, that is,

* Marsupial, I need hardly explain, signifies having a bag or pouch for carrying the young.

when sitting in tripod fashion on hind legs and tail When grazing, they support the forepart of the body on their short forelegs, and arching their great powerful tail, propel themselves along very materially by its aid; the great, seemingly disproportionate, hind legs being hardly used. When, however, it is necessary to move in earnest, the hind legs only are used, and the speed at which even a kangaroo rat can move on two legs (an animal not much bigger than a hare) must be seen to be believed. The central of the three fore claws on each hind foot is much larger than the other two, and is a most formidable weapon; it will easily disembowel a kangaroo dog,* or a rash and incautious sportsman, and great care should be taken in approaching an "old man" when at bay, or "bailed up,"† as the common expression is.

Then come the lesser of the kangaroo tribe, the wallaroos, paddy melons, wallabies, brush, swamp, and rock, kangaroo rats, &c., many of which have good marketable skins, though the price received for them is not very remunerative. All have a price set upon their ill-fated heads, of which I give details.

I do not deny that much has to be said upon the harm that marsupials do towards thinning pasture. Food is rarely too plentiful upon a sheep run, and it is a serious matter to have large "mobs" of kangaroos in one's neighbourhood. As to their decrease, it is estimated that

* A kangaroo dog, as far I can make out, should have a good deal of the Scotch deerhound about it, though the greyhound is frequently termed a kangaroo dog.

† "Bail up" is a common phrase for stopping a person for any purpose. It would seem to be derived from fastening up a cow for milking.

in 1881 there were more than six millions of kangaroos proper in the Colony, and, as at the end of 1889, their estimated number was not much over one million, five-sixths have been destroyed in eight years. Their habits, and size, render them more easy of destruction than the wallaby, who is estimated to flourish as much as ever, as his tribe total nearly as much as they did ten years ago; then, again, the value of the kangaroo skin is an incentive to their being hunted more keenly.

The wombat is a burrowing animal, and a price is also set upon his head. The native bear, or koala, is, I think, in appearance, the "low comedian" of Australian fauna. He is about two feet long, and with beady black little eyes, and a peculiar black leathery nose, which is in strong contrast to his grey fur; he is a very comical little fellow, his movements are painfully slow, and are characterized by an equally painfully evident anxiety as to his personal safety. I have mentioned his habit of giving utterance to distressing screams, of which he will give you a sample if you attempt to cut down the tree in which he is taking refuge. The opossum, I need hardly describe, has many enemies, owing to his valuable skin, and stands greatly in need of protection.

Then comes, I suppose, as odd a creature as is to be found, the platypus, as he is called "for short," known to science as the platypus ornitholynchus. Most people have seen a mole—if they will imagine one rather more than a foot long, of proportionate size, clothe him with short, rich, brown fur, substitute webbed feet for the powerful excavators of the mole, and provide him with a ducks bill, coloured a neat black, they will have a perfect picture of the platypus. The echidna is also an odd-looking creature, like a rudimentary porcupine with a bill—it is the ant-eater of Australia. The "flying fox," a huge bat, eighteen inches or more across the wings from tip to tip, is very plentiful in the Colony; forming large "camps," and being nocturnal in their habits, they are very destructive in orchards, choosing the finest and ripest fruit.

Native dogs, cats, hares, and rabbits are, I need hardly say, imports, at one time or another; the native dog or dingo, creates terrible havoc amongst a mob of sheep. He is a little less than the average collie, and the perfect dingo is of a reddish, foxy, colour. The native cat grows to a large size, and a visit of one to the fowl-house is a melancholy business. I need not describe a hare, I think, though the Australian hare is, perhaps, on the whole, smaller, and less "gamey" in flavour than his English relative. As to a rabbit, most English people have seen one, a good many Australians probably wish they never had.

The irrepressible rabbit, as is well known, almost amounts to a curse in certain parts of New South Wales. They have legislated for, and concerning him, but being lost to all sense of decency, neither the Legislative Council or Assembly have any terrorizing effect upon his hardened nature. He has been flooded out, shot, trapped, poisoned, fenced out and around, at enormous expense, but in spite of all that is done, he "comes up smiling" like some undaunted feather weight, and, regardless of his uncomfortable surroundings, continues to obey the Divine injunction to increase and multiply, in a manner which has long passed into a proverb. They *may* effect the extermination of the rabbit, but I humbly think that it is very improbable that any uniform scheme will ever succeed, different districts will require different treatment. Some people may be tempted to ask, very pertinently, if nothing can be done on a profitable basis, with an animal whose skin is valuable, and flesh also excellent as an article of food. The chances are that in most countries something would have been done. I believe that an effort is being made to place some of the hares upon the English market.

Before finishing with quadrupeds, I might add, that it is estimated that there are over four thousand wild horses or "brumbies" in the Colony, which are, I need hardly say, exceedingly difficult to capture, and are shot, if possible, as they entice domesticated horses to follow them.

The proscribed animals, and the prices given for their scalps, which vary according to the district, are :—Kangaroos, 1d. to 1/-; wallaroos, 6d.; wallabies, 1d. to 1/-; paddy melons, 2d. to 1/-; kangaroo rats, 2d. to 6d.; wombats, 2/6; hares, 2d. to 1/-; eagle hawks, 2/6 upwards; native dogs, 10/- to 80/-; wild pigs, 1/-; opossums, 1d. to 2d. Certain men are appointed in all districts to examine scalps, and the funds are paid out of an assessment fund, which is also subsidized by Government. In 1889, over £50,000 was thus expended, and, I might add, that the estimates given at the end of 1889 for the Colony were :—

Kangaroos	1,036,717
Wallabies	3,064,961
Native dogs	25,333
Hares	2,744,810
Wild pigs	3,354

for which the Department of Agriculture is responsible.

As to birds, the emu may, I think, be said to rank first among the birds of New South Wales, and I trust it will be long before it is extinct. Its dark-green eggs, which admit of being beautifully carved, are familiar objects in Australian shops. The eagle hawk is a magnificent bird, but very destructive to lambs, and it is, therefore, destroyed as far as possible. Of other notable birds, there is the great crane or "native companion," the lyre-bird, with its beautiful tail, the black swan at the head of a numerous family of wild fowl, and the "laughing jackass," often referred to in descriptions of the bush. Its proper name is the great kingfisher; it is of sober plumage, and distinguished by its hideous, mocking, laugh, which can be heard at a considerable distance. It would make the fortune of a pantomime "demon" if he could successfully imitate it. When a few of these birds get together at sunset, as they frequently do, to laugh, I suppose, over the events of the day, the noise made is something incredible. Then follow, the bronze-wing pigeon, leatherhead, more-pork bird, gill bird (excellent eating), bustard, scrub or brush turkey, and scores more, down to certain brilliant little fellows like the smallest of our English tits. All sorts of the parrot tribe also, which are fond of fruits, the cockatoos being especially destructive to maize, and by a system of out-posts, defy the shot gun. The laughing jackass, I might add, is an inveterate enemy of snakes, and, as such, is protected all the year round. Cormorants or shags are very plentiful, and a price is set on their heads. Many birds and their eggs, such as wild fowl, certain sea birds, bustard, brush turkey, lyre bird, &c., are protected from 1st September to 28th February.

The common quail is frequently met with, but its Californian relative, though introduced, does not seem to flourish. The pheasant has also been tried. I have been unable to find out whether the partridge has also had a fair trial. I should imagine they would do well, and failing the English partridge, the red-legged variety might be tried. All imported game birds are strictly protected during their breeding season.

Magpies and crows are common features in an Australian landscape. The former, though pied like the English bird, is in size and shape like our jackdaw. It has, in its wild state, a quaint and pleasing whistle, and can be readily taught to whistle a tune in captivity, in which it develops all the wicked ways and inborn devilry which seem to be the especial birthright of the magpie.

Of fish I have dealt elsewhere, so we will go on to the reptiles, of which there is a large and varied assortment, and among the principal snakes are the black, death adder, brown, tiger, diamond, and carpet snakes. The first three are all very poisonous. Of lizards there is also a large family, from the iguana downwards; the alligator abounds in Northern Queensland, but not in New South Wales.

A good many people have an objection to snakes, amounting, here and there, to what is termed a rooted antipathy; personally, I cannot say that they are very companionable, and one has to be careful, especially in the hottest weather, when they are most active and venomous alike. In common with many thousands, I have slept "out" in all sorts of places, in snake infested countries without injury, but then it is always well to examine blankets, boots, &c., before using them. I think that, as a rule, reptiles, and such things as centipedes, scorpions, &c., do not wander about at night, still, if they happen to be out late, they are not particular where they sleep. "Fossicking" for snakes is a pastime I do not recommend. After being "prodded," they have a knack of turning up, in the vilest of tempers, where least expected. I have had more than one narrow escape at this pastime.

The death adder has a somewhat suggestive title, but I have heard experts place the black snake first as regards fatality of bite, and, when annoyed, it is terribly vicious; in fact, any poisonous snake fully roused, and striking out time after time, is an exceedingly interesting sight. Instructions how to act in case of snake bite, are printed, and circulated generally, throughout Australia, and they are worth remembering, for a man struck by a poisonous snake out in the bush is in a bad plight. I believe that bites have been successfully treated, of late, by hypodermic injection of nitrate of strychnine: whether this has been tried in the case of the hitherto deadly and antidote-defying Indian cobra, I do not know.

The iguana* is occasionally a formidable looking reptile, measuring sometimes five feet or more in length, in shape like an alligator. It is non-poisonous. It is at home in the water, can shuffle along at a fairly quick rate on land, and can climb a tree: so it is not devoid of useful accomplishments. It will eat young birds, small fish, and in

* Although generally termed the iguana, the great lizard of Australia and the Cape differs from the iguana proper, of Central and South America, and its proper name is, I believe, the monitor. In the bush it is called a "gohanna."

rabbit-infested districts is, I believe, protected, as it enters the burrows and makes a meal of the youthful rodent. Its skin is handsomely marked, it is dainty eating, and the fat is reckoned a great cure for stiff joints, &c. Sometimes, if you come upon them suddenly, they will "bail you up," hissing vigorously, and distending themselves in a somewhat startling manner.

Of frogs, in localities suited to batrachian requirements, there is no lack, and a light sleeper would be much troubled by their musical efforts. Some of the green variety are of great beauty.

Then follow the insect tribes, of which I hardly think I can be expected to do more than mention a few of the most evident, as, perhaps, the entymology of Australia is not very widely known, even to the most learned and scientific.

I think the centipede is entitled to pride of place in point of size. I believe they are found as long as twelve inches;* the largest I have ever seen measured was eight. The style of insect is well-known, as we have it in a very much milder form in this country. It varies in colour, and its bite is much dreaded. It is very plentiful in dead wood, and it is well to keep an eye upon a camp fire in the evening, as the heat drives such gentry out of the wood, and they are not averse to quartering themselves on the bystanders. I have seen a very lethargic and silent gentleman suddenly endowed with an appalling fluency of language and abnormal activity, simply through

* I, of course, refer to Australian centipedes. I have seen specimens of the Brazilian centipede well in excess, I think, of twelve inches in length.

getting a large centipede up, what is termed "the leg" of his trousers. Scorpions are to be found, and are very vicious; with their tales curved over their backs, armed with a huge sting ready for instant action, they look what they are, venom personified.

Tree and ground spiders, or tarantulas (which, in New South Wales, are termed, very often, triantelopes), are very abundant; and there is a black spider, with red spots, which has a terrible reputation. I have noticed, on the river side, a very peculiar specimen of the spider tribe, in a small grey spider, which progressed as easily on the surface of still water as on the ground.

Locusts and cicadas are very plentiful, the latter, especially in the early summer, making a deafening noise. Some of them are very large, handsome insects, of bright green; the larva, a fat whitish grub, is dug out of trees, which an expert can soon detect, by certain traces, as containing them. Sometimes as many as thirty, or more, can be got out of a small tree. They have powerful nippers by which they eat their way along, completely honey-combing the tree trunk. They make a splendid bait for fish, and are a dainty morsel to the black fellow. Of handsome butterflies and beetles there is no lack. There is a hornet, but the wasp seems to be lacking. The bee is somewhat smaller than the English specimen.

The Colony is rich in ants, and if the due consideration of the ways of these indefatigable insects really confers a moral benefit upon gentlemen of inactive habits of life, and inculcates wisdom, there is, undoubtedly, ample material for observation. First of all, in point of strength and size, are the soldier and bull dog ants—red and black in colour respectively, and three-quarters of an inch long. They are, I think, the most courageous of created beings. If you come upon one, and threaten him with your stick, he opens his nippers, and defies you, in the clearest formic language possible, to "come on." They are very tenacious of life, and seem, like the Scotchman's dog, as if they "couldna get eneuch o' fechtin'." Their sting is a thing to be remembered. I have never found a nest of any size, but on any disturbance near their quarters, they rush out like dogs upon a tramp. Clay hillocks, and huge beds, are the works of other varieties; then there is a much smaller ant, and to have a number crawling over you is like being burned by red hot embers. Again there are the white ants, which eat through most things, from telegraph poles to Government records, but sheet iron is, fortunately, not as yet included in their dietary scale. It is on account of this pest that galvanized iron telegraph poles are used in Australia.

Black flies in the bush are a terrible pest; sand flies, in their haunts, and mosquitoes, are also troublesome. There is a "special brand" of the latter, called "Scotch Greys," which are very bad after rain; they make a humming noise, are larger than the ordinary mosquito, and would madden a rhinoceros. Still, notwithstanding such trifling drawbacks, sunny New South Wales is a glorious country.

CHAPTER XXI.

HOW TO ACQUIRE LAND — THE LAND LAWS OF THE COLONY — WHAT TO DO — BUSINESS OPENINGS — THE SMALL CAPITALIST — UNDEVELOPED INDUSTRIES.

The intending emigrant will, no doubt be, before all, generally desirous of knowing how he can be placed in the way of obtaining land in the Colony, and this I will give as briefly as possible, of course, recommending him to get further local information in the proper quarters, should he wish to become a land owner in New South Wales.

First of all, the Colony is divided into three divisions, a maximum area being fixed in each for purchase or lease by one person, in view of the conditions under which settlement may best prosper in each division.

These comprise :—

1. THE EASTERN DIVISION, which is a belt including the littoral, extending from north to south of the entire Colony, and in breadth from 150 to 200 miles inland from the coast.

2. THE CENTRAL DIVISION is next, of course, to the eastern, and is a belt running north and south, or, more

strictly speaking, S.S.W. and N.N.E., about 200 miles or more in width.

3. The WESTERN DIVISION includes the rest of the Colony.

In the above, CROWN LANDS open for selection, with certain exceptions, of which more hereafter, may be taken up on terms of conditional purchase, residential or non-residential, and conditional lease in the first *two* divisions, and upon certain terms of leasehold, known as homestead leases, in the western division.

The area any one person can take up is as follows :—

(*a*.) In the EASTERN DIVISION, a minimum of 40 acres, and not more than 640, may be taken up on conditional residential purchase, 320 being the maximum for non-residential purchase, and, in addition to the first-named maximum, adjoining land, if available, may be taken up on what is termed conditional lease (see later) to the extent of a further 640 acres.

(*b*.) In the CENTRAL DIVISION the minimum is also 40 acres, but the maximum that can be conditionally purchased and leased on residential terms is 2,560 acres. In this, as in the eastern division, the maximum for non-residential purchase is 320 acres.

(*c*.) Only specially proclaimed land in the WESTERN DIVISION is open for conditional purchase, the general system being one of leasehold, or what is termed homestead leases. The minimum is 2,560 acres, the maximum 10,240 acres. A homestead lease may be chosen from vacant land, or land held under annual or occupation lease, with certain exceptions.

The CONDITIONS under which the land is allotted for conditional purchase are :—

1. In the eastern and central divisions. *Bonâ-fide* residence for the first five years ; fencing of a substantial nature, of a description to be specified by the Land Board, to be erected within two years, or a sufficient reason given to the Board if this is not done.

2. Non-residential purchasers must fence within one year of the acquirement of the land, and must effect improvements upon it within five years to the value of £1 per acre, exclusive of the fencing.

3. In the western division, the conditions for homestead leases are, residence during six months continuously each year for a period of five years, and fencing.

The method of APPLICATION and COST OF TAKING UP LAND, are as follows :—

Mark a corner of the land, and consult with the land agent at the Land Office for the district in which your proposed selection is situated, to see if it is open for selection, and classed as ordinary lands. This is an important point, as well as application in the right district. Then lodge a formal application with the Land's agent. paying 2/- per acre deposit, which application is, as soon as possible, dealt with in open court, due notice having been given to the selector and objectors, if any.

If all is in order, a certificate of confirmation is given, and the land surveyed at the expense of the selector, at a cost about from £4 for forty acres, to £18 for 2,560 acres. Three months after date of this confirmation, residence must commence, and it is imperative to observe this, and also the due payments of all instalments.

All persons of, and above the age of 16 years, may apply for land on conditional residential purchase, but no one under 21 years on non-residential terms. Simultaneous applications are dealt with by ballot, preference being given to prior applications. No one who has made an original residential purchase, can make another, unless he holds a Land Board certificate stating that he has either fulfilled the conditions of his purchase, or that, making it in his own interests, he was compelled to vacate the land. No one who has made a non-residential purchase can make any other, residential or the reverse, except to complete the area allowed him. Every conditional purchase must be made solely in the interest of the applicant.

For ordinary lands* in the eastern and central divisions, the standing price, under ordinary residential conditional purchase terms as described, is £1 per acre, 2/- of which, as I have stated, must be paid as deposit on application, the balance of 18/- is payable in instalments of 1/- annually, the first to be paid at the end of, or three months after, the third year from the date of application for the land, and so on yearly, with interest added at 4 per cent. When the Land Board has certified that the conditions of purchase have been fulfilled, viz., of residence of five years, fencing, and payment of all due instalments, the whole of the balance due may be paid up forthwith.† For

* Lands specially exempt from conditional purchase, are lands reserved for town and suburban land, for village sites, for any public use, land within population areas, or occupied under the provisions of the Mining Act.

† Of course, at a great saving of interest.

ordinary land, under non-residential terms, the cost is double, viz., 4/- per acre deposit, and 2/- annual instalments. Formal declarations of fulfillment of conditions have to be made at stated periods.

Next to purchasing, comes, of course, leasing, and CONDITIONAL LEASES, as already stated, are granted in the eastern and central divisions to the residential purchaser. These leases have a term of 15 years from date of application, at a rent to be determined by the Land Board or Land Court, to which appeal, in such matters, can be made. Rent is payable yearly in advance, and, pending determination, an annual rent of 2d. per acre is payable on application. The condition of fencing, or other improvements in lieu thereof, attaching to purchase, of land apply equally to conditional leasing. The lessee may, at any time, convert it wholly, or in part, into an additional conditional purchase.

For HOMESTEAD LEASES, in the western division only, application must be made to the Crown land's agent for the district, *personally*, and a deposit of a 1d. per acre paid. If improvements on land taken up as homestead leases are not *Crown* property, the would-be lessee and the owner are given three months in which to come to terms over them. If they fail to do this, the Land Board appraises the value, and determines mode of payment. If they are Crown property, the Land Board, in every instance, determines the value. A homestead lease has a term of 21 years from the date of application, this being divided into three periods of seven years each, the rent during each period being determined by appraisement by the Land Board. If the land has been satisfactorily improved by the lessee, a further seven years may be granted.

IMPROVEMENTS, in lieu of fencing, on conditional residential purchases, are to be on the scale of 6/- per acre on an area of 1,280 acres, or £384 on over 1,280 to 2,650 acres, during three years, and within five years 10/- per acre up to 1,280 acres, and £640 over 1,280 to 2,560 acres. If the conditional purchase in non-residential, in five years, improvement to the value of 30/- per acre, must be effected. Improvements (amongst which partial fencing is included) in the case of conditional purchases, are understood to mean anything placed upon the land of a permanent and substantial nature, necessary for the beneficial occupation of the soil.*

Having now summarized from the Crown Lands Act the basis upon which ordinary Crown land may be bought or leased, I will give exceptions of tenure, and cases in which certain land is specially dealt with.

SPECIAL AREAS are understood to apply to tracts of land upon which a higher value than £1 per acre has been placed by the Land Boards, and the price varies—of such lands the maximum which may be purchased is 320 acres in the eastern, and 640 in the central and western divisions, the minimum in each case being 40 acres.

SPECIAL LEASES are for land wanted for such purposes as erecting works, machinery, special treatment, or cul-

* A decent frame house would cost, I think, '£60 to £80, but locality makes all the difference. A good bush carpenter can do wonders, and a man is not judged in the bush by his house or clothes.

O

tivation, &c. Applications for such have to be made to the Land Board. No lease must comprise more than 320 acres, or be granted for a term exceeding fifteen years—terms are named when the lease is approved of.

SCRUB LEASES are given upon special terms, when land is infested with scrub, or noxious vegetable growth, and it may be declared scrub land whether vacant or under lease. The conditions of scrub leases mainly are, that each holder shall clear, and keep clear, so much of the land within a certain time.

RESIDENTIAL LEASES ON GOLD OR MINERAL FIELDS, so proclaimed by Government, are granted with the concurrence of the mines Department officials; they do not confer upon the holder any right to gold or minerals contained in the land. He can only work for such, like others, if possessed of authority to do so, which is obtainable from the Department of Mines.

LEASES OF INFERIOR LANDS. In either of the three divisions, inferior or isolated land may be leased upon special terms, by application to the Under Secretary for Lands.

ANNUAL LEASES. Crown Lands, which may not be already occupied under the Lands Act, may be let on annual lease on application, or by tender, as may be, in blocks not exceeding 1,920 acres. There is no limit to the land which one person may thus lease. The system gives whatever no security of tenure, such land being open to be taken up on conditional purchase, leasehold, &c., at any time.

ARTESIAN WELL LEASES offer encouragement to the owner of an annual or occupation lease in the western division, to bore or search for water, the discovery of which, in a satisfactory quantity, entitles him to a lease carrying security of tenure, for such period as may be approved of by the Governor, and at the same rent as that charged for the existing lease.

PASTORAL LEASES AND OCCUPATION LICENSES apply to a large section of land in the western and central divisions.

Much Crown land, previous to the passing of the Land Act, of 1884, was let to squatters on Pastoral Leases, as they then were, which gave them no security of tenure. The consequence was, there was always considerable friction between them and free selectors, giving rise to a good deal of "dummy" selecting, and a host of attempts generally, to dodge the then existing land laws, upon the part of the squatter and the selector alike.

The Act of 1884, however, divided the runs into two halves—the Leasehold Area and the Resumed Area—the former to be held on certain terms for ten and fifteen years ; the latter to be open for selection as before—the tenure of the first to be known as a Pastoral Lease, that of the second as an Occupation License.

In 1889 a further enactment was made law for the benefit of the holder of a Pastoral Lease—which leases had now elapsed in the eastern division—as it conferred upon him, in the central division, the right, upon application, of a renewal of his ten years lease for a further five years, if sufficient improvements had been effected to justify such a concession, with a separate appraisement for rent every five years. While in the western division a lease of 21 years was legalised, capable of renewal for a further seven years, if, as in the central division, sufficient improvement had been wrought on the land. An appraisement for fixing the rent being made every seven years by the Land Board, with right of appeal, as in all such cases, to the Land Court.

Such being the laws with respect to tenure of land, the following items may be of interest :—

VOLUNTEER CERTIFICATES are occasionally referred to. The explanation is that under the Volunteer Force Regulation Act of 1867, which has since been repealed, certificates were issued to men who had been efficient for a certain period, entitling them to a free grant of 50 acres of land. These certificates are still good as regards any land open for conditional purchase.

TRANSFERS—In the case of conditional purchases, no transfers can be made until the full term of residence has expired (except in case of death, insolvency, &c.), but additional conditional purchases may be transferred, providing that the original purchase is transferred with them, the term of the latter having expired. A small registration fee is charged by the land's agent, and if the transfer represents an absolute sale, stamp duty is charged.

SALES BY AUCTION OF CROWN LANDS—Crown lands are put up to sale at auction on two systems. The ordinary, by which payment must be completed within three months, and the deferred, by which payment by instalments, with interest added, is spread over a term not exceeding five years. Town lands cannot be sold in blocks of more than half-an-acre, suburban lands in more than 20 acre blocks, nor country land in blocks exceeding 640 acres; at the same time, not more than

200,000 acres may be thus sold in one and the same year.

As to the SYSTEM of WORKING the Crown Land Act, that of 1884 repealed all previously existing Acts, and divided the Colony into the three divisions already specified, and there are further subdivisions of land districts, and land-board districts. Of the former there were at the end of 1889, 91, and in each there is a Crown Lands Agent, to whom applications for selections, payment of instalments, &c., are made. He forwards all needful matter to the Land Board, and these Boards really conduct most of the administering of the land laws. There are 14 of them, each having control over a certain number of the before-named districts. An appeal against any decision of the Land Board lies with the Crown Lands Court. The headquarters of the Lands Department, with the general staff, is, of course, in Sydney.

Such, upon the whole, is all that refers to Crown lands, which may interest or inform the reader. I have carefully compiled the foregoing from the Crown Lands Act, and, though slight errors may have crept in, I think there is sufficient to afford a general idea how to set about acquiring land, as well as shewing the law with regard to Crown land generally, throughout the Colony. Of course, there are large private holdings in New South Wales, to which such Acts as I have quoted do not apply, many of them originating with grants of land, such as the notorious " Macarthur " grants, which were made in that liberal style which usually characterizes the action of those who give away what does not belong to them.

Of the area of the Colony under crop there is about one two-hundredth part only, or less, probably, than one million out of one hundred and ninety odd million acres comprised in the extent of New South Wales. So much for agriculture. No doubt the would-be selector will ponder over the above for a while.

I hardly suppose that any one intending to emigrate to New South Wales, imagines that there is beautiful land awaiting mere selection, without any trouble at all in finding it. Such is not the case. He will also, at first, I trust, form a definite idea as to what branch of pastoral, agricultural, or general business he thinks of taking up, assuring himself as to his fitness for the same, and his means and ability generally, to give his choice a fair trial.

First of all, if he thinks of sheep farming, it will be necessary for him to spend sometime as "jackeroo," or, better still, as I have elsewhere suggested, gain experience as a station hand, and at droving, &c., as well. This he should—nay, must do, I think, before he can gain even an adequate idea, if he is fresh from England, upon the subject of the capital required to make a fair start, and make up his mind as to whether the life is suited to him or not. Many more may think of raising or feeding stock upon a smaller scale, farming, market gardening, dairy-work, fruit-growing, pig and poultry raising, &c., in any of which one may do well. But I cannot, of course, pretend to tell a man how he is to make a fortune, or even if he will be certain of a good living in any one branch. If I can only put him in the right way of thinking about, and looking at, making a venture in the Colonies, I shall do all I hope to effect.

Australia is, I fear, just at present, feeling severely the effect of the land boom of a few years back, and matters may not be re-adjusted for, perhaps, a year or so. The land, I should explain, over which so much speculation took place, was principally city and suburban land, which rose to absurd prices, and as so many people are centred in the cities of Australia, the usual reaction of such "booms" is much more severely felt than would be the case if the bush was more thickly populated.

I will assume, however, that besides those who intend to take up land and employ their capital in agricultural or pastoral pursuits, there may be many who, having some small capital, would like to know if there is nothing in Sydney and its suburbs that they could acquire in the way of a small business, which would render them a fair return. To this I say, certainly, there are often numerous little businesses to be picked up cheap. I have known people with less than a £100 at their command do exceedingly well.

In Sydney there are several agents for the sale of businesses generally, who advertise liberally in the daily papers. I would certainly recommend anyone who is desirous of investing, to see what they have for sale. They often have bargains to dispose of, and generally, I think, the fairest possible treatment is experienced at their hands. People, of course, who embark in an enterprise new to them must not be surprised if they are not very successful; but those who have any business at their finger ends can do well upon the whole, or, at least, make a living, with only a small capital. If the applicant promises well, business agents will frequently advance money towards the purchasing and acquirement of a business; so, altogether, from some experience, I think the small capitalist is likely to get along fairly well *if possessed of a knowledge of, and capacity for any business.* Thus also, the wife, if a couple without much encumbrance, have a little money to invest, can contribute to the increasing of the common stock, by taking up some light business.

I can do little more than briefly enumerate the general industries of the Colony. Wool, mutton, tallow, &c., are the staple articles, certainly far and away above all others, and of these I have written, I trust, sufficiently to give a general idea of them, and to stimulate full enquiry, under the heading of "Live Stock Resources of the Colony."

I must leave the intending emigrant to fight all for himself the mighty question of Free Trade *versus* Protection, in deliberating whether it will pay him to try farming in the Colony, or the cultivation of fruit, &c., not only with a view to supplying local demand, but, perhaps, with a hope of finding a foreign market. Sugar, too, is a commodity which will, no doubt, play a leading part in his deliberations, especially if he will look at some reliable figures on the amount that Great Britain draws annually from the beet fields of the Continent of Europe, leaving the cane fields of Greater Britain to take that luck which is generally described by the prefix of "pot."

There are cane fields on the northern rivers of the Colony, but whether the duty of five shillings per cwt. on raw sugar imported into the Colony gives them full scope and encouragement, I cannot say.

Tobacco has been cultivated in New South Wales for twenty years, a large quantity being manufactured in Sydney. The Colony stands rather high as regards the consumption of tobacco, it being estimated that each inhabitant annually uses more than 50 ounces. Lately, however, I believe that tobacco has been cultivated to an extent sufficient to meet local requirements, while there is not at present any outlet for it in the shape of a foreign market.

The Excise levy a duty of 1/3 per lb. on Colonial manufactured and cut tobaccos, and 2/6 per lb. on cigars and cigarettes turned out of Colonial factories. The import duties on tobacco are 3/- per lb. on manufactured, and 1/- per lb. on unmanufactured. Cigars and cigarettes pay 6/- per lb.

Wine growing is one of the New South Wales industries of which I cannot treat in a discursive manner; but I think that all that may be done in Australian wines, will, for the most part, have to be done in a foreign market. Careful attention may make the trade a very valuable one, and if the wines were better known by the wine consuming public, they would be better appreciated. The middle and lower classes of Great Britain do not incline to cheap claret (in some cases not without reason), and I think that middle-class Australia, of British stock, that is, is still less likely to do so. As time goes on, more especially, tea, I think, will gain ground, rather than lose it, and he would be a bold man who would suggest depriving the Australian of his great stand-by, a cup of tea. I have remarked that cider or perry might be made in many districts, and its use as a beverage might be as cheap, and perhaps better than so much tea. Colonial beer is largely brewed, it must be remembered, mostly from imported malt. The excise duty is 3d. per gallon.

I have drawn attention to the Illawarra district as being the dairy of New South Wales, but I do not think a fortune is readily made at the business, as dairy farms are fairly plentiful on other than the South Coast line. While travelling through the Illawarra district, small farmers have grumbled to me about the very poor price they get all-round for their butter from the much-abused middleman. Our winter months are their opportunity, as I am sure their summer surplus would find a market at that season of the year in England, and it would be a boon to a class that must work hard for a living. A good many butter factories are established in the suitable districts, their production, owing to its more even quality, fetching a higher price than farm produce.

The production of silk, or sericulture, as it is technically termed, has been brought before the Government notice. The industry is one in which Italians would be necessary to work it, and, I believe, it is being tried at a settlement called New Italy in the Richmond River district. Whether it is politic to encourage an industry for the sole benefit of Italians, or any other alien community, it is not for me to say.

CHAPTER XXII.

FORESTRY IN THE COLONY—NATIVE WOODS—THE WATTLE-TREE AND ITS CULTIVATION—IRRIGATION AND CONSERVATION OF WATER—MINING—BROKEN HILL—"PROSPECTING," "REEFING," AND ALLUVIAL WORK—OTHER MINERAL RESOURCES OF THE COLONY.

Reckless deforestation is, too frequently, a crying evil in a new country. The effect it may have upon the face of the earth and the properties of the soil are rarely considered ; while, apart from the waste and destruction of, perhaps, useful timber, little or no heed is taken about the replenishing of the denuded forests ; the destruction of the magnificent Kauri pine in New Zealand is one melancholy instance of this.

I have sketched the mournful aspect of the extensive paddocks, with their ghostly crew of withered trunks of ring-barked trees, if, here and there, a few had been spared, a clump, for instance, to crown some rising knoll, putting aside the mere question of appearances, it might have afforded some sort of shelter for stock, and done something, perhaps, to mitigate the scorching blasts of the hot winds.

The planting, too, of certain districts, might work a great and beneficial change, such, for example, as has been wrought in the Landes district, in the south-west of France; but the subject is so vast, and requires so much technical knowledge, that I hesitate almost to refer to it, lest it be thought that I took upon myself a task to which I am wholly unequal, and for which I am alike unqualified.

The exports of timber to Australia from Scandinavia, and later, from British Columbia, have been of vast extent. The enormous quantity of weatherboard houses and buildings generally, offered a large market for this class of timber, and even if Australian woods were as well suited as those of the northern lands in question, those who ask why rely upon imports so much? must remember the difficulty and expense of inland transit, handling generally, sawing, &c., compared with the facilities offered for sending logs down Norwegian torrents, or rafting them on broad Canadian rivers.

The principal hardwoods found in Australia are the blackbutt, iron bark, turpentine, messmate, woolly-butt, blue, spotted, and gray gums, white box, peppermint or red wood, stringy bark, and others, and to fully appreciate the hard nature of some of the afore-mentioned, the amateur should try his powers as an axeman upon them, and by some experience in handling them, gain practical knowledge of the immense weight of a few, at least, in comparison with their bulk. The soft woods contain amongst them the red cedar, silky, swamp, and forest oak, &c. Many of the above, in addition to being used in rough work, are beginning to be found of value for ornamental and cabinet-work purposes.

There are numerous regulations now in force with respect to timber and State forests generally, and what is far more to the point, the New South Wales Government has secured the services of a gentleman who did most excellent work in forestry matters in South Australia. He has not long been placed in the position of Director General of the Forests of the Colony, and judging from the style in which he has commenced his work, I think it argues well for this special department meeting with the care and attention it deserves.

The cultivation of certain of what are termed the wattle-trees,* may be briefly instanced to show what a comparatively valuable industry lies in a quarter from which little might be expected by the casual observer.

Certain varieties of the wattle-tree supply a bark which is greatly used by tanners, and is known, "in the trade," by the name of mimosa bark, of which it is important to remark that the demand is, as far as I can learn, in excess of the present supply. In South Australia, attention is being paid to the proper cultivation of the suitable varieties, and also, to some extent, it is practised in Victoria, which latter Colony instituted a Royal Commission upon the subject, upon which much that is useful might be written, but, as I have said, I merely wish to briefly draw attention to the industry. Several able lectures were delivered in Sydney upon the subject of wattle cultivation, and, as is not unusual under such circumstances, there was a little impetus given to the matter, and it threatened, not exacly to be overdone, but to be taken up with lack of judgment.

* Properly speaking, they are acacias.

The bark can be stripped from trees in State forests and timber reserves, by payment of an annual sum for a license or permit, and a royalty. As to whether there is any provision made for the planting of fresh trees, I am not aware. Only trees of a certain girth are allowed to be stripped. Proper cultivation of the wattle will, no doubt, pay exceedingly well, if the locality chosen be suitable for providing fairly cheap transport to the market, or port of shipment. If it ever happens that meat-killing centres are established on New South Wales railways, here is the bark for tanning, and it is not unreasonable to predict a very considerable local demand, in addition to foreign markets being always open. A peculiarity about the seeds of the wattle is the extreme hardness of their outer shell, so much so, that seeds may remain a considerable time in the earth without germinating. Bush fires, through heating the seed, greatly aid the sprouting, and in artificial sowing it is necessary either to heat the seed by burning brush, or else to soak it in hot water. The trees will live in the poorest soil, and with an annual rainfall as low as 16 or 20 inches. They do not attain any great size, and are five years, about, before they are fit for stripping.

If talk, in overflowing abundance, was alone required to ensure the success of anything, irrigation in New South Wales would have been raised to the highest possible pitch of perfection; talk, however, though good in its way, unfortunately is not sufficient, and though so much has been said, the outcome from a practical point of view is very disappointing.

The winter of 1889 was a disastrous one to a portion of the Darling district, and Bourke, an important township on the river, at the terminus of the Western Line, 503 miles from Sydney, was a great sufferer. The Darling rose to a height of 40 feet above its summer level, the district around Bourke, was flooded for a breadth of 40 miles, and the "record" flood of 1862 was, I believe, surpassed.

A very superficial look at the map of Australia will show what a gigantic watershed the Darling possesses, and how numerous and widely reaching, the feeders are that add great volumes of water, in time of flood, before Bourke is reached, from which point it flows another 400 miles before, at Wentworth, it joins issues with the Murray.

Such rains as fall in Queensland and in the north of New South Wales, soon change the rivers from their summer aspect of a chain of water holes, to a resistless torrent, and how wide the area is, and how far-reaching the tributaries are, may be realized when it is said that the people of Bourke knew of the coming of their enemy, many days before it was upon them.

From 1862 to 1889, is nearing a generation in point of time. Surely the reader feels inclined to say, some provision must have been made in all that time to best meet so probable a contingency. No. The "giant strides which the Colony has made," to quote a favourite phrase, had contributed little or nothing to the conservation of liquid treasures, to the means of converting an enemy into a most useful friend. Bourke was much in the same defenceless state probably as it ever was. Its inhabitants set to work to dam the approaching flood—to obstruct it, that is—with an amount of energy not unusually displayed by people of all nationalities, whose property, if not actually their lives, is in imminent peril. All was in vain, and Bourke, suffered as it probably will in the next, and the next great flood.

The well-known "Irrigation Colonies," which owe their origin to the Chaffey Brothers, being outside the Colony, have no place in this history; but, I believe, it is intended to start an "Irrigation Colony" in New South Wales on a similar basis; by the time these lines are in print it may have been done. Then, again, there are, no doubt, immense subterranean stores of water, which may have lost some of its valuable properties, but that is a matter for scientific research. Irrigation leases* have been instituted with a view to encouraging boring for such hidden treasures. But, after all, it is easy to find fault; the thoughtful traveller must look below the surface if he can. All things are not, by any means, what they seem. Magnificent estates may mean mortgage; the finest property, financial trouble. It is the custom in stereotyped descriptions of warehouses, factories, and centres of industries generally, to rhapsodize concerning colossal wealth, and profit, "beyond the dreams of avarice." How often is it the reverse? The poetic fervour which leads a writer to describe in glorious paraphrase the ships of Great Britain, sailing over every sea, might suffer considerably by his having a few shares in some of them.

What has all this to do with irrigation? Well, it simply means that we must consider, and a very important matter it is, too, in what position the squatters are in New South Wales generally. Can they afford to spend money

* See chapter on "How to Acquire Land," &c.

on irrigation, or support important movements for advancing their industries generally? It is a question that is an extremely difficult one to answer, and yet as impossible to gainsay the reply. The ledgers of the many banks are the best authorities, but they are not open to public inspection. It certainly would be interesting to know what proportion of owners of "runs" in New South Wales are wholly free from the control of banking or similar institutions, and possess the means, and readiness, to improve their business and their properties. Is it unjust to attribute an apparent lack of progress to some such cause? Have the banks too great a hold upon property for the general good of the Colony?

Mining is another matter upon which much might be written, as in the case of the two other subjects upon which I am so bold as to hazard a few remarks in the present chapter. It has, however, far different features. The "gold fever" is an ailment beyond the power of the physician. The seeking for hidden treasures is often a life-long dream.

Perhaps, in all the mining annals of the Colony there is no greater instance of good fortune than that which attended the observant and persevering men who brought to light the hidden treasures of Broken Hill, a name familiar enough to most people now-a-days, as the richest mine, perhaps, in the world.

Nine years ago the rocky outcrop of the Barrier ranges was a feature of an out-of-the-way sheep run, termed by the blackfellows Wilyu-Wilyu-Yong, scarcely noticed on the map of the Colony. Now there has sprung up upon

P

the somewhat desolate spot, a city of 20,000 inhabitants. No canvas mining town or collection of nondescript shanties, but a handsome well-built city.

It was during '83 that Charles Rasp, a boundary rider on the Mount Gipps "run," pocketed some specimens of the rugged outcrop, and took them to the manager of the station, Mr George M'Culloch, and the matter ended in leases being secured for seven blocks along the line of lode. The interest in these was amalgamated into a company or syndicate, under the name of the Broken Hill Mining Company, comprising, besides Messrs. M'Culloch and Rasp, five others.

The luck was not all one way at first, and as two members sold out, it was necessary to reform the syndicate into one of fourteen shares, which, since 1885, has been famous as the successful Broken Hill Proprietary Company, and it is satisfactory, I think, to note that some at least, notably Messrs. M'Culloch and Rasp, held on from the first, when success by no means seemed certain. When mining ventures have resulted in such gigantic out-turns in so comparatively short a time, it is not to be wondered at that many stories are current as to the early vicissitudes of the mine.

A glance at the map will shew that the mine is situated in the extreme south-west corner of the Colony, and is most easy of access from Adelaide by rail and steam tramway; from a commercial point of view, it must have proved an immense benefit to South Australia, rather, perhaps, than to the Colony to which it rightly belongs.

As to the possibility of similar finds, I can quote from

Mr. Coghlan's* work, the following:—"Old workings, which had been abandoned years ago, under a prevailing idea that they were valuable only on the surface, and which had scarcely, in any instance, been tested to a greater depth than 200 feet, have been re-opened with very encouraging results." The foregoing applies to gold, but with regard to silver, he writes:—"Sufficient time has hardly elapsed since the important discoveries of silver deposits were made, to enable all the principal mines to be properly developed."

The "fossicker" or "prospector" may be called the pioneer of mining. A pick, shovel, and tin dish constitutes, besides his "swag," his chief machinery. He is always on the move, and on the occasion of a "rush," he or his mate will be off to try their luck.

Roughly speaking, there are two styles of seeking gold, the alluvial, which may be defined as washing the deposits forming the sides and bed of a creek or gully, into which the gold may have been borne from the decomposed or disrupted outcrop of igneous rock; and "reefing," which, as the name implies, is the quarrying, shafting, and working generally, of quartz veins or reefs, the produce being dealt with by the stamping machine.

Alluvial gold, for reasons which it would be out of place to give here, is generally found in a pure, or nearly pure, state. In quartz veins such is not the case, hence, in addition to the stamping or crushing, it requires treatment by amalgamation with, and the subsequent sublimation of quicksilver. In "reefing," therefore, which requires capital, the great idea is to find "payable gold,"

* The "Wealth and Progress of New South Wales," already referred to.

and get a good price for your mine. The alluvial digger can work, and may make a haul, with his pick, shovel and cradle, as his sole outfit.*

A locality, even private land, may be proclaimed a gold or mineral field in the *Government Gazette*, upon which being done, mining licenses are issued to "seek, work, or win" gold and minerals thereupon. The Minister for Mines and Agriculture is at the head of the Department of Mines, which includes a staff of local surveyors, wardens, warden's clerks, mining registrars, and bailiffs.

"Fossicking," or "prospecting," is not, upon the whole, a very profitable pursuit, and is by no means devoid of hardship—getting back "stone broke" from a disappointing field, through a rough country, is not always pleasant, but generally the life has it charms, and most old "fossickers," like gamblers, are certain of things turning up "trumps" at last.

The coal trade in New South Wales is so extensive, that I can do no more than very briefly refer to it. The railway journey to Newcastle is only 4 hours, while the South Coast mines at Bulli, Wollongong, &c., are also convenient for a visit from Sydney. A colliery has not so very long been started at Helensburgh, on the South Coast Line, not 20 miles from Sydney, and a visit thereto would show the stranger what an impromptu "bush" township is like. Iron has been found in immediate proximity to the South Coast mines. Exports of kerosene shale are, I believe, rapidly on the increase. Copper is found in certain parts of the western division of the Colony. Tin and lead ore is also plentiful. In short, there is no lack of mineral treasures in the Colony.

* Diamond drills, and boring machines, the same being government property, can be hired by the public on certain conditions.

Chapter XXIII.

A CHAPTER FOR BUSINESS MEN — THE SYSTEM OF IMPORT BUSINESS — THE APPOINTMENT AND CHOICE OF AGENTS — RENTS OF OFFICES, WAREHOUSES, AND SHOPS—GOVERNMENT CONTRACTS — THE WHARVES OF SYDNEY — WHARFAGE CHARGES—CUSTOMS AND EXCISE —PROTECTION OF PATENTS AND TRADE MARKS.

Australia offers a very considerable market for English goods, the imports for the year ending 1889 amounted to £68,000,000 sterling, for the whole of Australia, of which, the sum of £22,500,000 is credited to New South Wales alone. It is, at the same time, our most distant market, and thus, though cheaper fares and quicker passages offer inducements to the merchant, manufacturer, or his traveller, to become personally acquainted with the country, and see for themselves how business is done, and, perhaps, how it might be more advantageously conducted, those who desire to open up, or extend a business in Australia, have, mostly, to take their chance, with the agents they appoint. A personal visit might have saved many men not only severe losses, but the satisfaction of seeing a business progress, which they have given up in disgust.

Briefly, the import business is conducted on two bases, indent and consignment, the former referring to goods which are actually ordered on certain conditions, as the word indent implies. Consignments, the word itself explains, they are shipments sent out by the manufacturer or merchant (sometimes a joint venture on the part of both) on speculation, for sale to best advantage; the manufacturer, if the parcel is shipped on his sole account and risk, frequently receiving an advance upon the goods to the extent of one-half, or two-thirds their value. Upon the sale of a consignment, all charges for freight, shipping, customs, wharfage, cartage and storage, and the merchant's selling commission, are deducted from the gross proceeds, and the nett results are not always altogether satisfactory. A modification of indenting has been introduced by the convenience offered by the cable service, and, in certain goods and produce which fluctuate greatly, "c.i.f. offers" are cabled, the term signifying that the prices sent, include the cost, freight, and insurance of the merchandize offered; these are liable to acceptance within a stated time.

But I will suppose that a manufacturer, or his agent, is about to visit the Colony, or Australia generally, and what I have to say applies to the several Colonies alike. I think I have given him all information he will require in deciding as to his mode of residence, and probable expenses in the Colony. As to travelling out of Sydney, in only very exceptional cases, if, indeed, in any, will he need to do so. Sydney is exclusively the centre of the import business; from Sydney it is that the travellers of the importing houses supply the inland stores with their requirements;

except, perhaps, the Riverina district, some of the trade done there being competed for by Victoria. To go into detail, a fair amount of retailing in the bush is also done by hawkers, who, in some cases, have well-appointed waggons. I have met them of many nationalities, English, French, German, Jewish, Maltese, Javanese, and Hindoos, among the number.

Furthermore, it is presumed that our new acquaintance does not intend to settle in the country, as an agent, but simply wishes to found a business, or extend one for himself or his employer. His first care, therefore, will be to grasp the system, or general idea, pursued in the selling and distribution of imported goods, so that he may find what middleman, or class of middleman, is necessary, or whether he can be dispensed with or not, before the retailer gets his goods. He will find the following styles of business houses:—

(*a*.) The merchant or general importer of all kinds of goods, who has his sale rooms for samples, also his travellers, perhaps more in the town than country, who, if he finds difficulty in dealing with a consignment, may employ:—

(*b*.) The broker, with whom he will divide his selling commission.

(*c*.) The importing houses, "soft goods" men, wholesale grocers, &c., who do the principal trade with retailers in town and country.

Through the hands of one, at least, of the above, if not occasionally through those of all three, does the bulk of imported goods pass before they come to:—

(*d*.) The retailer, or shop and store-keeper.

And, no doubt, our friend will give a good look round, and judge for himself as to what each has to say. I might most respectfully add that, at the outset, until he sees his way definitely to make any business proposition, he will do well to keep details of prices as much as possible to himself.

Should he consider it advisable to appoint any one of the A., B., or C. class as his agent—it is most probable his choice will rest with the first or third—he will, no doubt, have an eye to the commodious nature of the sale-room, and the attentions paid to customers by the salesmen, and others of the office staff with whom they come in contact. The style of travellers employed is another important matter, also if they are well received, and are genial in their manner, for it must be remembered by him that it is such men, and not the principals, who will really make his business "go," or the reverse. Fnally, let him notice how those that call at the office on business are attended to. A badly-attended office counter is not only an annoyance, but it frequently argues want of management generally.

Finally, in appointing an agent, he must remember that if he selects a general importer or broker, large or small, a more extensive field is open to him for business, for the reason that, supposing his "line" to be any article used by grocers, a general importer can sell to *all* wholesale grocers ; whereas, if he selects a firm of wholesale grocers as his agent, his sales, for the most part, will be limited to their connection, though that might be fairly extensive, and a certain and regular sale might from the first, be commanded.

As to endeavouring to dispense with a middleman, of course, our friend is at liberty to try it, and sell to retailers; and, here, what I said about keeping back details of prices comes in, for retailers are often glad to have such information, as it enables them to cut down their wholesale men; but, in the end, if our friend has to fall back upon the middleman after all, it is somewhat awkward for the retail trade to know his best terms.

Anyone starting in business as an agent for any English export house, will find it necessary to appoint a minimum amount, that is, to decide to sell not less than a certain quantity of his goods, so as to prevent retailers from dealing largely with him, otherwise he will get into trouble with " the trade," who will look upon him as an opponent, and not buy from him.

The foregoing few remarks, I trust, will not be unwelcome to anyone who may feel undecided how to go about matters when first landing in Australia. The next care will be his letters and cablegrams; if he can arrange an address before leaving England to which they may be sent, so much the better. If he must send them to the General Post Office to be called for, let him cause his English address to be placed in parenthesis under his name,* or his letters may miscarry. If he has to cable to England, let him register a "cypher" address at the Telegraph Department of the Post Office forthwith.

The question of rents of offices, warehouses, &c., is one upon which it is difficult to give exact information, so much depends upon the locality. Pitt street, near the General Post Office, is considered fairly central for offices,

* Thus, Mr. John Smith, (of 999, Gracechurch Street, London).

and here I have known £3 weekly paid for a ground floor single office. If position is not of importance, there is plenty of office accommodation to be had fairly cheap. Nearer Circular Quay is affected by shipowners, shipbrokers, wool-shippers, &c., being near to the Custom House, which is on the quay, and the Exchange, an unpretentious building, situated a short distance up Pitt street, which may be called the chief commercial street in Sydney, as far as the General Post Office, beyond which it is occupied by shops. George and King street contain the greatest variety of shops. Bridge street, a cross street near Circular Quay, is the home of many of the inter-colonial steamship companies. York, Clarence, and Kent street are more favoured by Manchester warehousemen, hardware, and wholesale people generally. Sussex street, down by the wharves, is great in dealers in produce, &c. Shops in the best streets are fairly dear, £500 and £750 a year, and upwards, for an ordinary size of shop, while in the less frequented city streets and suburbs, a house and shop may be had for £4 to £5 weekly. Warehouses will run from £4 upwards for weekly rental.

The requirements of the Public Works Department for railway plant, bridge work, &c., of course necessitate large orders to the English and other markets, as, with the exception of building certain carriages for passenger and goods traffic, New South Wales is almost entirely dependent upon external supplies, and upon the present system of obtaining these, 1 would make a few comments.

The Victorian Government does not employ their Agent-General in the matter of obtaining the requirements of their railways, or any consulting engineer, with his accompaniment of commissions. They call for tenders in the open market, and invite influential local firms to forward plans and specifications to their London houses, and for all these Government tenders there is exceedingly keen competition. They, the London houses, canvas the manufacturers, and send in their tenders at the lowest prices obtainable, with the usual marked cheque as security, in case they are successful, for the due completion of the contract, and not only do they tender for the cost of the material, but also for delivery thereof. The competition, which, as I have said, is keen, provides that everything is done at the lowest possible rate, so the Railway Commissioners have nothing to do but take delivery of and pass the plant. The risk of rejection in the Colony is, I grant, a somewhat harsh condition, but if the Victorians can get plenty of manufacturers to accept the conditions, I suppose they are right in making them. Of course, any manufacturer can tender direct; but, as there is the shipping, freight, and agency wanted in Melbourne, he finds it best to leave this in the hands of the merchant, who adds a small commission for his trouble.

A mistake is made frequently, I respectfully think, in calling for many tenders, that sufficient time is not given for their return, *i.e.*, to enable those that tender to institute due enquiry in foreign markets. Thus, if tenders are called for the making or duplication of a portion of a line, the brickwork, tunnelling, cutting, &c., can be worked out on the spot; but if bridgework is included, and, more especially, if the specification is not an ordinary one, the price must be estimated with a considerable margin, if there is not plenty of time afforded to get prices in the English or Continental market. This would be not only fair and reasonable as far as contractors, merchants, and manufacturers generally are concerned, but also to the interests of the railways, and those who find the money for them.

Furthermore, it may be said, I think, with perfect truth, that all manufacturers have a better chance in open competition. No man can go through a long business or professional career without having imbibed certain prejudices, and experienced certain disagreements, which may result in the "taboo" of firms, who should be entitled to bid for a share in the business of the Colony.

I should deeply regret if any remarks were, by any chance, misconstrued into references of a personal nature. Nothing of the sort is intended, I deal with the system generally; I deal with it because I think it needs especial reference, and I cite the Victorian system, because I think it is, in the most complete manner, the fairest "all round," it gives all manufacturers a chance, and to the Public Works Department, it means buying the best in the cheapest market, which I take to be a sound business policy.

An effort was made to establish a locomotive works in New South Wales, but it fell through, for the time being at all events; the labour troubles may have had something to do with its collapse, as such were alleged to be the bar to the development of the wealth of iron, which, with coal close at hand, is one of the richest natural endowments of the much favoured Illawarra district.

All tenders are opened by a Tender Board, of which, the Secretary for Public Works is president, the Under Secretary for the same is vice-president, and the remaining members are the Engineer-in-Chief for Harbours and Rivers, the Commissioner and Engineer-in-Chief for Roads and Bridges, the Engineer-in-Chief for Railways, the Director of Military Works, the Government Architect, while the Chief Clerk of the Public Works Department is secretary. Three members form a quorum, and the board-room is open to the public while tenders are being opened and declared.

The office of the Agent-General has more than once been discussed in the Leglislative Assembly during the past two years, and questions have been raised as to whether it would not be advisable to shorten the term of office. Upon this I do not wish to offer any comment.

Of the wharves in and around Sydney, there are public, or Government, and private sufferance wharves. Of the former there are three, the fine frontage of Circular Quay stands first, then there is the Cowper wharf in Woolloomooloo Bay, and Darling Harbour further west than Circular Quay, and situated on a southerly-running arm of the Harbour. The first-named has ample draft of water for all ocean-going mail steames. The "P & O," Orient, Messageries Maritimes, and Norddeutscher-Lloyd have their loading berths here, being moored alongside their respective lock-up sheds. There are also numerous jetties running out from the quay, whence the harbour steamers leave for the most part, and there is a ferry for the conveyance of horses and vehicles to the north shore. In the height of the wool season also, many of the large sailing vessels load at Circular Quay. Cowper wharf is the loading berth for the San Francisco steamers, and the principal place for discharging timber, and immense quantities of blue metal from Kiama, on the south coast. The private sufferance wharves extend from the Circular Quay westwards, around Dawes Point, to Darling Harbour, and afford fairly good accommodation, but the *jetties* are, in most cases, without sheds to protect cargo, as it is brought out of the ship, from sun or rain, and, I think, there is room for improvement in this way.

Wharfage rates are charged on all goods landed on any wharves. On much rough, heavy, stuff, the charge is 1/8 per ton weight, or measurement. In some cases package rates are charged from 2d. to 6d. each. Cartage is effected for the most part by "trollies," as they are called, similar to what are known as "lorries" in England. The draught horses are much lighter than those seen at British seaports, notably Liverpool.

The Government graving docks are at Cockatoo Island, $2\frac{1}{2}$ miles west of Circular Quay, and comprise the Fitzroy and Sutherland Docks. The latter is as large as, if not larger than, any single graving dock yet constructed, and can accommodate probably the largest vessel afloat.

As to tariffs, although the policy of the Colony for the present is Free Trade, a good many imports are liable to duty, including :—Bacon, beer, biscuits, butter, candied fruits, candles, cement, cheese, chicory, cocoa, coffee and tea, galvanized iron, preserves of all kinds, sugar, rice, sago, tapioco, wines, spirits, tobacco, &c.* There are

* Since the above was written, the Parkes' Ministry has been defeated, but the new tariff is not to hand in time for insertion in this edition.

bonded and free warehouses with fixed rates for rental, receiving and delivery.

The number of ships which entered at the Sydney Custom House in 1889, with cargo and ballast, was 3,254, representing 2,632,081 tons. Inward and outward pilotage is compulsory, the charge being 4d. per ton. There are good tug-boats, and towage rates are not dear.

As to the other ports in New South Wales, the coast is deficient in good harbours. Newcastle comes next to, though a long way after Sydney, and is the chief loading port for many vessels that bring general cargoes to Australian ports, and are chartered to take coal to San Francisco, Chili, or Peru. Wollongong, 50 miles south of Sydney, the principal town in the Illawarra district has a nice little artificial harbour,* but in bad weather the entrance is difficult. Bulli, famous for its coal mines, seven miles north of Wollongong or so, has jetties for loading coal, but they are entirely unprotected, and, if bad weather comes on from any easterly point, it is necessary to cast off and stand out to sea.

Patents and trade marks, and their due protection, are a matter of great concern to the generality of manufacturers. It is a great pity that there is no Intercolonial Patents and Trade Marks Act, but there is not. The Patents Law Amendment Act was the last effort made to protect the creations of the inventor in New South Wales, and became law in 1887. Letters patent for any inven-

* Vessels of 16 feet draft can be accommodated in Wollongong Harbour, and, I believe, they expect soon to take all up to 18 feet draft.

tion cost £5; the office is in Chancery square, Sydney. Trade marks are protected in New South Wales by the Trade Marks Act of 1865, and their forgery rendered a misdemeanor. Shippers of anything bearing a trade mark should always see that it is registered. The Government fee for each registration is 3 guineas. In 1879, there was also introduced a "Copyright Act," to secure copyright of printed matter, designs, &c., produced in the Colony.

Business hours generally are much the same as in England, perhaps a trifle earlier, and not so late. The luncheon hour, from 1 to 2 p.m., is strictly observed, so are the public holidays, which are not a few. The cost of clerical labour I have discussed in the Chapter on "Wages in Town and Country."

CHAPTER XXIV.

DISEASE AND EPIDEMICS IN NEW SOUTH WALES — SANITARY QUESTIONS — MUNICIPAL SHORTCOMINGS — SYDNEY HOSPITALS.

In seeking a new country for the purposes of health most especially, it is essential that the traveller should know whether, in the new world in which he is to make his home, he runs any undue risk of contracting certain ailments and diseases, from which, unfortunately, even the fairest lands are not exempt, but upon this subject I have but little wherewith to intimate the traveller.

Generally, I think, the bush is very healthy. The population is scattered, and an epidemic has, therefore, little chance of spreading. The people lead temperate, outdoor lives. The plain fare does not tempt one to practise gluttony; while, on the other hand, a healthy appetite supplants sauces and made dishes. Like the Spaniard, they rather eat to live, than live to eat. Early hours are the rule, and accident is more to be feared than disease. Sufferers from rheumatism *might* not be well suited in some parts of the mountains, but, though liable to it myself, it did not trouble me during many months on the mountains, and more exposure than most visitors would, perhaps, care to undergo. One pest of the bush and plains is "Sandy Blight," or inflammation of the eyes—it is, I believe, called "sandy" owing to the pain being exactly similar to that which grains of sand upon the eyeball would cause. It is also known as "bung-eye," because, as an Irishman would say, when you open your eyes in the morning, the lids are tightly closed, and require no small amount of fomentation to get them open. By taking it in time it may be easily checked, and I advise no one to neglect it for even a day. A good lotion is sold at nearly all bush stores. "Queensland Sores" or "Barcoo rot" are, I believe, generally attributed to excessive thinness and poverty of the blood, caused by the great heat and an absence of vegetable diet, with salt meat as the principal item on the bill-of-fare. One's hands and arms thus are easily "barked," and the sore is very slow at healing. The "yolk" or grease of wool is also a very bad thing to get into a cut, and visitors should be careful of handling freshly-shorn wool.

In Sydney, however, sanitary matters are, perhaps, not altogether in a satisfactory state. There is, I think, great room, and still greater need, for reform. A good deal of money has been spent on sewerage, and a fine sewer has been constructed, with an outfall into the ocean a few hundred yards north of Bondi Bay; but the most perfect system of sewerage does not mean everything. A sufficient staff of thoroughly competent health officials should be appointed, whose recommendations should receive immediate attention, indeed, as far as possible, they should have considerable discretionary power vested in them, and not be subjected to wearisome debate at the hands of that gilt-edged bumbledom, of which choice material, municipal councils are, not unfrequently, largely composed.

Diptheria and typhoid, both much to be dreaded, the latter cutting off so many, as it does, in the flower of youth, play frequent and terrible havoc in Sydney and its suburbs, and I will proceed to give some instances of what I wish to convey when I say that health officers should have the utmost possible power vested in them, and not be tied down, and their efforts frustated by municipal bumbledom.

Early in 1890, a sharp outbreak of typhoid fever occurred in a portion of the suburbs of Waverley and Randwick, perhaps the healthiest of any localities in and around Sydney. The milk supply was suspected, and a house to house visitation was made by the medical officers' instructions, to ascertain from what source supplies were drawn, and the affected or infected houses were found to have been supplied by a dairy in Randwick.

On the premises of the dairy in question, there was a well which was condemned, a considerable time before the above outbreak, by the medical officer, as being unfit for use. The Municipal Council of Randwick were asked to order it to be closed, or rather, so august and important body was, I suppose, "respectfully recommended," but, whichever was done, no notice was taken of the matter. All this formed the subject of a special report to the Legislative Assembly by the Medical Officer of Health, in which he commented strongly upon the amount of sickness and suffering caused by this omission, oversight, neglect, or whatever it may be termed, and one would think it would have roused people to action. I was, however, residing in Waverley at the time, and do not remember any notice being taken of it, or that the strong language in which the report was worded evoked any special comment from the single-minded gentlemen composing the Legislative Assembly.

The same report also disclosed another charming specimen of official disregard for the public health. This was in Waverley, a suburb adjoining that of Randwick, that hotbed of municipal genius.

A portion of the highest ground in Waverley, the loftiest, in fact, for some miles round, is reserved as a public park, and at each entrance there is the usual string of bye-laws which makes the passer-by half afraid of venturing into the sacred precincts of such enclosures. There, presuming, I suppose, that bye-laws were applicable only to the common herd, the local council allowed the savoury contents of the scavengers' night carts to be buried, the soakage from which, owing to the nature and formation of the land, made its way into the foundations of houses, built in the immediate neighbourhood, and much sickness was traced to this shocking disregard of the laws of hygiene. All the foregoing is a *modified* outline of the Report of the Medical Officer for Health, presented to the Legislative Assembly.

Another instance of disregard of the representations of qualified men.* An old hotel situated in George street,

* Having lost certain notes, I am unable to state whether the hotel had really been condemned.

north, suddenly collapsed like a house of cards, two lives were lost; by the merest chance it happened that more were not sacrificed, as a large company of time-expired blue-jackets had slept in the house a night or so before the accident. Then certain people in authority woke up, and remembered that certain buildings had been condemned by the city architect, and they were railed round forthwith. I suppose it was necessary that they should receive ocular proof that such places might tumble down before they even put a barrier in front of a condemned building.

What, therefore, I have to say, in view of the foregoing, is, if a thoroughly qualified man points out the necessity for a thing of vital importance being done, the neglect of which may involve risk to life and limb, who are the members of a municipal body that they should say him nay? or, if they do not do so in so many words, ignore or question his recommendation. If a doctor of medicine declares certain water to be dangerously infected, are they to say he is wrong? If a city architect declares certain buildings to be unsafe, must they wait until one comes about the ears of the passer-by before they take action in the matter, or credit the expert's verdict upon them?

"But," blusters forth Mr. Alderman or Mr. Councillor Bumple, "this is all nonsense, I must consider my ratepayers' interests." Certainly, sir; but if you haggle over strangling disease in its infancy, do you consider your ratepayers' interests? not to mention the expense, suffering, probably severe bereavement you may spare them. Your negligence makes a far greater hole in public funds; and what about the hospitals, which will be filled to overflowing? The fact is, gentlemen, it is too often your own vested interests, as you call them, that you really consider, and not those of your ratepayers. You, many of you, own property, and do not like to see it condemned, or improvements demanded, or sanitary measures enforced with regard to it; it may be only your neighbour's, but next time it may be yours. It all costs money, all means outlay without proportionate return to the owner of the property. You are an owner of property, and if you make money out of a rookery, why, you argue, should you not continue to do so? Then, the medical officer, surveyor, or sanitary inspector is somewhat chary of speaking his mind; you are, many of you, possessed of considerable influence, you can make it "hot" for an over-zealous official, and, sometimes, I fear you do. What is wanted, gentlemen, is someone whose position and qualifications are such that he shall not be afraid of speaking straightforwardly to you, and with authority. A medical officer of health, I most respectfully think, should be placed in authority, with assistants if need be, and be in no way dependent upon, or allowed to devote any time to, private practice, and he should have considerable discretionary power. Good men, well paid, are urgently required for such work.

Passing along Macquarie street north, by the building where spirited patriots discuss the affairs of the Colony, we encounter a low wall, surmounted with iron railings, to which is added a chaste fence of galvanized corrugated iron. Natural curiosity incites us to step into the roadway. Piles of masonry meet our view over the comely barrier. Pillars with ornate capitols. What are these architectural treasures so zealously guarded from the public eye? One feels almost as the traveller does, who, blundering through the fastnesses of a central American forest, suddenly comes upon the handicraft of a vanished people, a bye-gone race. Did some Antipodean Aztecs reign in semi-barbaric splendour before the primitive blackfellow came? Oh, no! That is the Sydney Hospital, or will be, when finished. It has for long remained incompleted, why, need not be told here. The completion has, I believe, been decided upon; when finished it will very likely be deemed obsolete in point of design. In the meantime, the "accidents" and "general" wards, for the most part, are in a two-storied, weatherboard building, very cold in the winter months, and as one glances down the long rows of beds, each with its more or less helpless occupant, the contingency, or possibility of fire, is not pleasant to contemplate.

What with the weatherboard and more substantial buildings, the Sydney Hospital has 236 beds, while there are 65 beds at an outlying branch, solely devoted to diseases of the eye. There is, amongst others, a ward for diseases peculiar to women, which is constantly full, and ailments of this nature seem very prevalent in the Colony. Its situation near to the wharves and harbours constitutes it the "casualty" hospital, and it is a matter of regret to see that no provision is made for the better conveyance of those who have the misfortune to be injured in the streets, &c., such as is now in vogue at some of the English general hospitals, viz., the ambulance waggon. The hansom cab is the usual means of very rough and ready transport, much gratuitous suffering being caused thereby, as well as longer detention in hospital.

The other principal hospitals are the Prince Alfred, in the University Domain, with 450 beds, and provisions for isolating certain infectious diseases. There are four private wards within its walls.

The St. Vincent Hospital is in Darlinghurst, and is under the care of the Sisters of Charity. It is a general hospital, and contains 175 beds. The Coast, or Little Bay Hospital, at the north entrance to Botany Bay, 11 miles from Sydney, is for infectious diseases, and has 270 beds.

There is a branch of the St. John Ambulance in Sydney which, however, is, as it appeared to me, hardly as well supported as it might be. Useful knowledge, such as the Association teaches, would be especially valuable in the bush, where accidents are liable to occur very many miles from any medical aid.

The principal cemeteries in the neighbourhood of the city, are at Rookwood, 10 miles distant, on the local line, and at Waverley, the latter beautifully situated on the coast, and sloping gently towards the Pacific. It is well worth a visit.

CHAPTER XXV.

TYPES OF AUSTRALIANS — THE RISING GENERATION — HOW THEY TALK IN AUSTRALIA — EDUCATION — THE CADET CORPS.

Those born of British stock have, for the most part, a wandering and venturesome nature, and it is well, therefore, that they are hardy plants, apt to thrive exceedingly in widely differing lands, generally bearing transplanting well. Even the cautious, wary Scotchman has been known to wander south of Tweedside, leaving the artistic, but not peculiarly remunerative surroundings of his native land, to make himself exceedingly comfortable amongst Sassenach surroundings, as well as in foreign lands. The visitor, therefore, to what is known as Greater Britain, is pardonably curious, if he is anxious to see whether Colonial born men and women have changed, in attributes of mind and body, from the British born, to-day resident in the Mother Country. There has been ample time for New South Wales to produce, if she is to do so, a distinct type of the Australian born man and woman. But we have, I think, to bestow more than a casual glance at a gathering in Sydney, or the bush, before we notice any substantial difference.

As there are different climates in the Colony, so are

there varying types of the native born. The Sydney people show, frequently, signs of town life, both sexes "age" somewhat early, and are, perhaps, not such long livers as might be expected. The colder air of the mountains produces rosy cheeks enough, not to say florid complexions; still, with the men, those that are, what we might term "stout," are usually obese to an extent which plainly shows that obesity is a disease with them, the majority being, as a rule, wiry, rather than powerful in their build. Then come the hot, dry plains, where the inhabitants are naturally spare, and when much exposed to the weather by outdoor life—

    Shadowed by the sun's dark livery,

the title "cornstalk" is, in many cases, applicable to the young Australian, for he is frequently, in New South Wales, above the average height, and possessed of greater slenderness, and less "shoulder" than one would like to see; in fact, at the inter-Colonial athletic meetings, the prizes mostly fall to the more hardy Victorians and New Zealanders. On the other hand, I have seen not a few men, young and old, born in the Colony, who would be easily mistaken for typical Englishmen.

 I have said that they age much faster, do not seem to wear quite as well as the average of people "at home," but on this point I would not like to give a very decided opinion, as in the cases in which I have especially noticed a comparative collapse at an early age, it may have been due to much hardship, of which, at times, there is quite enough in a bush life. Taking him on the whole, I think the bushman as I have before remarked, is a temperate man, his diet is spare—people must not judge colonial men and women by what they see of Sydney—and, generally, I do not think he is given to excessive drinking, by any means; perhaps, if less tea were drunk, more wine in the vine-producing districts, and a modicum of good cider where the apple is abundant, it might be better for the native.* Still, he is very enduring, a little flour, tea and sugar, and the ubiquitous, ever useful "billy" will carry him a long distance, and tea is so portable, and cheap a means of making a stimulating "brew," that I think it will be a long time before it finds a substitute; at the same time, I know of my own experience what it is as a useful and portable stimulant.

In manner, the young Australian is frequently accused of not being over polite, and he has been blamed for want of respect and reverence for older people, a complaint which I believe is not confined, at the present day, to Australia. He is accused frequently of "blowing," or bragging; in this I do not know, from my own experience that he stands alone. I have often seen Young England set him a very bad example. An argument, for instance, will often spring up about the country, the Britisher grumbling about everything. The natural retort under the circumstances is, "If it is such a beastly country, why the—that is to say, why did you come here?" In this way I have found not only young men, but much older men, who ought to know better, behave most rudely. Such bring undeserved contempt upon their countrymen, and are, generally, among the first to level abuse at what they

* The word native is generally used to describe a colonial born person. Blackfellows or aboriginals are the titles given to what are usually termed "the natives."

term the absence of manners amongst Australians generally. As to my own experience, I have found an abundance cf genuine good fellowship and kindly feeling in the bush, which I should be ungrateful in ever forgetting.

Certainly about school boys, of what are termed "tender" years, there seems to be a good deal of "cheek"—the word is slangy, but is exactly expresses what I mean, and generally, I think, it intelligible, which really is, perhaps, the main object of language. This fault also may be general. Those whose experience of large schools dates back some while, may be accused by those who choose to quote the Latin of the fag-end of an hexameter line, of being a class praising accomplished time. It may be that in past days a boy was better taught to realize that there were other people in the world to be considered besides himself, a fact which the Australian youth is sometimes apt to forget. However, they develop early, and very juvenile Romeos may be seen paying courtship in somewhat lofty and condescending fashion, both on the crowded "block" and at the more sequestered garden gate, to Juliets so youthful, that the sympathising onlooker almost fears that love's young dream may be rudely dispelled by that short, sharp, and decisive form of punishment, not unknown in the nursery. So the candour and ingenuous freshness of boyhood especially, is rapidly becoming very rare, but it is, I think, highly probable that the Cadet movement, which is now in force in all public schools in the Colony, may do great good in teaching young Australia how to spell the two words, "discipline" and "obedience."

As to the English spoken in Australia, I believe it has already been remarked how correct, as a rule, it is, and I think it is free from any distinguishing accent or provincialism to a marvellous extent, while the tone of voice is pleasing and well modulated. In Sydney, however, more particularly the young girls, especially of the lower classes, are apt to affect a Cockney twang in pronouncing the letter *a* as if it were *i*, or rather *ai* diphthong. Thus, the refrain to a well-known song will be pronounced as follows:—

> Is this a dream?
> Then wiking would be pine;
> Oh! do not wike me,
> Let me dream agine.

Another transgression is to term the plural "you" "yous," as "yous are busy." Of phrases more or less peculiar to Australia, as well as single words, are "push" for crowd; to "shake" instead of to steal; a "bit of a lad" expresses a wild young person of either sex; a "radical" is a thorough blackguard, of course I mean in Australia, where the political term is unknown; to "turn dog" on anyone is to betray him, and this atrocious libel upon the best friend of man, and, perhaps, the most faithful of created beings, is caused, no doubt, by the awful parodies on doghood one sees in the public parks; to "shepherd" needs no explanation, but it is generally used to express taking care of any person or thing; to "run" is to play upon anyone's credulity; to "nark" signifies to annoy; within "cooee" is what sailors term within hail, though it has a wider range, as a blackfellow's "cooee" can be heard at a long distance; "a dead bird" expresses anything useless or defunct;

to "give it best" is to confess one's self beaten, while the victim to a gang of sharpers owns that he has been "taken down;" to get in "a scot" is a very usual term for displaying temper; a "scotty" person is not one who hails from the land of cakes, but a quick-tempered individual;* a "blackfellow's game" is a left-handed tribute to the intellectual qualities of the original owners of the soil, and signifies a foolish act or pursuit; to "go bung" signifies commercial failure; "tucker" is the universal name for food; and a person is very generally referred to as a "cove;" the term "cockatoo" farmer, or "cockie," as he is frequently called, may sometimes puzzle the new chum. The expression is, I believe, derived from the out-of-the-way places in which some of them live, just as the cockatoo nests in remote and unfrequented localities.

Next as to the use of undesirable epithets and express-ons occasionally described as "cuss words." The average Australian, whatever his position may be, is capable of improvement, not that one meets with the cold-blooded profanity, which is so commonly used in certain parts of America; but many expressions of a more than questionable nature are somewhat generally used, and boys, and even young children, have very often a stock of bad language in active service, by far too plentiful, which, I suppose, did not originate with them.

Of Larrikinism I have written elsewhere, it is a very deplorable feature in Australian life. There is an utter absence of all that is manly in most of the actions of

* I have elsewhere mentioned the expression "to barrack" as meaning rowdy partisanship.

larrikin "pushes." They simply combine to set the law at defiance, and, in the present state of the Executive, they succeed. I have stated that people are fond of theorizing about its cause. Home influence, or rather the want of it, is blamed; and, no doubt, that has something to do with it. The fine weather permits of the children being much in the streets, where they pick up, in the way of language and ideas generally, a good deal that is hurtful to them. As time goes on they get work, at, perhaps, good wages; they leave what, possibly, was never much of a home to them, in the real sense of the word. They learned early to regard restraint as irksome, and they become very soon their own masters, except at their daily work. They live together, and having between them, for they make common cause in many ways, plenty of pocket money, they want for little to aid them in "turning up" wherever there is harmless amusement, for them to convert into riot and disorder. It will be a memorable day for Australia when any decided and vigorous step is taken to break up its larrikin "pushes."

With regard to schools for public and private education there is no lack, and in the bush, everything possible is done to see that the education of children, even in the most widely scattered districts, is not neglected. A good education is a goodly heritage—if a father can give his son nothing more wherewith to fight the battle of life—it is a great thing. There are in the Colony 2,300 public schools about, and between three and four hundred private schools, headed by the Sydney University, with which is affiliated three colleges and a grammar school. The University, in addition to endowment funds, enjoys a magnificent bequest, from a gentleman named Challis, of £200,000, which endowed, amongst others, many professorial chairs, the salary attaching to which is handsome enough to command the best talent available. The cadets, to which I have already referred as being enrolled at the public schools, number about 6,000, are armed with a suitable rifle and bayonet, wear a neat uniform, and have an annual encampment.

A step, most decidedly, I venture to think, in the right direction, is the establishment of an agricultural college, termed the Hawkesbury Agricultural College and Experimental Farm, near Richmond, 38 miles from Sydney, where it is intended to give a practical education to young men, in all matters connected with every branch and detail of agriculture, and it may be that some protection may be afforded to home-grown produce to make it worth the while of many young men to qualify for a calling, useful to themselves, and beneficial to the Colony.

Young Australia is not much of a traveller. He has none of American restlessness in him, or of the common desire of the Britisher to see foreign lands. If he believes that travel is a great education to a fairly observant man, he does not practice it. The annual outing, common to the Englishman, is not so much in vogue in Sydney; a few days at Easter or Christmas is all. In the bush, were it not for "overlanding" or droving trips, I think the young fellows would not move about much. In a chapter headed "An Idle Man in Sydney," I have endeavoured to show that there are plenty of splendid excursions from the Harbour City; but if Young Australia has the means of enjoying a holiday, I fear his ideal of one is "Cup week" in Melbourne.

CHAPTER XXVI.

AN IDLE MAN IN SYDNEY — HORSES AND CARRIAGES, AND THEIR COST — AMUSEMENTS — NEWSPAPERS — EXCURSIONS FROM SYDNEY, NEAR AND FAR — TASMANIA — NEW ZEALAND — THE SOUTH SEAS — CHINA AND JAPAN.

Of those that betake themselves to Sydney for a greater or less term of residence from motives of benefiting their health, for change, or other reasons which concern themselves alone, there may be many who feel loathe to leave the fleshpots of the city for the solitudes of the bush, and would therefore like to know what manner of amusements there are. Of these, some I have briefly touched upon, racing especially, in writing of sport in New South Wales, others, such as they are, which may be accounted diversions in any sense of the word, I will endeavour to chronicle.

Before, however, I proceed to do so, I wonder if Sydney and its neighbourhood will ever become in any way popular with Anglo-Indians as a temporary or permanent place of residence. I am not, for obvious reasons, going to institute a comparison between Sydney and London, as cities, but in point of climate, the former is likely to suit them exceedingly, and, I think, anyone who has no special ties in England might do worse than seek retirement in New South Wales. At all events, they might, with advantage, try a holiday in Australia, for which the "P & O" Company did provide, no doubt they do now, a specially low return passage between India and Australia.

Owing to my experience of India being but slight, I might, as is common with people who speak or write from first impressions, be incorrect, but I think that there was, some years ago at all events, a good deal of foolish prejudice agaiut Australia and its people, arising principally from the extremely high opinion that many Anglo-Indian officials entertained respecting themselves, their abilities, position, and importance generally: some modification of which would argue the possession of greater good sense and taste alike.

First, I will assume that the visitor to Sydney may have a few letters of introduction, and in time he will have no occasion to complain of dulness, especially if he have any introduction from naval friends. He may also be able to gain an introduction to one or more of the Sydney clubs—The Athenæum, Australian, Reform, New South Wales, Union, or Warrigal—the style of which, generally, may somewhat surprise the English visitor.

At the outset, our friend will, no doubt, think of getting a horse, and even if no horseman "at home," he will probably not be long in Sydney before he will yearn after making his appearance in the afternoons on the South

Head road or in the Centennial Park, and study to make himself an accomplished cavalier. As to keeping a horse in Sydney, livery stable charges are high, and a man can board for what a horse will cost weekly "at livery." The best way for anyone with limited means would be to advertise for board where there were horses kept, or where he could get stabling, and if he is not above looking after his horse himself, it will cost him about 10/- weekly for feed. Horses, on the whole, in Sydney are not turned out in "Rotten Row" style; in the bush they seldom trouble about grooming them at all.

And what is a fair hack to be bought for? Well, most people who have had the least to do with horses know that it is an awkward question to answer; but, with luck, I should say from £20 to £25. There are daily auctions at the several marts, where bargains are to be had, good and bad, and sometimes really good, useful horses may be picked up "dirt cheap." I have seen a useful horse bought for five and six pounds; and, in the bush, have joined in a raffle for an equine wonder which was valued at £2, and changed hands immediately afterwards at an advance of 2/-. Many people, however, have, I dare say, found that bargains in horseflesh are like a good many other things in this world, *viz.*, they do not invariably fulfil the bright promise of their early youth.

The buggy is *the* vehicle of Australia, and is a most useful one. There are any number of them for sale, and if no great amount of money is to be expended, they are to be had at prices to suit all pockets. English dog-carts are to be had in Sydney, as also colonial made. I have seen a good locally-made dogcart, and useful horse, knocked down for £26.

I do not especially recommend anyone to get saddles made when going out to Australia, say for use on a station. For bush work a large saddle with big knee pads is used, and they are fitted so as to buckle on a swag. For the town they are modified considerably as regards the pads and build of the saddle. The curb is a good deal used in Sydney, but the snaffle is the usual "bit" of the bush.

I have already touched on cricket, rowing, football, &c. In the former, there will be an ample field for the visitor, who is an expert, while the Association or Rugby Union man will, I fear, find not so much employment. Yachting is a very favourite amusement, "our harbour" being especially adapted for it: the two leading clubs are The Royal Sydney Yacht Squadron and the Prince Alfred Yacht Club. Sailing clubs are numerous, but the rowdyism of some of the crews, on Sundays especially, might be mitigated with great advantage. The coast line of the Colony is not favourable for deep sea yachting. But such localities as the Hawkesbury or Broken Bay are exceedingly beautiful, and suitable for a boating trip. As also is Middle Harbor, for those who do not care to go outside "the heads."

The idle man will, above all things, want his newspapers, and of these I think he will have little cause to complain. There is, first, the *Sydney Morning Herald*, very well written, if a trifle grandmotherly in style. The *Telegraph*, also, is a very good newspaper, though, at times, disposed to be mildly hysterical, while Protectionist matters are championed by the coruscations of the *Star*, which makes its appearance in conformity with the custom observed by the planetary system generally, as an evening paper. Two other evening journals, the *Echo*, and the *Evening News*, not always very powerfully written, are amongst the daily productions. The leisure of the early Sunday morning may be enlivened by one of two newspapers, *The Sunday Times*, or an opposition journal, which bears the not entirely original title of *Truth*. The sporting interests of the community are catered for by the *Referee*, which can be "appealed to" every Wednesday morning, the descriptions of the boxing contests being "done" in gorgeous paraphrase, and with a wealth of more than oriental metaphor. For heavier and more general reading and illustrations there are issued weekly, *The Sydney Illustrated News*, *The Town and Country Journal*, and the *Sydney Mail*. For caricature and vigorous work, if occasionally a trifle robust, the *Bulletin* is about as good as any of its kind anywhere.

If, during the Sydney summer months, the mountains pall upon the visitor, he must not think of the sea-side, for it will be muggy somewhat, and not exactly as bracing as could be wished, and there are no Scarboroughs or Brightons to enliven it. He should think of Tasmania, which is only about two days steam from Sydney. and is very well-worth exploring, Hobart being a charming little place; or, going further afield, he can make the New Zealand tour in a month or six weeks, visiting Auckland, Wellington, Christchurch, and Dunedin, and the inland wonders, lakes, passes, and snowy peaks, to his heart's content, while during December and January he can join a charming and not expensive trip from Dunedin, of some twelve days, to the wonderful Sounds of the West Coast, which equal in grandeur the most sublime of the Norwegian fiords, and returning, he can look in at Hobart for a stay, or continue his journey across Tasmania. Once a month, an opposition steamer, "The Jubilee," runs from Sydney to New Zealand, a very comfortable boat, which reduces the usual fares of the Union Steamship Company about her date of departure. The fares vary, so I might mislead if I gave prices. As to the Union Steamship boats, they deserve the highest praise for comfort, and appointments generally, while they take care that their passengers shall live like "fighting cocks." I might add, by the way, that I am personally unacquainted with the exact mode of life affected by fighting cocks, but it has long been a favourite synonym for the best of everything, and that is what I wish to express.

Auckland, at the north end of the North Island of New Zealand, is about two degrees south of Sydney, and from four-and-a-half to five days steam to the eastward of it. Wellington, the capital, is on Cook's Straits, at the extreme south-end of the North Island, about 300 miles south of Auckland. Christchurch, with its harbour, Port Lyttleton, is half-way down on the east coast of the South Island. Dunedin, is about 400 miles south of Wellington, while the Bluff, for Invercargill, is the southernmost point of the Island, opposite Stewart Island, famous for its oysters, thence the Union Company's steamers leave for Melbourne direct, or calling in at Hobart for a few hours. I trust to be pardoned for these trifling details, but I was once asked whether New Zealand was not a favourite Saturday to Monday resort of the Australians !

The excellence of the coasting service of Australian steamers is well worthy of comment. From Sydney there are frequent steamers to Melbourne and Adelaide, and northwards to Brisbane, and the coast towns up to the Gulf of Carpentaria. Such steamers as the "Aramac," and "Arawata," belonging to the Australian United Steamship Company, are as fine and well-fitted, as any ocean-going steamer need be.

Then in the winter time a splendid month or six weeks can be spent amongst the Islands of the South Seas, to us here in England, even in these days of so much travel, not very much known. New Caledonia is only three-and a-half days distant, by the large steamers of the Messageries Maritimes Company. The Feejee group is five or six days. Then the New Hebrides the Samoan group, and others can be visited, and at no great expense. A visit in the autumn should be avoided, that is, of course, in the antipodean autumn.

Finally, in three weeks from Sydney, we can travel to Hong Kong, by one of two well-appointed lines of steamers, thence to see such as we can of the wonders of the Flowery Land, or in four or five more days set foot in Japan, of which, perhaps, of all the lands in which I have travelled, I look back to with the greatest pleasure. So, if Sydney has not old world cities and countries close at hand, the sojourner "within her gates" will not lack many wonders and charming scenes to recompense him for occasional wanderings.

CHAPTER XXVII.

NEW CHUMS—THEIR PROSPECTS IN AUSTRALIA — WHAT CAN THEY DO? — LETTERS OF INTRODUCTION.

There are not a few young men who annually leave England, their friends, and such influence that they may, through them, possess, and set sail for the Antipodes, trusting, Micawber-like, that something will turn up, a large proportion seeming to have some vague idea that things generally have a happier and more frequent "knack" of "turning up" in the region in question than elsewhere, and, not unfrequently, they appear to entertain an equally hazy notion that there may be more scope for them, they know not exactly how, or in what direction, in so vast a country.

I do not wish to decry the spirit of adventure—far from it—or insinuate that pluck and perseverance are not in fulness of time, as virtue is said to be, duly rewarded; but I do not want to see such laudable qualities wasted, and their possessors doomed to the hard lines that frequently await those who venture to Australia in search of fortune.

* Letters of introduction, generally, form a material part of the outfit of the new chum, and I have, as, no doubt, have many others, very frequently heard it said of

---

* These remarks are not inspired by any feeling arising from personal disappointment.

a young fellow on the eve of setting out to a foreign land : " He has such splendid letters of introduction." Again, I have no wish to discourage in any way that somewhat rare commodity, disinterested good nature; but those who have travelled to a fair extent must all have had some experiences of letters of introduction which have been given in good faith, with equally well-intentioned statements as to their probable value which is generally far from realised. To those that travel exclusively for pleasure, the matter is not one of such great moment; letters of introduction serve to identify them, and can be used, as they should be given, with discretion; it rests with the bearers of such to do honour and credit to their friends, the givers of the letters, as well as those to whom they are addressed.

It is with those letters that commend the bearer to the care of men in Australasia that I wish principally to deal. They are given very often with comfortable promises, with words which, though uttered in good faith, are too seldom realized. " This is a letter to my friend Brown; he is a good fellow, and an influential man, and will do something for you." A few such letters and such promises—a very few—have, I fear, sent many a man to experience disappointment and bitter reverses.

Take " my friend Brown ; " he is, no doubt, all that has been said of him; but, to freely translate the well-known line of the Latin poet, " Times change, and change us likewise." He has gathered about him fresh cares, incurred new responsibilities during his residence abroad. The problem " What am I to do with my lads ? " is not confined to England; it may be an anxious one for him to solve. When he receives a letter, asking him to find employment for a new arrival, what could he say? What, in good truth, should he, if he spoke the truth, say? Something like "My good sir, I know scores of men in Sydney, Melbourne, &c., who want something to do badly." He promises to do his best. But I cannot refrain from saying that I fear that people in Australia, occasionally, do not much care to be the recipient of such letters, and no one can blame them. Young fellows have too often foolishly ventured to the Colonies, and I will not say forced themselves upon people, but in the too frequent extreme necessity which follows their ill-judged step—as sunshine follows rain—have been thrown upon the bounty of those to whom they may have been introduced. Let those that venture take all the letters they can get, but I beg of them to implicitly rely on none.

Now, concerning the chance of those who have some recognised trade, calling, or profession as a stand-by. I have written as fully as I can, in other chapters, but there are many who go to Australia who, unfortunately for themselves, have been brought up to no special calling, or, having been placed to the same, neglected their opportunity. These, most especially, I ask—what do they imagine they will do?

Have they any idea that they will try clerical or office work? Well, for every situation of the kind open in Sydney, and, indeed, other Australasian cities, at a wage of at most two pounds weekly, there are scores of applicants, the greater portion of them men trained to business, and possessed of local knowledge. Just as many to the full, if not more than would run after a similar situation in England. What chance has the new arrival?

Very well, they elect to try "the bush"—they have no choice! Seriously, what can they do there? Perhaps some are, worse luck, town bred. Can they groom, harness, ride, and drive a horse? Yoke up and drive a team of bullocks? Kill, skin, and cut up in reasonable time a sheep, or steer, or work ten hours daily as roustabout in a woolshed? Have they any knowledge of handling stock? Can they split rails, cut billets, rough it, and do the innumerable odd things that happen in the course of a bush life? Well, hardly, they are not exactly possessed of all the foregoing accomplishments, (which there may not be very much in after all), but could soon pick them up—which I have no doubt they would—but in the meantime the Australian bush lad is bred to all this from his childhood. So it is a precarious matter getting manual work in the bush. Then at present there are the railway lines with pick and shovel, hammer and drill work. Can they not do better at home?

Many may be possessed of a sum of money which they hope to turn to better account in a new country than in the old. To this I have also made special reference elsewhere. But do they expect to find people less sophisticated in the colonies? Such is not the case. Throw a stone into yonder pool, and watch the ever-widening rings that ripple outwards from the plash. There are just as many "rings" in the business world of Australia, and "wheels within wheels" as multitudinous as in the most complex piece of mechanism ever constructed. If, therefore, their aim be to invest money in business, a little of a watching and a waiting game will not be played in vain.

One class of man remains, the ne'er-do-well, and why Australia should have been selected as the place of shipment of such I do not know. It is a great injustice to the country, and brings the name of Englishmen into discredit, and if such considerations do not weigh with the relatives of any erring black sheep, better anything, for *his own* sake, than such a step.

Much has been written and said about Australian hospitality, and some of those whom I have heard speak of it, seem to expect that if they were to visit any of the colonies absolutely unknown, and without introductions, they would be received with open arms. Such an idea is absurd, a man must know, it is due to his family that he should know something about the stranger he admits to his family circle. Hospitality in the past, has also, I fear, been abused, but even now, the visitor, in the bush especially, will, I think, have nothing to complain about his treatment, and those who can least afford to give, will often give most freely.

Go to a cheap restaurant in Sydney to see how "seamy" a side there is of Colonial life. Look at the wearied, drawn faces of not a few poor fellows coming in to spend their last sixpence on a good meal. They have walked the streets all night, or struggled for uneasy snatches of sleep in the public parks. Go into such places in the darkness of night, or the grey of earliest dawn, and see among those who lie and lurk there, hopeless and homeless, many, who with brightest hopes for the future, came out to find only hard times and bitter disappointments in the Antipodean Eldorado. This is no fancy picture by any means. I wish to discourage no one—but I want to depict things as they really are.

Chapter XXVIII.

SYDNEY SOCIAL LIFE—LARRIKINS—AND LARRIKIN " PUSHES " — AND OTHER MATTERS.

The eminent author of "Oceana" has placed it on record that he failed to see in Antipodean society, any special features distinguishing it from that which he had experienced in England. What Mr. Froude expected to find he does not, by any hint, whatsoever, allow his readers to conjecture, but I should have imagined that an experienced traveller would have been prepared to find things much the same as at home. That which that bibulous old warrior, Captain Costigan, was wont to term the "hoighth of poloit societee," has little variety about it. If I were asked, however, to name any distinguishing feature in the amusements of Sydney society generally, I think I should at once say picnics, and an amplitude of public holidays favours this social organisation. Fine weather is not the least important item necessary for the success of a picnic, and it may be generally relied upon in Sydney. Then if the destination be Chowder, Clontarf, or some more sequestered bay or inlet, there is the pleasant sail upon "Our harbour," which is a host in itself, whether it is the occasion of the annual outing of the "Baby Brotherhood of the Blue Ribbon," with band playing and banners flaunting or a complimentary picnic tendered to a prominent rowing man, or pugilist, or any other great and distinguished person.

It is, perhaps, in the lower walks of life that we should rather look for the unconventional, the picturesque in attire, ideas, and conversation, and I think I may select the "larrikin" as deserving our especial notice.

The expression is, no doubt, familiar to English ears, and, as many people are doubtless aware, it originated, at least so the common story goes, with a Melbourne policeman—not long departed, by the way, for "that undiscovered country" where the general impression is, I believe, that policemen cease from troubling, and "moving on." He, like many other eminent men, was of Hibernian origin, and among a few trifling mannerisms that clung to him—to whom do they not?—was the habit, not uncommon amongst his countrymen, of modulating the harshness of the Saxon tongue by the occasional insertion of a vowel between two consonants.

"What are these lads charged with, officer?"

"They was lar-r-i-kin', your washup."

And so, as Columbus found a new world, did Police-constable Allen, for that, I believe, was his name, create a new word for the use and benefit of his fellow-countrymen.

The real larrikin is, for the most part, a hard-working youth, and he, and his comrades form themselves into "pushes," a common term in New South Wales, and equivalent to our slang expressions of a "crew" or a "crowd." These pushes are named according to the locality their members inhabit and affect. There is, for instance, the Woolloomooloo "push." The younger generation living in the rocky neighbourhood of the Argyle cut, near Circular Quay, constitute the "Rocks push," and in Balmain, as the gentlemen that compose it are for the most part professionally engaged in the slaughter-houses, their faction is named with a grace and elegance of diction, which is, I think, beyond praise—the "liver push."

I have said that the larrikin is, as a rule, hardworking. He wants money, and when he goes forth in search of pleasure, he is not unfrequently particular about his dress, or "clobber" as he prefers to term his wardrobe. Here comes a larrikin dandy, younger, perhaps, than the rest of his "push." Physically, he is not a marvel of strength, or symmetry. His complexion is colourless, and, save for freckles, characterless; and, as yet, there is no promise of a moustache to tone down a spacious, shapeless, mouth. His manner and bearing generally, would indicate that he has seen all that is worth seeing, done all worth doing. Life, it would appear, he is beginning to find hardly worth living. His attire is new. A soft felt wideawake crowns his seat of intellect; his collar and scarf are of the latest fashion. His waistcoat is adorned by a silver chain, extending from pocket to pocket, bearing many "tokens" and ornaments depending therefrom. His coat, of neat black cloth, (he is not partial to colours), is distinguished by general brevity as regards cut, and as you gain a back view of the wearer you think it might have been made longer with advantage. Probably he is desirous that you should notice that what he would term the "seat of his pants" is not marred by any unseemly patch. The sleeves, too, are short, and terminate in a good deal of wrist, and large, loosely dangling hands. His "pants"— note them with envious eye—are tightly fitting above, in sailor fashion, increasing in width as they descend, till they almost hide his precious boots from view. They have tiny, but high heels of the French pattern, and are eyelet holed down to the toes. His gait is deliberate, and savours somewhat of that of the stage-policeman.

And has this gorgeous creature no mate? Does he waste his sartorial sweetness on the desert air? No; there is the "larrikiness" or "larrikine," as, I believe, it is intended to term her. She has much the same walk, is dowdy, and needs no description. She is, above all, outspoken, and her phraseology is vivid in the extreme; at fourteen she is as unsexed as if she had spent a century in vice.

Larrikinism is a foul blot; it is a standing disgrace to Australia. The most vigorous denunciation that the ablest writer ever penned falls short of doing justice to the subject. San Francisco has its hoodlums, Liverpool its "high rip" gang—or had it—its roughs and "corner men," but in both cities the disturbing, law-defying element is local. In Sydney, such is not the case. No public place is free from the hideous pest. Open air amusements, such as music, must give way to larrikinism. In the parks, on the harbour, the yells, the filth and blasphemy of the larrikin are the salient features of a public holiday. School children, and those who safeguard them to a picnic or outing, never know but what a day of intended pleasure will end in the aim and object of larrikinism—a riot. One would have thought that such unspeakable outrages as those known as the Woolloomooloo and Mount Rennie affairs would have stirred up any community to action, but no. The police are confessedly helpless, and, beyond complacently theorizing as to the cause of larrikinism, the Sydney folks have not attempted to cope with it.

Is the foregoing overdone? I have desired to be moderate. The subject may be a safe one upon which to launch abuse; with that I have nothing to do. I have had a very fair personal experience of individual larrikins, representative young men in their way, and not as a journalist seeking sensational "copy," by which I mean that I was honoured with confidences which were not overcoloured in view of beer or notoriety. This gave me a good insight into what larrikinism really is.

Of other social matters there is not much that I can say. I do not know that Sydney is better or worse than other cities. That which we term the "Social evil" does not much offend the eye, and is but little in evidence—Waterloo-place and certain other leading London thoroughfares by night or even in daytime would be a revelation to a Sydney native, though no doubt in Sydney there may be much room for improvement.

I have, in the course of some remarks upon sport in New South Wales spoken of gambling as being fairly prevalent in the colony, and, indeed, in Australasia generally, to what extent I could not say, for the reason that I have no pretence whatever to a sufficient knowledge of the subject to allow of my offering an opinion upon it. But there is, undoubtedly, or was, amongst such blots as mar the pages of social life in the colony, one that is most evident even to those who may care to scan them in the most casual manner, and that is not unfrequent defalcations amongst trusted officials in public and private positions.

S

More than once I have remarked upon the multiplicity of banks, and of the abundance of clerical employment which they provide; they have lately furnished some grievous cases in which their employeès have been defaulters to a very serious amount, and in an important government department more than one unpleasant revelation has been made. This lamentable state of things would argue either that a very different system of supervision is necessary, or, which is the more probable, perhaps, of the two, that the means offered to men in such responsible positions, for wholesale speculation, are of a varied and most extensive nature, in which they are accorded support, if not encouragement, at the hands of men of self-styled respectability and standing. It is sad enough when peculation is committed to a small extent in the case of a too-frequently ill-paid clerk, when money is taken to stay some pressing want, some great and present necessity; in such the cause and effect are evident; but when a man who need feel, as far as the world can judge, no such pressure, one is apt to think that the lost thousands might tell strange tales. Verily, if there were no receivers, there would be no thieves.

CHAPTER XXIX.

THE MODE OF GOVERNMENT—THE LEGISLATIVE COUNCIL AND ASSEMBLY—LEGAL AND ECCLESIASTICAL MATTERS—THE POLICE FORCE—THE IMPERIAL AND LOCAL FORCES IN THE COLONY.

No doubt some interest will be taken with regard to the mode of government pursued in the colony, so a few particulars concerning the system thereof and kindred matters, will, I trust, not be out of place.

First of all comes the governor of the colony who is appointed by Her Majesty the Queen at a salary of £7,000 a year with a residence at Government House, Sydney, and a summer resort at Sutton Forest, situated on the tableland, some 90 miles from Sydney. He is also Commander-in-chief of the naval and military forces in the pay of the colony, by virtue of his office, as well as the Governor of Norfolk Island, which he has to visit once during his tenure of office, which is for five years. In the absence of a Governor, the Lieutenant-Governor, a permanent official, takes his place.

Next comes the Executive Council under the presidency of the governor, with the government representative in the Legislative Council as the Vice-president, the Premier and ministers forming the body thereof. Then there is the ministry for the time being, the Premier, who is also at time of writing, Colonial Secretary and Registrar of Records, receiving an annual honorarium of £2,000. The Attorney-general with a like sum, while the Colonial Treasurer, with ministers for lands, Public Instruction, Mines and Agriculture, Post-office, Justice, and Public works are rewarded by £1,500 annually.

The Parliament is composed of the Legislative Council, and the Legislative Assembly, the former having about 70 members. They are elected for life, bankruptcy or criminal offence alone annulling the appointment. No salary attaches to the position, which is much coveted. The members are entitled to the prefix of Honourable *within the Colony*, and the letters M. L. C. affixed to their name signify members of the Legislative Council. The Legislative Assembly is composed of 137 members, who are each paid £300 annually for their valuable and disinterested services, and, in addition, they have a free pass, in the form of a gold token bearing the Royal Arms, over all the government tramways and railways throughout the Colony. The affix of M.L.A. signifies that a gentleman is a member of the Legislative Assembly. The qualifications for such a position, are, that they be 21 years of age, natural born, or naturalized subjects of Her Majesty the Queen, not holding any office, other than political, under the Crown, or a Crown pension. Elections are determined by ballot. Each Parliament is limited to three years, the present commenced in February, 1889.

There are 74 electorates in the Colony, the number of free and independent electors being about 280,000.

The qualifications are simply—over 21 years of age, and natural born, or naturalised subjects of the Queen. Each electorate under 3,000 returns one member; 3,000 to 5,000, two members; 5,000 to 8,000, three members; over 8,000, four members.

The machinery necessary for keeping legislation going and attending to its wants, provides some very snug "billets." The staff attached to the Legislative Council consists of eight persons who enjoy an average salary of about £440 a year, that of the Legislative Assembly, from the Speaker, with £1,500 a year, consists of 14 gentlemen who average the very comfortable salary of about £550 annually, while the joint staff of librarians, draftsmen, reporting staff, &c., of 18, average fully £475 a year. Then there are the house-keepers, messengers, and servants, generally, and taking into account salaries of ministers and members, the ministry and Parliament cost the Colony quite £70,000 sterling a year.

As to the merits of the Legislative Assembly, for they are supposed to do the brunt of the work, there is certainly no justification for extravagant praise. Its great feature is "talk," not unmixed, occasionally, with personalities. Very many of its members seem to come each with their own axe to grind, and terribly blunt and useless some of them are which they aim at knocking into shape upon the very expensive grindstone the Colony pays so much to support. Few seem prepared to give another the credit of possessing any sound ideas, and as to any concerted action for the furthering of public business, it is frequently wanting.

Next there come the many governmental departments, headed by that of the Colonial Secretary, each with a large and well-paid staff, and here I might mention that the revenue, generally, is derived from customs, excise, stamps, sales and rental of Crown lands, railways, post and telegraph departments, water and sewerage rates.

As regards ecclesiastical matters, State aid to churches was abolished in 1863, but it was continued in favour of those then in receipt of it, which number not very many ministers of the Church of England, Roman Catholic, and other denominations. The greater part—nearly one-half—of the population are Church of England, perhaps rather more than one-fourth belong to the Roman Catholic.

Sydney is the seat of the Bishop of Sydney, who is Metropolitan of New South Wales, and Primate of Australia and Tasmania, while, in addition to the diocese of Sydney, there are five others in the Colony, *viz.*, Bathurst, Goulburn, Newcastle, Grafton and Armidale, and Riverina, with about 880 churches and 720 schools or dwellings where public worship is conducted. The city is also head of the Roman Catholic Archdiocese of Sydney, and seat of the Archbishop, while the Colony contains six dioceses, *viz.*, Armidale, Bathurst, Goulburn, Grafton, Maitland, and Wilcannia, with about 360 churches, and 500 other places of public worship; in addition, there are many convents, excellent schools, and charitable institutions, all supported by voluntary contributions, for, to the best of my belief, the State gives no aid to Roman Catholic schools. Of other principal religious bodies, the Presbyterian Church of New South

Wales has, I believe, 280 churches, the Wesleyan Methodists many hundreds of meeting houses. An old-established and powerful organisation known as the Church Society contributes very materially to the support of the Church of England in the Colony.

For the administration of Law and Justice, there is the Supreme Court, with a Chief Justice and six Puisne Judges, including Courts of Lunacy, Divorce, &c., District Courts, Coroners' Courts, and Petty Sessions. Then comes the police force, which, including detective, mounted and foot branches, numbers about 1,600 men of all ranks throughout the Colony. The Inspector-General, as the chief is called, has £1,000 a year and allowances. Then come superintendents, inspectors, and sub-inspectors, at salaries varying from £500 to £250 a year. The other payments are :—

First class detectives	11/- per diem
Second class ,,	10/- ,,
Third class ,,	9/- ,,
Mounted and foot police—	
First class sergeants	10/6 ,,
Second class ,,	9/3 ,,
Senior constables	8/- ,,
First class ,,	7/6 ,,
Ordinary ,,	7/- ,,
Probationary constables	6/- ,,

with fuel, light, water, and quarters when available. Sydney and suburbs has about 550 police, the traffic, as I have elsewhere mentioned, being conducted by the Metropolitan Transit Commissioners' officials. About two-thirds of the police are mounted.

As the above might seem tempting to men in the

English force, I should add that I believe there are very many applicants for positions in the New South Wales police, though men belonging to Sydney are, I believe, debarred from joining the Metropolitan force. As to physical qualifications, the Sydney force is not a particularly stalwart body. The standard would be about five feet eight or nine inches, and chest measurement, I should say, low. For the mounted branch, a man must be before all, a really good horseman, pass a strict medical examination, and, upon joining, not weigh more than 11 stone. The head-quarters of the Police are at 109, Philip-street, Sydney.

The Fire Brigade is composed of a Superintendent, from the London Brigade, I believe, and a permanent staff of about 40 men. There are 18 to 20 volunteer fire brigades in the city and suburbs, who act as an aid to, and under the orders of the regular staff.

Coming to the question of the defences of the Colonies, it is pretty generally known, I think, that Sydney is the head-quarters and Naval depôt for Imperial warships on the Australian station. The twin-screw belted cruiser, "Orlando," is the present flagship, and the remainder of the squadron is composed of screw cruisers, gunboats, and the screw yacht, "Dart" for survey purposes. One way and another they spend a good deal of time in Sydney Harbour, but when the summer heats commence, the "Orlando" retires to cooler latitudes, protecting Melbourne during the troublous times of "Cup week," and thence to Hobart, and New Zealand. Then there are cruises to "the islands," and surveying work. Altogether, I should imagine that the Australian station is by no means disliked in "the service;" under the Imperial Defences Act, of 1888, five cruisers and two torpedo boats are in part completed, for the reinforcement of the Australian station.

A training-ship in Sydney, even on a small scale, might be very useful. There was a reformatory ship called the "Vernon," now replaced by the well-known passenger ship, "Sobraon" which has bid adieu to active service.

For local naval defence work, there are about 200 naval artillery volunteers, who are purely volunteers, a small amount annually voted them for working expenses, being all the cost to which they put the colony. Then comes the Naval Brigade, many of them old men-of-warsmen, about 350 strong, one company of which is in Newcastle. They have certain yearly drills, for which the officers are paid at a rate per diem. The petty officers and men from £18 to £12 per annum. The wooden steam corvette "Wolverene," given by the Imperial Government to that of New South Wales, affords the Naval Brigade opportunities for their drills, and cruises, as well as the Naval Artillery Volunteers. She has only sufficient of a crew to keep her in working order, and in case of her services being required she would be manned by the Naval Brigade. The colony possesses also two torpedo boats.

It is more than twenty years since the Imperial troops left New South Wales, and their recal gave rise to the present permanent force which was at first artillery and infantry, and then changed wholly into artillery, in which form, under the name of the Permanent Artillery it has since remained. It is entrusted with the defences of the coast, and the general military duties of the colony. Its members are for the most part housed in the very comfortable barracks in Paddington, a suburb of Sydney. The principal fortifications are at Middle and South Head, the former having splendid command of the entrance to the harbour.

This permanent force is composed of one field battery, and two garrison batteries, in all about 500 men, a very fine body too, but of late, for some reason or another they seem to have some difficulty in getting recruits, and, in fact, the standard was reduced to five feet six inches. Officers and men are well paid. The former receive, from Major and brevet Lieutenant-colonel who gets £450, to Lieutenants, £238, each with allowances, quarters, rations, &c., and £52 per annum, for groom. A gunner's pay is 2/3 per day, rations of bread, meat, and groceries, free kit, uniform, quarters, &c. Special rates of working pay, and rewards for good conduct, but no pension. Recruits must be from 18 to 40 years of age, and are enlisted for five years. They may re-engage for a further two or five years. A detachment of mounted infantry, and submarine miners complete the permanent forces of the colony. The uniform of the artillery is similar to that of the Imperial arm of the service, with the exception that a white helmet with the badge of a cross and stars, is worn. Officers wear gold lace. For fatigue dress, a jacket of blue serge, and broad-brimmed, grey felt hat, looped up on the left side, is worn. Drivers and mounted men wear "cord" breeches and tanned leggings. The mounted infantry wear karkhee uniform, brown leather bandolier and belts, "cords," tanned leggings, and grey wideawake. Engineers wear the Imperial scarlet.

NEW SOUTH WALES VOLUNTEERS.

Volunteering has experienced many reverses of fortune in New South Wales. The first effort made to raise a volunteer corps was, I believe, in 1851, and some years later a yeomanry troop was established, which, on its first parade in the Government House grounds, was ingloriously routed by a pet bull of the Governor's (I am fairly elastic as regards pets, but I think I should draw the line at a bull). It never survived the little affair, and, as the "Buffalo Brigade," was jeered out of existence. Now, volunteering has settled down by force of circumstances and Acts of Parliament combined, into a somewhat anomalous body which is officially termed the Partially-paid forces, and consists of engineers, submarine miners, artillery, mounted infantry, and infantry, with reserves of cavalry, artillery, and infantry, which are all well-paid for the time they devote to their duties. A number of reserve rifle companies are being formed, which are made a small allowance.

The training to become efficient, in addition to nine continuous days in camp, and three whole detached days' drill annually, is :—

    For Engineers ... ... 12 half-days and 10 night drills.
    ,, Submarine Miners 22 ,,
    ,, Artillery ... ... 16 ,, and shot practice.
    ,, Infantry ... ... 13 ,, and course of musketry.

A whole day is a parade of 6 hours; half-a-day 2 hours; and a night parade 1 hour. Commissioned and non-commissioned officers attend certain classes.

Payment for the above is made as follows :—10/- for whole days, 5/- for half-days, 2/- for night parade, 15/- for course of musketry, 10/- if a first-class shot, 5/- if second class, a bonus of £2 if efficient, and £2 for uniform. The officers are paid from £100 a year as commanding officer, with forage for one horse, to £25 for a second lieutenant.

The rules for the reserves are 12 daylight attendances, 20 night parades, shot practice for the artillery, and musketry for others. The uniform of the artillery is dark blue, of the infantry scarlet, mounted infantry and cavalry, Karkhee, grey wideawake, &c. The age at which recruits may join is from 18 to 40 years of age, the maximum for the reserves being 50, and they have to pass a more than cursory medical examination. The annual training and encampment is held at Easter time, near Sydney, for cavalry and infantry, while engineers and artillery take possession of the fortifications at Middle Head and elsewhere.

As regards appearances, the New South Wales P.P. forces compare very favourably, I think, with the average of British volunteer batallions. They seem, for the most part, to contain older and steadier men, and, no doubt, the medical examination keeps out many of the rather "weedy" lads that find their way into the ranks of our volunteers. The mounted men are particularly serviceable, but on foot are hardly so smart in their bearing as could be wished. No doubt, being so much on horseback has a good deal to do with this. The entire force, exclusive of naval volunteers and naval brigade, is rather over 5,000 men. Major-General Richardson, C.B., late 12th Foot is in command.

Upon the whole, I don't think that at least some portion of Young Australia looks with a favourable eye on "soldiering." I have often, when a young fellow in the bush has been a trifle glum about his prospects, tried to do a little amateur recruiting, but the reply very often was—" Oh, I couldn't do all that saluting business," &c. In short, his idea of the whole duty of a soldier would sometimes rather be that of the "comic" soldier or sailor of Adelphi dramas, who "cheeks" his superior officers in a manner more pleasing to "the gods" than true to life in the barrack yard or on the main deck. Still the young fellows in Sydney "rolled up" nobly for special constables during the labour troubles, and organized a splendid mounted patrol, but they do not seem to be able to raise a good brace of troops of cavalry, which, I think, they should be well able to do, seeing that nearly every young fellow, who can possibly afford it has his own horse.

CHAPTER XXX.

CONCLUDING REMARKS—CENTRALIZATION —LIFE IN CITIES—TECHNICAL EDUCATION—THE ABORIGINALS—"JOHN CHINAMAN"—ALIEN COMMUNITIES.

Reviewing the foregoing chapters which I have apportioned each to a subject more or less materially essential to that upon which I have, generally, presumed to write, I find naturally one or two small matters upon which I am tempted to make a few concluding remarks.

I have written, some may think, somewhat vigorously, upon the idea of young men going out to Australia when they are unfitted for colonial life, and trained only, if indeed they have received any training at all, to clerical work, which there is no need for me to state, is a drug in any market, but I feel sure that anyone who ' nows the colonies, even superficially, will confirm my statement that it is hardly possible to write too strongly upon such a subject.

It is an old, well-worn story no doubt, but the tendency to centralize the crowding together in large cities, which is as observable in Australia as in England, throws yearly a greater number of town-bred youths upon the market, who have never been in a position to acquire a taste for rural life, or likely to take kindly to it even if they were possessed of any aptitude for it. All this undue centralization, no one needs to be told, provides an overwhelming number of applicants for even the most paltry clerical situation, and threatens to overcrowd every profession, and to add to this, the work bench and the useful trade is frequently looked down upon, and sacrificed for the questionable position afforded by the office-stool. A life of worry and anxiety thus becomes the lot of many and many a poor fellow who, though his position may be a fair one, and he devotes all his energy to the due performance of his duties, can never feel that it is assured : as he must know, none better, that many would be glad of his " billet " at a less figure, and if his health suddenly, or prematurely fails him, which, under the circumstances, is not by any means improbable, there are not many firms nowadays like the dear old Cheeryble Brothers, not a few commercial magnates preferring to see their names in print for three-figure donations to fashionable charities, to exercising a little of that greatest of cardinal virtues, which is said to begin at home, though daily events go far to prove that its source is unfavourable to local development. The question then arises is there sufficient opportunity for technical education, by which stuff suitable for colonization may be turned out ? What chance is afforded the many for gaining useful experience of a rural life? The Hawkesbury College to which I have already alluded may be the beginning of a most useful, and extensive institution, as it stands to reason that knowledge is best acquired in the country in which it is to be turned to account. The idea of placing young fellows on English farms to qualify them for colonists is, as an idea, perhaps good, but I have had experience of some instances in which it would appear that such mysteries as top-dressing, sub-soil, drainage, &c., were best learned in the billiard-room of the nearest market town, and agriculture generally, by assiduous riding to hounds, or driving about the country in a well-appointed dog-cart.

I fancy some people may expect to hear a little about what are usually termed the "natives," the original possessors of the country. As I have explained the term, "natives" apply to Australian-born white men—the gentlemen who were in possession when Captain Cook made his appearance being termed officially, aborigines, and colloquially, "black-fellows." I regret I cannot say much about them, for the simple, and I trust, sufficient reason that, personally, I know very little of them, but such knowledge as I do possess, I will detail.

I have foregathered with men of many nationalities, including specimens of what poetic fancy has described as the noble savage; but the Australian black fellow does not occupy any conspicuous niche in my mind's temple of ethnological reminiscences. He possesses many traits in common with those who are supposed to have benefited by civilisation. He is not overclean; is given to the use of tobacco and the consumption of liquors, malt and spirituous, the latter for choice, when he can get them, it being illegal to sell liquor to a black-fellow. He is averse to working, and prefers to get along without recourse to honest toil if he possibly can. He is also, I fear, rather treacherous, and would not wholly object to stab a man in the back, just as his Christian brethren will sometimes slander a fellow-creature in like manner. Like many others, civilized and savage, he may have good *in him*, but he does not allow it sufficient scope, or permit it to shed its light upon his domestic circle, and associations generally, as much as could be wished.

In appearance he is frequently of middle stature, strongly built sometimes, and black as ebony. His head is adorned by a shock of straight tangled hair, which hangs over a low forehead, and jet black eyes glitter through the thick fringe in no friendly or assuring fashion. A full beard and moustache frequently hides the rest of his face. As to the partner of his joys and sorrows—or "gin," as she is generally termed—I am not an adept at describing female beauty, and will only say that the personal attractions of the average Australian gin may, with great reason, be termed an acquired taste. A benevolent Government allows the black-fellow blankets and tobacco; he has the privilege, like the law-makers of his colony, of riding free by rail or tramway. There is an Aborigines' Protection Board, and also an association which is endeavouring to establish certain missions for the benefit of the New South Wales Aboriginals.

Speaking of the Chinese, I shall not presume to enter upon what may be termed the Chinese Question, save by remarking that a poll tax of £100 is claimed from each immigrant from the Flowery Land. Captains of ships manned by a Chinese crew, or having Chinamen on board serving in any capacity, are under very strict regulations while in port, and subjected to a heavy fine if any one of the Mongols make their escape, while no vessel is allowed to carry more than a certain proportion of Chinese passengers, in accordance with her tonnage. There is a large number of Chinamen in New South Wales, from market gardeners, cabinet makers, "fossickers," &c., to merchants. One of the last-named, Mr. Quong Tart, is very well and most favourably known in Sydney, and as among his many gifts is numbered the ability to sing a Scotch song, it will, I think, be owned that he is no ordinary gentleman. As to the forming of distinct colonies of alien Europeans, I must leave the encouragement of such to wiser heads than mine. No doubt, those interested in the welfare of Australia will remember that, if ever she casts off from "the old ship," the presence of foreign elements in her midst may prove a rock ahead, as the recent question raised by the "Mafia" troubles in New Orleans may teach her.

And now, without any impassioned peroration, I conclude a lengthy, though pleasant task, in the earnest hope that what I have written may not fail in being a source of some interest, perhaps use, to those who may chance to think over "trying Australia."

FINIS.

THE Pioneer Life Assurance Company,
LIMITED.

CAPITAL £100,000.
(FULLY SUBSCRIBED.)

Life Assurance at LITTLE MORE THAN HALF THE RATES Charged by existing British Companies.

EXAMPLE OF COST OF ASSURANCE,
Age 40. Amount £1,000.

Average Annual Cost under existing British Systems - £32 5 10
Annual Cost under PIONEER System (after first year) £18 3 4
Saving to PIONEER Policy-Holders   -   -   - £14 2 6

Directors:

J. HENRY IREDALE, Esq., Chairman (Liverpool).
W. H. BROWN, Esq., Vice-Chairman (Bolton).

T. BAYNE, Esq. (Burnley).
GEO. BOHN, Esq., C.E. (Hull).
A. K. CANNINGTON, Esq. (Liverpool)
R. INGER DEXTER, Esq. (Nottingham).
A. H. JEFFERIS, Esq. (Manchester).
J. D. MURRAY, Esq. (Wigan).
T. W. OAKSHOT, Esq., J.P. (Liverpool)
THOMAS RITCHIE, Esq. (Belfast).
GEO. SENIOR, Esq. (Sheffield).
P. SPEAKMAN, Esq., C.C. (Runcorn)
W. H. WOODS, Esq. (Preston).

General Manager and Secretary:—E. L. LEWES.
Assistant Secretary:—J. CARLISLE M'CLEERY, F.S.S.

Manager, Agency Department:—W. T. OVERSBY, } 11, Dale Street,
District Manager for Liverpool:—JAMES LOWRY, }   LIVERPOOL.

Before applying elsewhere, Gentlemen capable of Influencing Business should write to the Head Office for Terms. To really Competent Men the PIONEER Company offers advantages otherwise unobtainable.

Head Office: 11, Dale Street, LIVERPOOL.

THE Pioneer Life Assurance Company,
LIMITED.

That existing methods of Life Assurance are a very expensive luxury may be readily gathered from the facts which will be found in the prospectus of the Company. Under the existing systems, a person aged 30, who "lives out his expectancy," will have paid (at existing rates, and including 4 % Compound Interest) nearly £2,000 for a life policy of £1,000. True, he may have received back a portion of the sum in "bonuses;" but the very fact that "bonuses" are possible, proves at once that the assured has been charged an excessive premium, and that when he receives a "bonus" he is simply receiving back a portion of his premium, which portion, in the first instance, he ought never to have been called upon to pay. Under the **Pioneer** system of Life Assurance this anomaly is impossible. The **Pioneer** system, as explained in the prospectus, is a system of Life Assurance pure and simple. It is not encumbered with Bonuses, Endowments, or any of the elements which have converted existing British companies into Banking concerns. It does not tell a man of 30, that, if "he lives out his expectancy," and pays his premium regularly, it will charge him £2,000 for £1,000, plus a possible bonus; but it says to him that, if he is willing to devote about about 6/- per week to the payment on a Life Policy, those dependent on him will, on his death, receive the sum of £1,000.

The *North British Economist* says:—"There is room found in the prospectus for a table showing the reserve fund, premiums and interest received, and claims by death and endowments of most of the leading offices; and the perfectly fair question is asked—Why these companies, with reserve funds exceeding, in aggregate, no less than eighty millions sterling, should go on demanding prices that fill out this income from premium and interest to nearly twice the sum paid in claims. As the imposing array of cyphers, which covers from east to west the costly show cards we see everywhere, grows and grows in importance as the integer in front of them from time to time increases, one often seems constrained to ask—Where is it all to end? The rainy day against which the millions are saved comes not—only the showery, occasionally, so far. Will it ever be otherwise?"

Write for Prospectus to the

Head Office:
11, DALE STREET, LIVERPOOL.

SILVER MEDAL, INTERNATIONAL EXHIBITION, 1886.

EDMONDSON'S
OLD ESTABLISHED
Fishing Tackle Manufactory,
BASNETT STREET, CHURCH STREET,
LIVERPOOL.

RODS, TACKLE, NETS, &c., Made to Order.

OUR OWN MAKE SPLIT CANE RODS,
Either Double Cane or Steel Centre, to Order.

Agents for Best RACKETS, TENNIS, LA CROSSE,
POLO, CRICKET, ROUNDERS, FOOTBALLS.

Makers of Flies for Norway, Sweden, Canada.

ALL VARIETIES OF TWEED, DEE, SPEY,
AND OTHER PATTERNS MADE TO ORDER.

TROUT FLIES in endless variety.

GREENHEART, CASTLE, CONNEL RODS, &c.

REPAIRS DONE WITH CARE & DESPATCH,
Having special facilities on the Premises.

Trout & Trammel Net, & Sea Tackle of every description.
ESTIMATES FOR YACHT'S OUTFIT.

HENRY WHITTY, Proprietor.
Telegraphic Address—"FISHING, LIVERPOOL."

ILLUSTRATED CATALOGUES GRATIS.

Awarded Gold Medal L'pool Intern'l Exhibition, 1886.

ENGLISH MANUFACTURED
TOBACCOS

RICHMOND CAVENDISH CO., Ld.,
LIVERPOOL.

SPECIAL BRANDS:—

"Pioneer" Golden Flake Cut.

"Richmond" Navy Cut.

"Richmond" Smoking Mixture.

Superfine Bird's Eye.

Golden Bird's Eye.

"Golden Brown" Fine Cut.

Bright & Black Plug Cavendish.

IN ALL USUAL SIZES.

PRICE LISTS ON APPLICATION.

Established over a Quarter of a Century.

A LIST OF SOME OF THE MORE IMPORTANT WORKS

PUBLISHED BY

EDWARD HOWELL,

CHURCH STREET, LIVERPOOL.

"**BEING AND DOING.**" A Selection of Helpful Thoughts for Daily Reading, cr 8vo, *cloth*   5/-

---

BOWES (James L.)—
    JAPANESE POTTERY, with Notes and Illustrations, *many beautifully executed photographic plates*, royal 8vo, *cloth*   £2/12/6
    A DE LUXE EDITION, on JAPANESE PAPER, with 23 *extra plates in gold and colours, half morocco* £6/6/-
        Only a few copies left.

CHRISTIE (Dr.)—
    BOOK OF REVELATIONS, 8vo, *cloth, (shortly)*.
    METHODISM, a part of the Apostasy, cr 8vo, *cloth*   3/6

COLERIDGE (T. S.)—
    AIDS TO REFLECTION, *cloth*   2/6
    NOTES AND LECTURES ON SHAKSPEARE, *cloth*   2/6

EDWARDS (President)—
    FREEDOM OF THE WILL, *with preface by Isaac Taylor*, *cloth*   2/6

FENBY (Thomas)—
    DICTIONARY OF ENGLISH SYNONYMS, *new edition*   2/6

GAMLIN (Hilda)—
    MEMOIR OF LADY HAMILTON, being an Old Story re-told, *numerous portraits, plates, and woodcuts, &c., half vellum*   £3/3/-
    CHRONICLES AND MEMORIES OF BIRKENHEAD (*shortly*)

LUND (T. W. M.)—
    A Sicilian Christmas Eve, *second edition*   1/6
    Behind the Veil, a Reminiscence of Influenza, *just out*   1/6

SMITH (Thomas)—
    Chairman and Speaker's Guide, *new edition*, 1892, 2/-

TAYLOR (Isaac)—
    History of the Transmission of Ancient Books, *cloth*   3/6

VERNEY (Lady)—
    The Grey Pool, and other Stories, *with portrait*, 7/6
    Essays and Tales, *with frontispiece (Claydon House)*, 635 p.p.   10/6

WHISHAW (A)—
    Sermons preached in the Church for the Blind, *cloth*   7/6

EDWARD HOWELL,

Publisher, Bookseller, and Dealer in Rare and Out-of-the-Way Books, Portraits, Old Prints, and Engravings.

100,000 VOLUMES IN STOCK.   CATALOGUES FREQUENTLY ISSUED.

BINDING BY SKILLED WORKMEN.

LIBRARIES PURCHASED in any part of the Country **FOR PROMPT CASH.**

CHURCH STREET, LIVERPOOL.

www.ingramcontent.com/pod-product-compliance
Lightning Source LLC
Chambersburg PA
CBHW022110230426
43672CB00008B/1337